JUST MARY

A Memoir

JUST MARY

A Memoir

MARY O'ROURKE ～

Gill & Macmillan

Gill & Macmillan
Hume Avenue, Park West, Dublin 12
with associated companies throughout the world
www.gillmacmillanbooks.ie

© Mary O'Rourke 2012
978 07171 5409 8

Index compiled by Helen Litton
Typography design by Make Communication
Print origination by O'K Graphic Design, Dublin
Printed and bound in the UK by MPG Books Ltd,
Cornwall

This book is typeset in 12/15 pt Minion.

The paper used in this book comes from the wood pulp
of managed forests. For every tree felled, at least one
tree is planted, thereby renewing natural resources.

A CIP catalogue record for this book is available from
the British Library.

5 4 3 2 1

To Feargal and Maeve, Aengus and Lisa, and their six lively children, Jennifer, Luke, Sarah, Sam, James and Scott

But most of all to my lovely Enda

CONTENTS

PROLOGUE

Saturday, 26 February 2011

It's a dry, warm day, after a couple of weeks of really uncertain weather. I have joined many others in St Dominic's Community Centre in Kenagh, Co. Longford, where the combined count for Longford and Westmeath is being held. It is about four o'clock in the afternoon and it's clear by now that I have lost my seat as one of the Fianna Fáil representatives for the constituency. My active political career is ending here, in this spacious community hall.

So, who is with me? I have driven here with my older son, Feargal, who intended to travel down from Dublin for the count anyway, but who came early when he got the news that all was not going well. Here with me also is my lovely niece, Gráinne Lenihan, daughter of my late brother, Paddy Lenihan, who died just four short months earlier. Gráinne and I are soul sisters on many issues and, like my two stalwart sons, she worked hard for me in that General Election. My younger son, Aengus, is here too and has been in the count since 8.30 a.m., along with Mícheál Ó'Faoláin, a dear friend who was in charge of so much in my election campaigns and who had ordered all the people keeping the tallies to arrive as early as possible that morning.

Was I on the floor with despair? No! As I said to everyone in the centre, I was disappointed but not devastated, and that is the most accurate way of describing how I felt. I decided to adopt Avril Doyle's mantra, which always made such an impression on me. She had been defeated in one of her election campaigns in Wexford and she said, 'Hold on, what's all the crying for? No one died!' Deep within me, that is really the way I felt. I had lost my husband, Enda. I had lost my two brothers, Brian and then Paddy. These deaths, as well as the very poor prognosis for my dear nephew

Brian Lenihan in his battle with pancreatic cancer, weighed heavily on me (Brian would pass away less than six months later, of course), and I had an immeasurable amount of grief within me. Losing a parliamentary seat, whilst catastrophic in career terms, is clearly not in any way comparable with the loss of such dear loved ones from one's life.

When I had arrived at St Dominic's in Kenagh, I met all the team who had worked so hard for me, along with Mícheál and my great friend and valiant Director of Elections, P.J. Coghill. As the outcome became ever clearer, I found that my job would be to console them, rather than theirs to console me. I think that is what keeps one strong on such an occasion: it certainly kept me strong. I went through the motions. I did the national television and radio; I did all the local TV and radio stations too. I stayed up on the balcony, looking down, keeping up a positive front. But the numbers were already written up for me — literally — and I was about to be eliminated.

Now, I had form in this. Back in 2002, I had lost my seat after 20 continuous years in the Dáil. I had subsequently gone into Seanad Éireann, appointed by the then Taoiseach, Bertie Ahern, and had indeed enjoyed a highly productive five years as Leader of that house. But on this occasion, the defeat was somewhat final. I knew that the end of my active political life had arrived — but I did not intend it to be the end of my active, living life. In the cards and the letters and the phone calls that followed, so many said to me, 'Enjoy your retirement'. I didn't intend to retire, however. I didn't feel like retiring. I wanted to do things; I wanted to be involved; I wanted to continue to have a voice.

That night, we all went back to my home in Athlone. Throughout the evening, many other people called in, those who had been less directly involved in my political campaign but who were all dear friends who had contributed in other ways. Among these of course were Mícheál Ó'Faoláin's lovely wife Maura, and my close friends, Hugh and Celine Campbell, and Niall and Angela McCormack. We had a few glasses of wine or a few gins and again, my job was to talk things through with everyone, to reassure them and allow them to reassure me. Eventually they all left and it was just my son Feargal and I. He wanted to stay with me, but I insisted, 'No Feargal, I like my own company. I'm happy to be on my own.' So, finally alone, I sat down in my familiar easy chair in my familiar living room with all my familiar things around me. And I found myself thinking back to when the long odyssey of my political life had first begun. I went back, back, back . . .

I went back to 1944. I was a young child, seven years old, and living in the town of Athlone with my mother and father, my sister Anne, who was four years older than me, my brother Paddy, who was six years older and my brother Brian, who was seven years my senior. It was a night of great excitement in our home town, because the chief of the Fianna Fáil Party, Éamon de Valera, was there to give impetus to a General Election campaign which had lacked lustre until that point. That evening we had all been brought by our parents to the town centre of Athlone, where de Valera spoke from a platform outside the church in what was then called the Market Square (now more often called St Peter's Square). Huge crowds, huge excitement, huge commotion and, to my childish eyes, the huge, imposing figure of the man in the long black coat, there in the Square. He was talking and talking — in a funny voice. A high-pitched voice, I remember thinking at the time, and with an odd emphasis on certain words.

After that, it was everyone back to our house in Gentex (the Athlone General Textiles factory complex) and a whole crowding in of all of the Fianna Fáil faithful to meet at first-hand 'the Chief', there, in our home. My sister Anne and I were told to go to bed, but our brothers, being older, and politics being then as now very much a male world, jostled in to the dining room-cum-living room with the others. And then the door was firmly closed. The drinking began and the serving of tea and sandwiches; and the tumult of the talking and the shouting rose and fell and ebbed and flowed throughout the night.

In our shared bedroom, my sister quickly fell asleep, but for me the excitement of it all was far too great for such a thing as sleep. I soon crept out of bed and up the long, dark corridor to the noisy living room and the vibrancy and clamour which, even at my very young age of seven years, drew me irresistibly towards it. I lay down on the ground at that door, knowing that there was no need for anyone to use it as a passage to the bathroom, as there was a bathroom on the other side of the living room, which I had heard people going into. As I lay in that dark corridor, pressing my ear to the door, it seemed to me that I was living in the middle of huge excitement, and that I was part of it all, even though I was outside of it.

Voices rose and fell. Laughter boomed out. Arguments broke out and animated discussions waxed and waned. There was the clinking of glasses, the acrid smell of cigarette smoke (at that time, smoking was allowed always and anywhere). It seemed to my childish senses and my very young mind that this was real life. This was the tumult and the talk that I wished to be part of. And there and then, I determined that I would be part of it, of that excitement which was unfolding in our house. Not only that, however: I knew that I wanted to be involved in this sort of life in the years ahead. I wanted to be someone who knew about politics, who was part of the political world and to whom politics meant as much as it did to those gathered in our house that night.

Finally, tiredness overcame me and I crept back to bed and pulled up the covers around me. But my mind jumped and sprang for a good while after that, and I was still awake to hear people departing loudly with 'Goodbye' and 'Slán Leat' and 'Slán Abhaile'. And then, a single sound remained — the odd intonation and timbre again of what I knew was the voice of Éamon de Valera.

Back to the present, and me sitting alone in my home in Arcadia in Athlone on that night of February 2011, contemplating the end of my professional life in politics. Was I very sad? No, I wasn't. I knew I had worked at politics all my life, had given it my very best shot and now I was back in the house where my very happy domestic life had played out, where I had lived from the very beginning of my marriage with Enda, the only man I ever loved and who had brought such happiness to me and to our family. Wrapped in the warm mantle of happy memories, I felt somehow safe and secure. As far as my life in politics went, of course some of the memories were good and some were bad, but undoubtedly my journey began on that very far off day in 1944, as the seven-year-old with the lively mind who wanted to know all that was going on. And I find myself in 2012 at age 75, still wanting to know all that is happening in political life and in life in general too.

After that day of the count in Kenagh, I decided that I was going to write a book about my life. Not a high and mighty book — how could it be? — but an ordinary book, detailing my life in and out of politics over the years: one which would aim to shed some light on the key events of a long career in public life. I hope that those reading this narrative will find that I have been able to go some way to achieving that aim.

Chapter 1

AN ATHLONE CHILDHOOD

My father was a County Clare man, P.J. Lenihan, from Lickeen, Kilfenora. My mother was from Drumcliff in County Sligo. They met as students at University College, Galway, where my mother was doing a BA and my father was doing Arts and then later a Law degree. Both bright, full of life and highly intelligent, they quickly fell in love with one another.

My father was the son of Patrick Joseph Lenihan Senior of Kilfenora, Co. Clare. My paternal grandmother Hannah, née McInerney, had died when the children were all very young: they were four boys and one girl. My father, the eldest, was barely ten years old at the time. After a suitable interval of time, my grandfather married the assistant teacher who had come to work with him in his two-teacher school. She was Sarah. Obviously I never met my grandmother Hannah, as she was long, long dead, but my step-grandmother, Sarah Lenihan, was a formidable woman who often visited us in Athlone and put the fear of God into my young heart and, I feel sure, into those of my siblings too.

The mortuary card of my paternal grandfather, P.J. Lenihan Senior, shows a stern man with an unwavering gaze. Records from the time show that he was a leading figure in the fledgling Irish National Teachers' Organisation (INTO) trade union in County Clare and one of the greatest adherents to their cause. From what my father used to tell us — and this was confirmed by my aunt Maura, the only girl in the family — he was a strict father. All the children were expected not just to do their lessons but to excel at them, as well as doing whatever work was needed around the house, yard and so on — no one was to be spared. I often thought about how my father must have felt, losing his mother at such a young age and how this must have affected him throughout his life, despite the calm sense of order which his stepmother Sarah imposed in their home.

My mother, Annie Scanlan, on the other hand, grew up in a household without a father. My maternal grandmother was left a widow when she was a young woman in her mid-twenties with several youngsters clutching to her skirts and a child in her womb. Her husband, my grandfather, Bernard 'Brian' Scanlan, had been stretchered home to her, fatally wounded, on a door from a pub in Sligo town, where he had got involved in a row over Charles Stewart Parnell. He was a member of the UIL (United Irish League), a group of small farmers. Remember that this was a time when Lloyd George's enlightened social welfare reforms were not yet fully in place in Ireland. There were very scant pickings for a widow with six young children and another baby on the way, and twelve acres of rough land at the foot of Ben Bulben.

My grandmother was lucky in one respect, however, in that she had a cousin who was head of the Ursuline Convent in Sligo. So she was able to send each one of her five daughters — May, Tattie, Chrissie, Annie and Bridie — there for their secondary level education. Of all of them, according to written and spoken evidence of the time, my mother was the star pupil. A small incident will tell its own tale. She did a very fine Leaving Certificate, achieving first place in French in Ireland, and secured a scholarship to UCG. However, she had not studied Latin and at that time there was, over and above having the Leaving Cert, a matriculation examination which one had to sit to get into university, and this examination had a compulsory Latin component to it. Undaunted, however, my mother elected to do her matriculation in September. And so between the months of June and September, she studied Latin with private tuition and managed to pass all elements of the September exam. Throughout my life, I have often thought what a remarkable feat it was, for a young country girl from County Sligo, to set such a goal for herself and to manage to win through at it. She surely showed great resolve and great determination.

My mother's family were strongly republican and all of them, young and old, took the anti-Treaty side during the debate in the early 1920s and in the Civil War. In fact my uncle Roger, then a young man of just 15 years of age, was actively involved as a runner for the republican side, and had to be smuggled out of Ireland and sent to Australia to be resettled there, because the Treaty side were after him. My father's family on the other hand, and my paternal grandfather in particular, would have been strongly in support of Michael Collins and of the Treaty. Indeed, when he was a student in UCG, my father and a group of other devil-may-care students rode out to Athenry on their bicycles to assist the men at the Barracks there in fending off an imminent raid by anti-Treaty forces.

This aspect of our history was to come back to haunt me a few times during my early political life, when small-minded people would toss back at me my father's family's allegiance to the Michael Collins tradition, regardless of the fact that by then my father had fully embraced Fianna Fáil. On these occasions, I was always able to counter such innuendo by reminding them about my mother's family in County Sligo, about the bravery of my young uncle Roger and his commitment to the anti-Treaty movement, and about my Aunt Chrissie, who became the life-long President of Fianna Fáil in Sligo and was revered at her funeral as such. That usually silenced my detractors — although then again, the same facts were also used to taunt me in other situations!

My father and mother married young, starting their new life together in Dundalk, Co. Louth. My father entered the civil service at Higher Executive level and began in Revenue. Both my brothers — Brian and then Paddy — were born in Dundalk, and then, following a promotion for my father, the family moved to Tralee where my sister Anne was born. My father was promoted once again and posted to Revenue in Dublin Castle. My mother often spoke to me about what these moves involved for the family and how disruptive they were — but that was the life they led. My father was lucky to have what would have been regarded as a good middle-class job, and in some senses this is why my mother didn't get the opportunity to use her qualifications, except for early on when she taught for a few years in Loreto in Bray (and had vowed that if she ever had daughters, they would be sent there to school).

The final move for our family came whilst we were living in Sutton, Co. Dublin. One day my father came back from work and announced to my mother, 'We are on the move again, Annie. We are going to

Athlone.' An exciting opportunity had arisen. My father was nothing if not full of adventure and he had decided at once that we would meet this one head on.

This change in professional direction for my father came about because Seán Lemass, who was then Minister for Industry and Commerce in a Fianna Fáil government, had met him while he was working in Revenue in Dublin Castle and had liked the cut of his jib. Accordingly, when a government initiative involving the setting up of factories all around the country was being put in place, Lemass suddenly thought of P.J. Lenihan, the civil servant he had met during the course of his work and whom he thought was a go-ahead young man. He contacted my father, proposing that he take leave of absence to go to Athlone and start up a plant specialising in textiles, to be called General Textiles Limited. My father jumped at the chance.

And so, with three young children and a fourth — myself — on the way, my parents arrived at the old Ranelagh Protestant School opposite the railway station in Athlone. That was in 1936, and my father would work day and night to get the fledgling factory off the ground, while we were reared on the site of what was to become a thriving plant employing a thousand people. He quickly established himself and started to recruit staff, while life assumed a pattern too for my mother, with now four young children to mind. She was very ill after my birth, but was lucky to have the devoted services of a young girl, Bridget Sharkey from County Louth, who came to live with us and in many respects became a surrogate mother to us all.

My father was busy and outgoing, with an attractive personality which drew people to him, and so it was a natural evolution that he became involved, and quickly assumed a permanent role, in civic affairs in Athlone. He was persuaded to run for the town council, initially as a Chamber of Commerce representative and Independent. Later he decided to take on the mantle of Fianna Fáil, not for any ideological reason, but out of loyalty to Seán Lemass, I imagine.

At this time Athlone was part of the constituency of Athlone–Longford, which was represented by the TDS Erskine (Hamilton) Childers, Thomas Carter and Seán Mac Eoin. It was Childers who 'serviced' Athlone and so about once a month he would visit the area, arriving by train with his bicycle. I would be sent, as a very young girl — just six or seven years old — over to the railway station to meet him and would accompany him as he wheeled his bike up the road to our house in the Ranelagh. There my father, who had detailed in his notebook for the TD all the queries which had come in from constituents over the previous weeks, would go through these with Childers, who would in turn note them in his own book. Then up Childers would get and on his bike and away around the town, calling at all of the addresses faithfully compiled and given to him by my father. Much later, he would come back to our house, fortified by the many stories he had heard and the many cups of tea he had been given. Then it was time for me to do my job again, accompanying him back over to the railway station until he got on the train, put his bike in the luggage carriage and away he went. It all sounds so old-fashioned now, but it wasn't really. There was a great deal of dignity in the exchanges between my father and Erskine Childers, and in turn between the TD and his electorate, those who had solicited his presence. There was a strong sense of the unspoken contract which existed between them all. Around that time, 1943 to 1944, there were two elections within eleven months, and Erskine Childers, who was returned for both of them, continued to put in his regular appearances in Athlone.

In the years which followed, life carried on seamlessly in our busy household. My father was clearly devoted to his work and no matter what the vagaries of the night before, would get up at 6 a.m. without fail, wash and shave himself and walk down into the bowels of Gentex, as the factory was called, to meet the workers coming in for the first shift of the day. The number of employees — many of them female — increased exponentially and for many years, Gentex was the economic mainstay of the town of Athlone and the rural hinterland around it. The factory complex was continually being added to with, for example, huge sheds being erected — the bleaching, dying, finishing and spinning sheds — but for my father, with his advanced ideas on social practice among workers, the facilities on offer for employees were an equal priority. There was a resident, full-time nurse on the premises and a doctor visited at regular intervals. Right throughout the 1940s and beyond, there were workers' councils and recognised trade unions in place in Gentex — at a time when such structures were only beginning to be introduced in other workplaces throughout Ireland. I know now that my father was very much influenced by socialist thinking, and he never failed to put such principles into practice in so far as he could.

Looking back now from a world in which women are expected to use their education and to enter the workforce, many may wonder how my mother managed to contain herself, with her brood of young children in the town of Athlone? It seems that she took up the card game of bridge, which at the time was starting to be a craze throughout Europe. She joined clubs and found friends to play with. And she mastered the game. So much did she master it in fact, that later, in the 1950s and 60s, she would represent Ireland at bridge conventions in Europe and beyond, travelling to such far, far places (to our young minds) as Lake Como, Vienna and London to fly the flag. In Seamus Dowling's *The History of Bridge in Ireland*, Mrs Anne Lenihan is cited as being a winner of the Lambert Cup, with her name 'frequently appear[ing] high on the leaderboard of major competitions'. Meanwhile, my father continued to be ever more involved in local politics, going from town council to county council, and becoming on many consecutive occasions Chairperson (there were no mayors then), both on the county council in Mullingar and on the Athlone Urban District Council.

My childhood was easy-going and because I was the youngest by so many years, I assumed a kind of 'busybody' role. When people came to the house to see my father about problems they had, I would always be the one to answer the door, bring them in and sit them down. I would say that my father would be with them in a moment and then dutifully go off and get him. I am certain that it was then that the belief was instilled in me that you were there to serve the people and that they should be treated properly and politely — and in my public life, I never forgot those early lessons. My father often explained how, for those people who came to him with a difficulty, their problem was the most important thing in their lives at that moment. I would notice that people generally seemed happier going away than when they had first arrived to see my father, as if the sharing of their troubles had helped them, and so this was something I strove for also in my work throughout my life.

Brian and Paddy were sent to the local Marist Boys' Primary School and from there to the Marist Secondary College, also in Athlone. Brian completed his schooling there, but Paddy was sent at a certain point to Garbally College in Ballinasloe as a boarder, as he was proving a handful at home. It was felt that he would benefit from the discipline and the control of Garbally, but he was to prove a handful there too, and he was threatened with expulsion on two occasions. On one occasion, the threat was actually carried out, but he was taken back again — a rare event, I would think! Paddy smoked from a relatively young age and perhaps took a beer or two as well, all of which at that time was regarded as wild behaviour. I remember hearing this and it passing over my head. But both of my brothers persevered to the end and came out with their Leaving Certs.

My mother was true to the promise she made herself in her first teaching job in Loreto Bray, and she sent my sister Anne there as a boarder at the age of 13. It sounds odd now but it was the norm then that, if you could afford it, after national school was over, you sent your children — both boys and girls — to boarding schools. And so in due course, I too arrived at the Loreto Convent in Bray as a twelve-year-old, when Anne was in her final year there.

I hated boarding school with a passion. Just as my mother had vowed to send her daughters to Loreto, I vowed that as regards any children I might have in future, I would never send them away. I missed my home; I missed my father and all the family; I missed my friends. I hated the cold; I hated the food; I suffered with the loneliness of it all. Yes, I made friends but somehow I never got over my wish to be at home rather than where I was. I became a prickly teenager, noted for being vaguely subversive and not at all like my 'good' sister, with whom I was constantly compared. But there was one sterling aspect about life in Loreto, and that was the way we were taught and with this came the realisation that learning could be exotic and interesting, and that there were worlds outside ours to be explored through books and through conversations and in classes. I loved the wonderful library there, where I could continue to enjoy the adventure and excitement of reading, which had begun in my home in my very early years. I developed a schoolgirl crush — we all had them — on a Mother Benedicta, who taught us Latin. Looking back now, I realise that she was a brilliant woman who instilled and fostered in me a love of the Latin language, of the *Odes* of Horace and so many other classical works. I enjoyed sports too, and in my last year was appointed captain of all the Dublin Loreto schools at netball. All of this side of school life was exciting and it made up in important ways for the barren loneliness of being a boarder, as I experienced it. It was always cold and we were always hungry: these were my two dominant impressions at the time.

My love of Latin flourished, however, and has stayed with me. I got Honours in my Leaving Cert Latin and indeed when I started my teaching career, it was Latin I wanted to teach. But of course it eventually disappeared as a subject from the general curriculum and is now taught in just a few chosen schools. I think this a great mistake because Latin is the foundation for all other languages and its concision, language structure and clarity of thought are qualities which would stand many a writer now in very good stead.

By the time I left Loreto Convent, Bray in 1954 at the age of 17, my brother Brian had concluded his law career at UCD. Meanwhile Paddy had begun studies in agricultural science, but left after one year to go to England. My sister Anne had completed her hotel management training in the college based in Shannon Airport, while my father and mother had purchased and re-established the family home in the Hodson Bay Hotel in Athlone. So life had changed utterly for me during my final years at school.

That summer of 1954, and indeed during the long college holidays in subsequent years, I helped out in the Hodson Bay Hotel: like my siblings, I was expected to work — there was no such thing as three months spent hanging around. I worked in the kitchen, washing dishes; I worked in the bar; I worked in the bedrooms. I can't remember if I received a regular payment, but from time to time my father would give me money — enough for me to get by on. I had friends in the area and we went for all of our entertainment to Athlone town and the nearby rural areas, where marquee dancing was the excitement of the day. A large tent would be erected in a field, miles from nowhere, and one of the foremost bands of the day would play until 3 a.m. There we young girls met our opposite numbers in the young fellows, and the encounters which followed were often strange, interesting and exciting.

I learned to drive when I was very young, just 16 or thereabouts. An experience from those days has always stayed in my mind as one of those key moments in my life, and very much indicative of my upbringing. I was barely 17 at the time and very useful to my father during the holidays as a driver. The railway station in Athlone had to be visited every day to pick up fresh chickens and fresh salmon, which would be sent via rail from Limerick and Monaghan and such places for the numerous weddings we hosted in the hotel and for which we had quickly established a good reputation. My father had a big, old-fashioned, two-tone Rover car and one of my first drives on my own was into CIÉ to collect boxes of fresh provisions. With some help, I loaded up at the station and then set out on the road again, to drive the three miles back to the Hodson Bay. I careered into a ditch, however, and got a right fright. There were no mobile phones then of course, but I went to a neighbouring house: that of Delia Donnelly, who ran a typing school — I knew she had a landline. We telephoned my father at the hotel, and I told him what had happened.

'Are you hurt? Are you alright?' he said. Fortunately I was fine.

'Did you hurt anyone?' was the next question.

'No, just a ditch.'

'Well then, you're fine. I'll be there for you shortly.' And so he was.

The very next day, without any hesitation, he sent me off again in the car. I have always thought how that was the right thing to do at the time, as I have been a fairly fearless driver ever since. It was a lesson well taught and a lesson well learned.

I had what was considered a good Leaving Cert — Honours in English, Latin, Drawing, History and Botany — a strange assortment of subjects. My parents could afford to send me to college and it had always been assumed I would go to UCD. I remember my father asking, 'What would you like to do, what would you like to be?' I had replied, 'I would love to be a journalist', but back in 1954, there were very few women journalists about. It is funny that I was always interested, and continue to be interested, in the world of media and journalism. Anyway, my father insisted that the first thing I needed to do was to get a good BA degree, and of course he was right. I was enrolled at UCD — which was then in Earlsfort Terrace — to study Arts.

My first term at UCD began in early October and it had been decided that I would lodge in Loreto Hall, which was a hostel for first-year students. I ended up staying there for the three years. Earlsfort Terrace was literally beside Loreto Hall, so if you had a lecture at 9 a.m., you

could get up at 8.55 a.m. and still be there on time — and that was the
way I lived those early days! I also developed a habit that has remained
with me throughout my life. I was not what one would call a steady
studier — although I was a consistent attendee at lectures and always
keen to absorb everything which passed within the confines of the
campus between the students and the tutors. My pattern of study had
quickly developed into that of a last-minute 'spurter', with a frenzy of
work in, say, the last six weeks before an examination, when I would
study flat out and really achieve results. Somehow my brain wasn't
suited to the long slog, but rather to the hard, frenetic, eleventh-hour
dash. To this day, if I have study or work to do, I will always leave it to
the very last minute, as this is what works best for me.

I liked the atmosphere of college life — there were always things to do
and people to talk to — but my enjoyment of those years was based
above all on my thirst for knowledge and the stimulation of learning. I
went to my lectures, even though I wouldn't have been a great note-taker.
In the first term of my first year, I took Latin, English and Sociology.
There would be 300–400 students in the English lectures, if you chose to
go, which I did — there was a wonderful English lecturer called Lorna
Reynolds, who later became a professor at University College, Galway.

My father's first cousin, the historian Robert Dudley Edwards, was
the head of History in UCD at the time. One day I was seated in this vast
lecture hall and in came Dudley Edwards with long, flowing, curly grey
hair, wearing his gown, as he always did. All at once, he boomed out at
the top of his voice, 'Is there a Mary Lenihan here?' I was mortified. I
put up my hand and when he commanded in that loud, resonant voice,
'Come with me', everyone around me started murmuring and
laughing. I followed him outside, where he questioned me, 'How come
you didn't join my History class?' I replied in a mumble and he just
said, 'You are to start taking History *now!*' And I did. Later on, I was
delighted I had followed his advice, as he was a wonderful lecturer.

I enjoyed hostel life, as restrictive as it was, certainly by today's
standards. My older brother Brian was living at that time in Dublin in
an apartment quite near me, with two other fellows. Any time you
wanted to stay out late, you would have to get permission, so Brian
would say to the staff at the hostel, 'I am taking my sister to . . .' — it
would always be a worthy place. Of course I wouldn't be going out with

him at all: I would be staying over at a friend's flat. In that sense, I was never restricted. I was reared in a house with two boys, so meeting the opposite sex wasn't a big novelty for me. Of course though, we girls would be eyeing up all the boys at college. I remember at one stage, I used to sit three seats down from Tony O'Reilly in the lecture hall!

I completed my first year and I always remember how my English lecturer Lorna Reynolds wrote to my father and mother, saying that I should continue English as I had got a very good mark. My parents were delighted and it was decided that I would do a 'Group 4' English, which was a complete English degree with an ancillary subject — French was mine.

I met Enda O'Rourke that summer while working in the Hodson Bay Hotel. I was just 18. I was playing tennis on the court adjoining the hotel and he was there with some of his friends. I heard him say, 'Who is that girl?' and we were duly introduced. I fell for him straight away. Two years my senior, he was interesting and a bit of a lad, but initially, it was above all a physical attraction: I loved his looks, his dark hair and dark skin. It was this physical liking which turned into love and led to us getting married. Throughout our long married life together, Enda and I never lost that sense of attraction and delight in one another.

The Crescent Ballroom in Athlone was the favourite place at the time for my age group to go. It was owned by the legendary Syd Shine (who is still alive today), and he played there with his band, the Syd Shine Orchestra. In the beginning I would just arrange to see Enda there on a Thursday night when the band was playing. We didn't have proper dates, with him bringing me there and so on, but we soon graduated to that. I remember standing outside just before we went in, watching people weaving in and out and dancing. I have a very vivid memory of them dancing old-fashioned quick steps and foxtrots, and so on. Enda and I went there on a regular basis. I had been out with guys in Dublin — harmless things, like walking home from English Lit. debates — but Enda was my first serious romance. I knew pretty quickly that he was the one; I don't know if he knew as quickly as I did. I also knew, however, that I had to finish my degree, as I had only completed one year.

After that summer, I went back to UCD and Enda would come up to Dublin to see me. It was quite intense and I would go home on a more regular basis because I had something to go home for. When I was about 19, we made the joint decision that we would break up for a while and see what happened. I don't remember being upset about it, so it must have been a mutual decision. We decided we should 'play the field' for a bit, just to see if what was between us was real. Looking back now, I suppose it was a pretty modern way of approaching the relationship. Before Enda had met me, he had had a girlfriend and I used to tease him about her. She was away doing a Physical Education course, which was very glamorous and up-to-the-moment, I thought.

During the period when we temporarily broke up, we both went out with other people, although not in a very serious way. I met a guy called Gerry O'Malley, who was a very well-known Roscommon footballer. He was quite a few years older than me, and very quiet and shy. We started to go on a few dates. From time to time, I would hear that Enda had been out with his girlfriend from before. Of course, we ended up getting back together again. I think we must have met somewhere and when we saw each other again, we knew that this was it.

I remember how Enda and I were out at something in Athlone — I must have been about 19 or 20 years old — and we both knew, without saying it, that we would be together for the rest of our lives. He asked me something like, 'We'll stay together won't we?' and I replied, 'Oh yeah, yeah.' And he then said, 'You know what I mean, don't you?' I told him that I did, and I asked, 'Forever?' and he said 'Yes'. I don't think he actually said the words, 'will you marry me?' and there was certainly no going down onto one knee or anything like that.

In those days, there was no such thing as living in sin — absolutely not. Now, you went pretty near to the edge from time to time, but you didn't take the final step. We are talking about 1950s Ireland, where the worst thing that could happen to a young, unmarried woman was to get pregnant. That really was the very worst thing — worse than failing exams or falling out with your parents or people throwing stones at you! I had sufficient awareness of the facts of life to know that it was very easy to tip into, and while we had a very sexual relationship, we always stopped short. It was constant self-denial, which was very frustrating. But you knew you had to wait until you had been to the church and had the ring firmly on your finger.

Meanwhile I was nearing the end of my time at UCD. In my final year, I studied Old and Middle English texts, such as *Beowulf* and Chaucer and so on, which were of great interest to me because of my background in Latin. I also loved Wordsworth. There were only 12 in my English class, among them the late Gus Martin, who would later become renowned as author and editor of some key educational texts, including the seminal *Soundings* poetry anthology for Leaving Cert.

I got an Honours BA, which was regarded as a good degree. When I was preparing for my final exams, a delegation from Newfoundland came over: it was like a hiring fair, and they were looking for people to teach over there. I went for an interview, and lo and behold, I was offered a job as a teacher in Newfoundland. I came home and told my parents that I was going to teach in another country. 'Well, you certainly are not!' said my father. Years later, I remember telling that story on RTÉ Radio 1 and afterwards getting a letter from a fella — a real Fine Gaeler, I assume — which simply said, 'Pity you didn't go to Newfoundland'!

Anyway, I didn't take the opportunity. My sister, who was four years older than me and had trained in hotel management, had recently married and was no longer running the Hodson Bay for my father as previously. He told me he had a job for me now and that I could take over from Anne. So I stayed at home and worked in the hotel for a good salary, also helping out my brother Paddy in the haulage business he had just set up. I had Enda in Athlone too of course, and that was all I wanted in my life. And I was delighted to be in my home town again.

| CARPE DIEM

I was 22 and Enda was 24 when we got married. Enda did the traditional thing and spoke to my father. My father was in Dublin on business and Enda and I went there and got the ring and then we met him for lunch in a place called The Bailey, which was a classy pub-cum-hotel. Enda told him, 'I want to marry Mary', and luckily my father agreed to it. Naturally, we got married in my local parish church and had the reception in the Hodson Bay Hotel. We went for two weeks' honeymoon to the Channel Islands, which was an unusual choice in those days. We had a lovely time, and the first morning we opened our door to happen upon another couple from Athlone who were staying only two doors down from us! I still remember that. We hired a car and went everywhere there was to go and did everything there was to do.

When we came home, we lived for a month in the Hodson Bay Hotel, as we were in the process of building the house which was to become our family home, and in which I still live to this day. My father had a couple of sites on the same road and he gave us one as a present, which was fine. We needed a county council loan to build the house, as I wasn't working at that time, and Enda was earning £10 a week with a wholesaler, Michael Hanley, in Athlone, working as a seller from the vans. He would take orders from the shopkeepers and then deliver to them when all was ready. We borrowed £2,200 from the council, to be paid off at £2 2s a week, which sounds quaint now no doubt, but was a huge amount of money in those days and in fact the maximum you could borrow at the time.

Once we got married, Enda and I wanted a family. My two brothers and sister had each married in their turn and within the year they all had had their first child, with child number two arriving the following year. So I thought it was only a question of getting married and you would have children as a matter of course. However, it isn't always the case, and it didn't work out like that for me. It wasn't because we weren't trying — we had a very active sexual life — but it just didn't happen. We used to wonder why, and every month I would think I would get pregnant, but I didn't. I didn't start to worry for about two years. We had a great social life and were very much enjoying ourselves. I remember how on Sundays, we would fly out of the house at 10 a.m. and not come back until midnight — we would drive to different towns and eat in hotels, and we thought we were wonderful and had a great life. And we did have a fantastic married life from the very start. I look back on our early years now with great joy. We had no responsibilities whatsoever: imagine — 22 and 24, and no responsibilities at all!

When we were about three years married and there was still no sign of a baby, I decided it was about time to do something about it. I went to my local GP, Dr Jim Keane, and he made an appointment for me to see a man called Éamon De Valera, who was the most eminent gynaecologist in Ireland. I can still remember the day I went to Dublin to see him. I was really quite modern: I went up on the train and then got a taxi. I can vividly remember sitting in the waiting room, surrounded by other women. I went in and told the great man my tale: that I was married and that we had satisfactory sexual relations. He asked me how often. How often? How often *not*!

Dr de Valera was a lovely man. He did all the examinations, including an internal and told me I would become pregnant soon; that he had no doubt about it. That must have been a standard line of his, but it gave me such great courage and hope. I remember thinking to myself, to his mind no doubt, a healthy 25-year-old girl and 27-year-old fella were sure to get pregnant. But they're not, and you read about fertility problems more and more now — but it was not publicly discussed then. We are talking about 1960s Ireland so needless to say, we had to keep this to ourselves: it was our secret. Enda had to go and give a semen sample in the Mater, where Dr de Valera had a clinic. Looking back now, I think, wasn't Enda marvellous to do it? Most guys wouldn't have done such a thing, especially in those days. I remember how, when

Enda got a letter saying that his semen was 100 per cent mobile, he exclaimed, 'Yippee!' and was most pleased with himself.

Dr de Valera had given us a thermometer so that we could take my temperature, and when it came to mid-month and my temperature rose, we knew we were supposed to make love then. Making love to order never suited us, however, and Enda used to say 'Oh God!' when I would announce to him in the middle of the day that we had to go to bed. It wasn't as nice because it wasn't spontaneous. Within six months, however, I found out that I was pregnant and I was very happy. So that ended that trauma in our lives for the time being — but I always think how well we managed it together.

At the start of my pregnancy, we went back to Dr de Valera and followed up on all the advice. I thought my bump would never get bigger: I couldn't wait for it all to happen, and wanted to be bigger and bigger and bigger. I had my son Feargal in Dublin's Hatch Street Maternity Home. Dr de Valera was my gynaecologist for the birth: it was the August Bank Holiday Monday and I can still remember him coming in, wearing his tennis shorts. Feargal was born on 3 August 1964. I had a very easy birth — I went in at 3 p.m. and I had him at 5 p.m. — but I do recall screaming during labour and the nurse saying to me, 'Oh please, you are going to upset the whole nursing home!' There were no such things as injections or the like: you just had your baby — not like now. On the other hand, I was kept in for ten days after the birth, as if I was sick, while now you are lucky to be allowed to stay two nights at the most!

Feargal was a lovely child, but very cross and crying all the time. I breastfed for a short while — maybe two weeks or so. I did my best, but it just didn't work out. When I first came home with my beautiful baby, I thought I had it made. I felt I had fulfilled myself. Most women feel the same, I think, because I believe that as a woman, you are programmed to have children — in my opinion that is the way your hormones operate and your body cycles move.

Looking back now, it is clear that I suffered from postnatal depression, but didn't know what it was, as nobody talked about such things in those days. I remember sitting in the living room with Feargal on my knee and the tears coursing down my face, and Enda coming home and saying, 'This can't be right, that you are crying — we have a lovely baby and a nice home', and so on. Reading about postnatal depression now, it is obvious I had all the typical symptoms. I had longed for a child and I now had a beautiful son — give me an Irish mother who doesn't want a son — I had everything I wanted, a loving husband, a lovely home, a delightful baby, and I was crying about it! I just felt that I would never get on top of it, of minding him. Gone were our lovely Sundays, and now I had to mind this little baby, who was crying morning, noon and night. I didn't feel the wealth of love I should have felt for him. But I got out of it very well, fortunately. Enda spoke to Dr Keane, who came to visit me. He referred me to a psychiatrist in Dublin: a nice, helpful man, who said that I had post-natal depression, and that I was a classic case. He gave me medication, which I took and I met him two further times, after which he told me that I had fully recovered. In all, it must have lasted for about four months and thankfully, I have never had any episodes of depression since.

I thought that once you had one child, they would just keep coming: that it was a matter of having babies to order. Particularly since my two brothers and my sister continued to have more children: they were all very fertile. But it didn't happen with me, and about two years after Feargal was born, I said to Enda, 'Isn't it funny there's no sign of another baby?'

When Feargal was three, we arranged for me to go back to Dr de Valera. I was still a young woman — I was only 30, for God's sake. The doctor did more examinations and then said that it could be that I might not have any more babies. I think he was a wily old fox and that, from the internal examinations and other tests, he knew more than he was letting on to me. He told me I might not be a very fertile woman and he asked me if we had thought of adoption. Afterwards I went back home to Enda and told him all this, saying that I would like us to adopt. Enda felt the same, so I went back to Dr de Valera and he began to set things in motion for us. It was all to be arranged through the St Patrick's Adoption Society in Dublin. We told our respective parents and families and were happy to go along with all the initial formalities. My brother Brian's wife, Ann Lenihan, was particularly supportive during this whole process and came along with me on many of the exploratory visits. She was and has remained a true woman friend to me.

Not very long afterwards — or so it seemed anyway — Dr de Valera contacted me to say that he had a client who was single and pregnant and that the background would suit us well. And then, on 4 September 1968, he rang me and told me that we had a baby son. I was delighted, because I had already been rearing a son and reckoned I would know what to expect. We went to Dr de Valera's clinic on the appointed day to collect our new son. Feargal, who was four at the time, came with us. There was a nurse there also, as Aengus was just five days old. I think it was because he was so tiny — almost newborn — that I thought of him as my son from the very beginning. He was a beautiful baby — he has remained a very good-looking man — with a head of dark hair and gorgeous, swarthy skin. I just loved him from the minute I held him; so did Enda. As far as Feargal was concerned, we did all the right things without realising we were doing the right things, because he held the new baby as well the first time he met him.

The three of us took Aengus home and Enda's sister came over and there was lots of fussing over him. That evening we put the cot up in the corner and put Aengus in the cot. He was such a good child. Aengus didn't cry much as a baby (although he became more spirited as time went by!): it was almost as though he was just happy he had found his mother.

Adopting Aengus was a momentous thing to do. It was unusual enough to adopt in those days when you already had a child: most people who adopted didn't have children. I realise that I may have made the process sound less complicated here than it was at the time — there were undoubtedly procedures and bureaucracy to be negotiated — but it was nonetheless far simpler then than it is today. Of course Aengus knows all about it: we told him in stages as he was growing up. When he was a young child, I got a book from Barnados, *How to Talk about Adoption to your Child*. I told Aengus that I had been sick and not able to have another baby in my tummy, but that another mammy who was not sick had the baby for me. They say you should start to introduce a child to the idea early and explain more when they start to ask more questions.

As time went by, however, we never emphasised the issue and it never really came into our lives very much again. Years later, in the early 1980s when Aengus was in his late teens, it came out that you could trace your mother and that you had a right to do so and to make contact and meet, as long as your biological mother was willing. Aengus was in his first year in college, I remember, and he had a very bad bout of glandular fever and was ill for almost 12 months. All he could do was mooch around; he had no energy for anything else. At this time, I remember telling him that he could look for his biological mother if he wanted to — that we would not take it amiss and would understand completely if this is what he wished to do.

I did not even allude to the matter again until some years later, on the eve of Aengus' wedding to his lovely wife, Lisa. We were in my apartment in Dublin and I said to him, 'I am sure you have told Lisa about your adoption?' He replied, 'Of course, Ma, she knows all that.' I then asked him if he had ever looked for his birth mother, and he said at once, 'No Ma, I didn't. I thought about it, but who could have been as good to me as you and Enda were?!' And I thought, what a lovely thing to say to me.

I was always very close to my Dad — I suppose it was our shared interest in politics and English literature that was part of the strong bond between us. One evening, when Feargal was about two years old, my father called into our house with a copy of *The Irish Times*. Pointing out an ad for Maynooth College, he asked me, 'Do you see this?' It seemed that the college was opening its doors to external students — up until then, only student priests had been able to study there. The first such course they were offering was the Higher Diploma in Education, which could be completed within one year, and they were inviting applications from mature students who had a BA, B. COMM. or B. SC. AG. 'Would you be interested in doing an H. DIP.?' was my father's next question.

I think he felt guilty that he had truncated my continuing academic career by asking me to work in the hotel. Aside from the teaching possibility in Newfoundland, I had originally wanted to do Law after I got my BA: at that time, once you had graduated, you could do an LLB in one year. 'But who would mind Feargal?' I asked him. He offered then and there to cover the costs of taking on someone to look after Feargal, and to put petrol in my car every week for the drive to Maynooth. That night, I talked it over with Enda and he said that I should do it if I wanted to. Enda was a very modern thinker, fortunately for me. I put an ad in the local paper, saying, 'Person going to Maynooth to do H. Dip. invites others to make a carload'. Three people replied and the four of us went up to Maynooth four nights a week, each of us taking our car in turn. On the journey back each time, we would have our own study seminars, comparing notes and swapping tips. Feargal was just beginning to talk and I can remember him saying, 'My mammy going to school'. Fortunately, I had been able to find a very good girl to mind him. I very much enjoyed doing the Diploma in Maynooth College. Years later, they would present me with a 'Maynooth Made Me' Award. We were so fortunate in our professor there, Brother O'Sullivan — a brilliant lecturer. Once I had completed my Diploma, I started to teach for a few hours in a local school. I had never really wanted to teach when I was growing up but once I started, I loved it. I would never have gone into public life if I hadn't done teaching.

When we adopted Aengus, I had to stay at home for a year, as you were not allowed to have any outside work during that time, so that you could give your full attention to the child. After my year out with Aengus, I went back to teaching, this time at St Peter's Convent. I stayed there for a year and then St Peter's closed and it was transferred to Summerhill, about two miles from Athlone. This was the time of Donogh O'Malley and the opening up of secondary education, and they were looking for teachers everywhere. When I started at St Peter's, they were so short-staffed that they were offering to pay for a housekeeper to look after my children, but of course I preferred to pay for my own childcare. As the kids got older and started going to primary school, I began teaching full-time. By this time, Latin wasn't a compulsory part of the curriculum any longer, and therefore I taught English and History. I relished teaching, particularly the constant interaction with young people, the privilege of being part of their growing-up years and the fun of the staff room.

My father died in 1970. He had served as a TD for Longford–Westmeath from 1965. After my father's death, I was asked to put forward my name as a candidate, but at the time, I declined. Later in my political career, some people would say that I walked into a seat because of my family connections, but that is incorrect. I did not 'walk into' my father's seat. As I have explained, since very early in my childhood, politics had been part of my life, and this continued to be the case throughout my teenage years and into my twenties and thirties. As a young schoolgirl, I was a dedicated member of the local Macra Fáil, as the youth branch of Fianna Fáil was then known: literally 'the young men' of Fianna Fáil. (This would later be given the more politically correct name of 'Ógra Fianna Fáil', i.e., 'young people of Fianna Fáil'). I remember helping out after school and in the holidays, in the company of other young devotees, sticking labels or stamps onto envelopes for posting. Politics had always been part of the family discourse and ambience, and at the time of my father's death, I was the Fianna Fáil Secretary, the Comhairle Ceantair, for my district. I was very much involved in politics and keen to become even more involved. If my father's death acted as a catalyst as regards my political career, it was in the sense that it made me even more aware of my desire to be deeply engaged in this area of life and the community. My family and I were Fianna Fáil: I neither knew nor dreamt of any other kind of politics.

At the 1974 elections, I was put forward as a local candidate. When I was canvassing in that election, I was Mary O'Rourke — I was never known as Mary Lenihan. The town was small and people would have known me. When I called at the houses of St Peter and Paul's Terrace, the kids who came to the door would say, 'Mammy, Teacher is at the door', so it was the teaching that helped. There had been one formid-able woman who had run before me in Westmeath — Aileen Mallon — but otherwise there were very few women putting themselves forward at that time. I was only in my mid-thirties then. I had great support from fellow political friends such as John Butler, who, I remember clearly, first came out canvassing with me at the tender age of 17. John and his wife Mary would later be amongst our closest friends. Again, I was so lucky, as Enda was very progressive and all for me going into politics. Now, he wouldn't have gone out canvassing, but he would ask people in the local pub to vote for me and use his other networks to gather support for me.

I can very well remember getting elected to Athlone Town Council in 1974. I don't think I ever had as big a thrill: for your own townspeople to elect you is a huge thing. I became a very committed local politician. During those early years, I was subsequently elected as Chairperson of the Town Council, which was a big accolade.

The town council had a nominee to the board of the then Regional College, which was still in its fledgling state. I asked Seán Fallon, the leader of our group on the council, for that board nomination. Although he was sadly not there to see the college open its doors in 1971, my father had during his time as a TD been a key figure in pushing for Athlone to be chosen as one of the sites for a Regional College. I had followed its evolution with great interest and felt that if I were to be involved in the board, I would be helping to further the work my father had started. The Fianna Fáil Party agreed and I took up my role with great gusto.

Also on the Athlone College Board was Labour's Tim McAuliffe, who had been a soldier-in-arms with my father when the college was being mooted and had also been Chairperson of Westmeath Vocational Educational Committee (VEC), which oversaw the launch of the college. Paddy Russell, a Fianna Fáil nominee from Westmeath County Council, was Chairperson of the Board and I was Vice-Chairperson. We had a small, tight membership and I greatly enjoyed those early years of my involvement. Indeed, when Paddy Russell departed to become a Tax Commissioner, I assumed the role of Chairperson.

Now remember, I was still quite a novice in public matters, but I worked hard at my brief. I never went to a council or board meeting without having fully read the relevant papers and so I was able, I hoped, to contribute with intent to every discussion that was held. It was a great apprenticeship for my later career in public life. I also partook in many an interview board and I found that extremely worthwhile and an interesting way to meet a lot of new people.

This brings to mind an amusing anecdote from the next stage of my political journey, which was my election to Westmeath County Council in 1979. I had been serving on Athlone Urban District Council since June 1974, but I knew that this county council business was a more serious matter. Anyway, it was June 1979 and the night before I was due to attend my first county council meeting. I had duly ironed my blouse (as tops were then called), as well as the boys' shirts for school and taken care of all the other household tasks one generally has to do on a Sunday night in a busy household. I was finally able to sit down to read the latest issue of *Cosmopolitan*.

As I turned the pages, I happened on an article about going to your first board meeting, which struck a chord with me at once. The recommendation was that you should speak up at that first meeting, even if you didn't have much to say: this would 'break the ice', so to speak, and mean that you would not be nervous the next time you had to address the room. So, armed with this strong advice, off I travelled the next day to Mullingar, the county capital (though we in Athlone quite plainly regard Athlone as the capital!). Anyway, I duly arrived in Mullingar, to be greeted by our party Whip on the county council, Deputy Seán Keegan, a well-respected senior Fianna Fáil politician. He had, he said, a bit of advice for newcomers like me: you should never speak on your first day, but you should wait about six months and then make an intelligent intervention, in the meantime simply observing all that's going on.

Going into that council chamber, I was already in a dilemma, weighing up these two pieces of conflicting advice in my mind. On the one hand, there was the recommendation of *Cosmopolitan*, read in the comfort of my own home on the night before: 'speak up at your first board meeting'; on the other, the wise counsel of the tried and trusted Fianna Fáil whip: 'whatever you do, don't speak for about six months'. We all sat down and our name cards were duly put in front of us: 'Councillor Mrs Mary O'Rourke' was on mine. Obviously, I was a junior member but everyone was most friendly, and I didn't feel in any way diminished or intimidated as I looked down at the agenda for the meeting. Seeing that there was an item on housing, I said to myself, 'Oh, I know something about houses. I live in one and I run one!'

When Item no. 5 — Housing — came around, I put my hand up and the Chairperson, a kindly man also named Keegan, said, 'Oh, Councillor O'Rourke wishes to speak.' With that, all heads turned in my direction and all 23 pairs of eyes rested on my face. I could feel the blush rising in me and my knees atremble. However, I reminded myself that as a teacher, I had already faced down much bolder recalcitrant pupils, so up to my feet I got and said some brief words about housing, based on what I knew about the matter. When I had finished speaking, there was a little murmur of general approval throughout the room and I knew I had made it. I had taken the initiative, I had spoken, and I would never be afraid again. I recount all of this here because I firmly believe that when an opportunity comes to one, the initiative should be taken.

As a scholar and one-time teacher of Latin, I have always felt that it is the famous adage from the Roman poet, Horace, which best sums up this philosophy: 'Carpe diem' — 'Seize the day'. Or, even more poetically, that line from Robert Herrick, the seventeenth-century English poet: 'Gather ye rosebuds while ye may, Old Time is still a-flying . . .' It is an attitude which has stood me in good stead at certain key moments throughout my life in politics.

My next major venture was in 1979, when I put myself forward for the Fianna Fáil National Executive, which was of course a big deal in political terms. I canvassed hard and used my family connections. My brother Brian Lenihan was in politics of course and by this time had been in the Dáil as a TD and Cabinet Minister for a number of years. Through him, I had been able to get to know many people at national level. Then as now, there were two ways to accede to Executive level: either via a vote on the floor of the Ard Fheis or by being nominated by the County Executive for your area. I went for the first option, and was over the moon when my bid was successful. I remember thinking, this is heaven, being on the National Executive! My brother Paddy was also elected, via the County Roscommon Executive. He and I used to go to monthly National Executive meetings together, along with Áine Kitt (later to become Áine Brady TD), who had been elected from County Galway. The three of us would duly meet beforehand on the first Thursday of every month in the yard of the Prince of Wales Hotel in Athlone. And of course my brother Brian, as General Secretary of the party, was also on the Executive at this stage.

Next, in August 1981, I made a successful bid for the Seanad. This too had come about as a result of my 'carpe diem' approach to life and politics. I had been at a Fianna Fáil National Executive meeting one day, when Charlie Haughey, who was leader at that time, had announced, 'We are short someone to go for the Cultural and Educational Panel. Is there anyone in this room who thinks that they are cultured and educated?'

And do you know what I did? I put up my hand and I said, 'I do.'

Haughey said, 'Right, Mary O'Rourke, so you can run on that panel, okay?'

It was that simple to run, but of course I then had to go and get the votes. I managed to do so however, and the first day I walked through the gates of Leinster House as a Senator was certainly an occasion to remember for me. I started to speak at every debate I could possibly participate in and I soon discovered that I was well able to put across my point of view, and that I could have an influence with what I said. I talked a lot on different Bills — especially educational Bills — as well as many other areas of concern. I talked a lot. At an early stage, I became Seanad Spokesperson for Education. That first six months we were under a Fine Gael government, with John Boland as Minister for Education. I remember him bringing two separate Bills along, one of them concerning the National Council for Curriculum and Assessment (NCCA). I had plenty to say on these issues and many others besides.

As soon as I got into full-time politics, as a member of the Seanad, I left teaching, and I didn't ever contemplate getting a teacher's pension. I didn't take a sabbatical or leave of absence — I just left. At the General Election in February 1982, I went for the Dáil but I didn't make it, so I put myself forward once more for the Seanad. I had to go around to all the local councillors and knock on their doors and say, 'I am Mary O'Rourke and I am going for the Educational Panel.' That was hard work, but I had a lot of moral and practical support from Enda, as well as from Mícheál Ó'Faoláin, Pat Kelly and Seamus Browne, all of whom have remained my great friends to this day. My second bid for the Seanad was successful: in fact, I got a huge vote. I wasn't too disappointed at that stage that I had not got into the Dáil, because, there too, I had very good voting figures which clearly augured very well for the next time. I also knew the February 1982 government was unstable and that it was likely that there would be another election soon. And six months later in November, this is what indeed transpired.

| MARLBOROUGH STREET

I got into the Dáil as a TD in November 1982. I remember clearly now how it rained for the entire three weeks of the election campaign. Each evening I would come home, soaked to the skin. Enda had set up a great HQ at our house, and every night there would be people there, checking off the registers and so on. No matter the weather, however — we had a very successful campaign and achieved a great result for me. In broader terms, we were now in Opposition to a Fine Gael–Labour coalition government, which was of course not so positive, but at least I felt that I would now be in a strong position to play an active part in strengthening the Fianna Fáil hand.

The three men in my life — Enda, Feargal and Aengus — came with me for my first day in the Dáil on 14 December 1982. We drove through the gates of Leinster House and went in, and they were all three in the gallery as the names of the newly elected TDs were called out. These were announced constituency by constituency and when it came to the turn of Longford–Westmeath, and my name was called, I remember thinking, 'I am a TD now!' It was at once a very exciting thought and a sobering realisation. I always took my duties of representing the people very seriously. Throughout my career, I continued to regard it as a very big responsibility, by virtue of the fact that the people had put their faith in you and that therefore you had to keep faith with them. Maybe it was that awareness which kept me on the straight and narrow; maybe it was also partly the fact that I had been a teacher, a role which brings with it a great sense of public responsibility.

That first day, after the formalities were over, Enda and the boys and I went into the dining room in the Dáil, which was very posh! There is a very good photograph of the four of us outside Leinster House that day, which later appeared in an article Bruce Arnold wrote for the *Irish Independent* about the new faces in the Dáil. In the picture, Enda, Aengus and I are smiling broadly, but Feargal, then a young man of 18, looks thoughtful and somewhat downbeat, as if he could envisage the road ahead for me and for our family and could see the kind of pitfalls which might arise.

One of the first items on the agenda for the newly formed Dáil was a debate on the committee system. John Bruton, who had been appointed by Dr Garret FitzGerald as Leader of the House (a post which was not continued thereafter), and who was charged with setting up the committee system, invited us all to participate in the ensuing discussion. I was sure to take the opportunity to voice my views on this occasion, remaining true to the strategy suggested in that *Cosmo* article of so many years previously, which had worked so well for me in the past — that if you speak early, you will lose your terror and be able to speak more easily the next time.

Here follows the complete transcript of that first speech I made in the Dáil, on 27 January 1983. Reading it back again almost 30 years later, I am struck by the extent to which much of what I was saying is still so highly relevant to political life today.

First of all, I am very pleased that it is on such a topic as Dáil reform that I have the opportunity to make my first speech in this assembly. Like many of the speakers from all sides of the House, most of whom I listened to yesterday, I am of the opinion that the present Minister has done a service, not alone to the House but to the nation at large, in bringing this very important topic to the floor of the House. In my span of public service at local authority level, at Seanad level and now at Dáil level, I am struck by one factor: that the public perception of people in public life is not good. However much we have contributed to that perception, however much of it has grown among the people themselves and however much the administration and day-to-day running of both the Seanad and Dáil institutions have contributed to it, they have all [had] their input, but we must play our part in rectifying this situation.

In my other life, when I was a secondary school teacher, I had occasion from time to time to bring groups of young people to this Chamber. When we would be travelling back home by bus or train, I was always struck by one factor. These young people never saw the Dáil as having any relevance to their lives. These would be girls of the age group of 16, 17 and 18 years, approaching voting age and the time when they would become citizens of their country in their full right. These pupils would leave school with 'A' and 'B' levels and the trappings that are taken as making a successful person nowadays — I would have my own remarks about that in another context — yet they would have no idea of how the Dáil system worked. Their visit here would not have given them any confidence in that system. They would go home without any further enlightenment. They saw the Dáil as a place where people came in and talked to an empty Chamber about unintelligible things which had no relevance to everyday life.

I see this debate as the start of making this Dáil assembly, with all its great importance in our history and its pivotal importance in our lives — and it must remain of pivotal importance — highly relevant to us. We can no longer afford the luxury of the present-day system in the Dáil. If we continue as we are, we have only ourselves to blame, if we become like the characters in *Alice in Wonderland*.

Much of the discussion document which the Minister presented to us yesterday is practical and, given the broad acceptance which this debate has achieved already, many of the points can be implemented without undue delay. I refer first of all to the points which seem to have been accepted among the speakers who spoke yesterday and today. The broadcasting of the debates in the Chamber would achieve much more care by speakers in their contributions in the Dáil. It would lead to much more thought being put into those contributions because one will know that at any given time, one can be heard over the airwaves. It would lead to a tightness in contributions.

This leads me to the second point, which the Minister touched upon in an underlying way. I refer to the length of the contributions. I do not want to appear presumptuous in my first speech, but as a result of my Seanad experience, I feel that too often people get to their feet to talk on and on, perhaps experiencing vicarious satisfaction, and of course there is always local consumption of what is presented in the media, but to continue to talk for the sake of doing so is ridiculous. I do not know whether the Minister envisages a cut-off point for contributions in debates, but I think it would be highly desirable. Apart from doing away with irrelevancies, it would allow many more people to contribute. Often I have sat in the Seanad, and probably it will be the same in the Dáil, hoping and hoping to get in while the debate went on and on. Therefore, a cut-off point would be highly important.

The committee system is the salient factor of this discussion document. I have read and re-read what the Minister has said about it, and I have read also about the experiences of the parliamentary system pertaining in Westminster. Generally speaking, the committee system appears to be a more effective way of running the nation's day-to-day business than the sometimes long-winded debates in the Dáil. I would like to enter a caveat on this point. There has been much talk of consensus politics and having the committee system whereby important issues of the day, particularly social structures and planning and also financial planning, would be discussed by Members of the House on all sides. This is highly important. I do not want to carp but I want to make the point that in a democracy, healthy tensions are very important. Naturally there must always be a Government, but also there must be an alternative Government with a coherent, planned Opposition policy. I would like to see a balance kept always and that the committee system would not be seen as everything being agreed upon. Listening to the speakers yesterday would give the impression that life would be very happy, and everybody would live very happily when the committee system would have had its say and we would all come in with set formulae to answer the problems of the day. Of course, life is not really like that, and perhaps that is just as well. It is important that the healthy tensions between Opposition and Government be always maintained, although not in a destructive sense. With other speakers I abhor utterly constant adversary politics, whereby because Minister Bruton would say something, Deputy Mary O'Rourke would say 'No, I do not agree with that'. That is silly and to the young people, it is outmoded and outdated. The normal, differing ideologies and intentions of the political parties and their different sets of policies should be allowed expression and the debate should take place following on the committee system. This is very important for democracy and we should keep it very firmly in our minds.

The second point, an underlying philosophical one, arising out of the discussion document presented by the Minister, is that if we discuss Dáil reform, we are in effect discussing Deputy reform: we are talking about ourselves. There has been much comment recently on radio and television that Dáil Deputies should be legislators, that they are getting their roles mixed and that we are being seen primarily as people who just go out to get things for people who would normally [not] get them, that we should be legislating and thinking of it. Both points of view are right. That is what I intend to do in, I hope, my long Dáil career, but I also believe that if we immune ourselves in the Dáil Chamber and we sit on committees and find ourselves talking to one another for ever, there is a slightly unreal atmosphere in that. When we find ourselves in this Chamber, in the corridors around this House and in committee rooms, we can grow in on one another and think that this is life, that life is Dublin, Dáil Éireann and Seanad Éireann. Life is part of this, but it is also down the country among your people, hearing their points of view.

How can I effectively contribute to a committee on education, in which I am interested, or on the environment and housing, which is my greatest interest, unless I have been listening to people, hearing what has gone wrong with their entitlements and what they want to see in house grants, loans, building, construction and roads? Each Deputy must get the feedback from people before he or she can come into this Chamber or go into a committee system and give their views. It is only by intermingling with people that one can do this. I would like this point to be on record. The Minister has not said anything about this but it arises out of his discussion document, which is the underlying philosophy of the role of a TD as perceived by the people, the media, but, most of all, as perceived by ourselves. If we ignore the highly relevant everyday life of people for what is, too, highly relevant, the committee system and the Dáil system, and we do not merge the two things, we will have lost an essential element of what must go into it. We must be practical in our legislation and we must not be in a cloud up in the sky.

Another point I want to make is in relation to the very valid point brought up yesterday about holidays … [Deputy Séamus Brennan] said he would like to see the Dáil holidays broken up into sections so that we would not appear to be away from our jobs for a long time, which is wrong if we are to govern the country and to be seen to govern it. The Minister spoke about the Estimates and about how it is ridiculous that we talk about the money when it has already been allocated. That is like a housewife going out to do her shopping when the money is gone and she cannot say what she can put into the supermarket trolley on that particular Friday. The same is true about the Estimates.

He brought up the point about the New Zealand example, where members of the House of Parliament can interject, not in an argumentative sense, but having five minutes on a discussion point, which can be taken up by another member and by the Minister and brought back when the point is clarified, so that the member who originally made the point could then stand up and contribute to it again. This is an ongoing debate where the member can [have] his or her input into that debate. This is very good because very often when one stands up and contributes to a debate, a very relevant point comes up later in the debate and one cannot get in again and answer that, because one has already spoken. The rules of the debate which state that you can only speak once and you cannot speak again [apply to] many of the debates which take place here.

I am in agreement with more time for Private Members' Questions, where matters of very important interest can be dealt with on a more relevant day-to-day basis. The Member would then have the satisfaction of having what was to him or her a very important matter discussed at that point.

With regard to future legislation and the committee system, I believe the Minister means that we would have at our disposal experts in various fields, who would come to the committees and give us their points of view. That is important because very few of us are experts in any particular field. It is important to call on the expertise of people who have spent many years in management, health services, the environment and many other fields. That can be very good for legislators. Existing legislation very often needs re-vamping. The Minister should look into this matter to see if it is possible, along with his hoped-for committee system for future legislation, to have a rethink on past legislation whereby it could be amended and brought again to the floor of the House to keep pace with what has occurred in the meantime. We are [in] a very fast-moving society and we appear to be two steps behind everyday life.

I must now take my own words to heart and not go on and on. The salient points of my speech are that the healthy tensions must remain between the Government and the Opposition. I welcome the committee system and the broadcasting of the debates. I am very glad as a new Member to have made my first speech on what I will be glad to say to my electorate, half of whom are young people, which is the case in all constituencies: 'Yes, I am your TD, I came to the Dáil as your messenger to relay what you have said to me.' The most important message I got from my constituency of Longford–Westmeath is this: 'Make your job more relevant: tune it, sharpen it, bring it to the point and make it more in touch with everyday life.'

I welcome the Minister's report.

I had another chance to reap the benefits of my 'carpe diem' mantra one Sunday afternoon in January 1983, in what I would realise later was to be a defining moment in my career in politics. In the early days of the New Year, Charlie Haughey as our leader had undergone another 'heave' and had won through once more. The next step for him was to choose his Shadow Cabinet. Anyway, it was a Sunday afternoon and I was at home when the telephone rang. I had been cooking the lunch, while Enda read the Sunday papers; the boys were out at football or rowing or some other sport. We had that most modern of marvels — or so it was in those days — an extension from the hall telephone to the kitchen. So I picked up the phone and took the call in the kitchen. 'Hello,' I said, 'Yes, it is Mary O'Rourke. Oh, hello, Mr Haughey, good afternoon.' (Needless to say at that stage, as a greenhorn in the Dáil, I always addressed him as Mr Haughey.) I knew that Enda could hear me and could imagine him cocking his ears to listen at this point, but obviously only my side of the conversation was audible to him.

In any case, Charlie Haughey it was, and he said to me, 'Tomorrow I am forming my Shadow Cabinet and I want you up here for 11 a.m. — I am going to make you Shadow Minister for Women's Affairs.'

Without giving it a second thought, I responded immediately, 'Thank you for the offer. But I don't want to be Minister for Women's Affairs.'

'Oh! And why not?' he said.

'Of course, I think Nuala Fennell' — Nuala was Fine Gael's Cabinet Minister for Women's Affairs at the time; she and I had befriended each other back in the 1970s — 'a very fine woman. But I don't want to be put in a cupboard, with "Women's Affairs" on a label on the door and to only get out whenever there are women's affairs to be discussed. I will always be discussing women's affairs, because I am interested in them and I am a woman — but I don't want to be pigeon-holed like that.'

'Oh, I see Missy,' said Haughey after a pause, 'Particular, aren't you?' And with that, he put down the phone.

Enda had gathered enough from what I was saying to deduce that I had somehow turned down the Taoiseach and, coming into the kitchen, he said, 'Well that's you f***ed then — you won't get another offer now, I can tell you!' So anyway time went on and we continued with our day, eating our lunch whenever the boys came back from their game and doing the usual Sunday things.

About three hours later, the telephone rang once more and it was Charlie Haughey again. 'Shadow Minister for Education, opposite Gemma Hussey, okay? Be in by eleven in the morning.' So there it was, I had been bold — but it wasn't until sometime later, when I had more experience in the Dáil that I fully realised just how bold I had been. To this day, whenever I think about or relate that incident, I still do not know from what part of my soul, mind or body I dredged up the idea and the audacity of that initial reply I made to Charlie Haughey on the Sunday afternoon in question. Yet wherever it came from, I did it and of course it shaped my life thereafter. It was an imaginative strike and one that I never regretted, as of course from then on, especially once I was appointed Minister for Education, my career took off in a big way. Once again, I see this story as an example of the importance of 'carpe diem', and as indicative of the way in which he who seizes the day can in fact win the day.

So there I was, duly elected as a TD for Longford–Westmeath, full of
hope and bounce and so much looking forward to my work in Dáil
Éireann. I went on to act as Shadow Minister for Education for four-
and-a-half years. It was very hard work. We would meet at 11 a.m. every
Tuesday. Charlie was every bit as rigorous with his Shadow Cabinet as
if it were a real Cabinet. There is no doubt that Haughey expected you
to work as hard as if you were a Minister in government. I really
revelled in the work, however. I enjoyed shadowing Gemma Hussey, a
very pleasant woman, with whom I have maintained warm relations
and indeed a friendship throughout the years. No doubt I made her life
hell on occasion, as she did mine at times too. But I like to think that
we both played the game as it then was, within the limits — she as a
full-blooded Minister and me as a full-blooded Shadow Minister.

———

In February 1987 the coalition of Fine Gael (under Garret FitzGerald)
and Labour came to an end in a messy way. Now blessed Garret in
retrospect often liked to represent this parting of the ways as a very
amicable one, insisting that they all remained great friends even as they
fell out. Perhaps it was the case, but what they presented to the public
seemed more like a rather acrimonious adieu, as Labour pulled out
over very necessary and indeed long overdue spending cuts.

Meanwhile, Fianna Fáil returned three out of four TDS in
Longford–Westmeath: Albert Reynolds, Henry Abbott and myself.
There had been a hugely entertaining incident involving Albert
Reynolds and me, which indeed he has delineated skilfully in his auto-
biography and which has gone down in political folklore as 'the Battle
of Tang'. Tang is a small village on the borders of Westmeath and
Longford, but technically it was part of my area for canvassing and
garnering the vote. On the last Sunday before the General Election of
February 1987, however, Albert and his cohort of followers decided they
were going to speak outside Tang Church after morning Mass. Since my
team and I had exactly the same plan, it seemed that we were set for an
almighty stand-off. I arrived at the church with my truck, my guys and
my microphone. Shortly afterwards, Albert arrived with his truck, his

guys and his microphone. We knew that the priest was nearing completion in the church because we had a scout going inside and keeping us informed. But we had no idea what was going to happen next — whether or not we were just going to go head-to-head and drown one another out, or whether someone would back down at the last moment. In the end, we both stepped back from the brink and agreed to stage a united front by addressing the church crowd from the same truck. Fortunately, we got a great reception from those assembled! I can't even remember now who got the most votes from Tang, but I know I was happy with the overall outcome and no doubt Albert was too.

While in that election, things in my part of the country had panned out very well for Fianna Fáil, it looked very uncertain as to whether we would win the day and Charlie Haughey would be returned as Taoiseach. The party had undoubtedly lost some important seats — a year earlier, Des O'Malley, Bobby Molloy and Mary Harney had left Fianna Fáil to set up the Progressive Democratic Party (the PDS), and of course that had affected the Fianna Fáil vote in some areas. But Charlie fought a great campaign. We had all of our position papers at the ready and a series of huge billboards in place in a timely fashion in the key locations. It was an election of the old style: Charlie barnstorming around the country; church gate meetings; intense canvassing day-by-day, night-by-night. Ultimately we emerged triumphant.

I had high hopes of being offered the job of Gemma Hussey, whom I had of course been opposite for over four years as Shadow Minister for Education. I knew very well, however, that I was still a rookie member of the Dáil and that there were many more in the pecking order ahead of me — but still, I had my dreams. The intervening weeks between the results of the election and the recalling of the Dáil were tense, with many forecasts in the papers and the media in general as to who would wear the crowns of Cabinet. One afternoon during this period, I was at work at my desk when I received a telephone call from Charlie Haughey's Private Secretary, Catherine Butler, inviting me to come over to see him. With my heart thumping, I duly made my way over and was ushered into Charlie's office. As always, he came straight to the point and offered me the post of Minister for Education. I could not believe my ears! However, my excitement was quickly tempered when Mr Haughey said to me, 'Now, I don't know if I am going to be appointed Taoiseach at all. It all depends on a few important Independent votes and in the main, it depends on Tony Gregory.' So whilst I had been offered the prize, I did not know if I would ever hold it.

On the fateful day of decision, we all filed into Dáil Éireann, where the usual spats began and the arguments raged back and forth. At the end of it all, Charlie Haughey emerged triumphant as Taoiseach, elected by Neil Blaney and Tony Gregory, with the casting vote of the Ceann Comhairle, Seán Treacy, the then Independent TD from Tipperary. So Fianna Fáil was in government — albeit a minority government, with Alan Dukes as leader of Fine Gael pledging to support us on condition that we adhered to a stringent financial path — the Tallaght Strategy — the one that he had wished to follow but had been deterred from by the Labour Party under the coalition government of the previous four years.

So we were off! That night, we went up to Áras an Uachtaráin and got our seals of office from the then President, Patrick Hillery, and again I was quite awestruck. My brother, Brian Lenihan, was also in government as Minister for Foreign Affairs, and it was noted that we were the first brother and sister ever to serve in Cabinet together. Such considerations were not at the forefront of my mind, to be honest. I had earlier gone over to the Department of Education in Marlborough Street, where the then Secretary, Declan Brennan, was waiting to greet me in the hall. I had to keep pinching myself to be able to believe that this was really happening — that I was now the Minister for Education.

Declan Brennan was a great, open, talkative man, very well regarded in civil service circles, and he and I were to chart our course together for the next few years in good tempo with one another. He brought me upstairs to my new office, and one by one, showed in the Assistant Secretaries to the Department of Education: the person in charge of Higher Education, the Secretary for Secondary Level Education, the person in charge of Primary, and so on and so forth. I thought they would never stop coming in and I remember saying to myself, how on earth will I remember all their names — how will I ever get to know them? But I kept my counsel, listened to everything and tried to remember as much as I could.

It must not be forgotten: I had never served in government before. I had never been through the portals of a Department before. I was from rural Ireland, albeit brought up in a political family and having won my spurs at two General Elections. I was finding it very hard to believe that I was now responsible for what I regarded and continue to regard as the most important portfolio in government. Each Assistant Secretary who came in presented me with a file giving me the details of the section of the Department of Education he (and they were all male) was responsible for: the facts, the figures and particularly the gloomy forecasts. These formidable files were piled up one after another on my desk and afterwards, I was left mulling over them, wondering how I was ever going to absorb all of the information in them.

That night, after the presentation of our seals of office, we had a brief Cabinet meeting in a stateroom of Áras an Uachtaráin, as is the custom. We were immediately told by the Taoiseach that we were facing into a very stringent financial situation. The spending Ministries — Health, Education and Social Welfare — were to be the most keenly targeted, Haughey asserted, and he concluded with an ominous warning, which I remember to this day: 'There will be blood on the carpets. It's going to be a tough time, folks, and if you don't like the heat, you'll have to get out of the kitchen.' I was just so junior, so untried, so green-horned, so naïve that I can tell you, I kept quiet at that initial meeting. On this particular occasion, it didn't seem like the time to put my usual rule of speaking up quickly into practice! I went back to my apartment that night, exhilarated and daunted at the same time, with my mind in a jumble. I felt that in what I had managed to achieve, Athlone had got its just reward. I felt proud and still very much overawed by what had been bestowed upon me.

However, grim reality was to set in very soon. In the period that followed, we had a series of further Cabinet meetings, day after day, each one laden with what seemed like increasingly dire financial news. Ray MacSharry of Sligo ('Mac the Knife', as he would soon become known) had been appointed Minister for Finance and it was clear from the off that he meant serious business. Each Minister was issued with a file containing details of the cuts which the Department of Finance wished to impose upon their respective Departments, along with more dire forecasts. Over a period of two to three weeks thereafter, a series of strong cutbacks were to be imposed immediately, over which really and truly we didn't have much choice: they were presented to us as a *fait accompli*. Of course you made your case against them as you could, but because the task was so huge and the time so short, neither Ray MacSharry nor Charlie Haughey listened to my bleatings or indeed to the bleatings of any of the other Ministers around the Cabinet table. I remember as a comic interlude one occasion on which Finance put forward the proposal that all trains for the West of Ireland should cease at Athlone!

During that time as Ministers for Health and Education, Dr Rory O'Hanlon and I were soldiers-in-arms together. We were in charge of two of the biggest spending Ministries and we were left in no doubt that these were where the financial axe was going to fall. Anyone who remembers Ireland in the late 1980s will recall that what is happening in cutbacks these days is mild compared to the hair shirts imposed upon all of us as Ministers by Mac the Knife. Intellectually, I knew that what we were embarking on was proper and correct if the country was to be saved from financial ruin, but another part of me registered that these cuts were going to be in my Department and that I as Minister would be held responsible for them, so you can imagine how I felt. As a former teacher, I knew the lingo and was all too aware of what these strictures from the Department of Finance would really mean in terms of teacher numbers, curriculum choices and overcrowded classrooms. So it was too for my colleague Rory O'Hanlon in Health. In a way, perhaps it wasn't such a good idea, putting a doctor in charge of the Department of Health and a teacher in charge of the Department of Education. We knew what the outcome would be. We could see only too well the forthcoming social, trade union, patient and parental unrest and what would unfold for us from this. But we had no choice but to put our noses to the grindstone and focus on day-to-day efforts at Cabinet to make our respective cases.

As regards Education and Health, it was clear that the main spending area was staff — teachers and doctors and nurses — and that inevitably, this was where cuts would somehow have to be made. Education costs could be cut by increasing the Pupil/Teacher Ratio (the PTR) and yet, despite all of the cutbacks my predecessor Gemma Hussey had imposed, she had steered clear of this one — and with good reason. My own teaching background informed me that this was a measure that would just not be worn by the teachers' unions. I knew in fact that parents wouldn't initially attach that much significance to the issue, until prodded to do so by the INTO, the Association of Secondary Teachers, Ireland (ASTI) and the Teachers' Union of Ireland (TUI), because to parents, if their child was in a classroom and being well taught, that was all that really mattered.

In April 1987, before the true implications of Ray MacSharry's proposed budget had become clear, I had to undertake my obligatory tour of the teachers' unions' Easter conferences. As a former teacher, I knew already that these conferences were like enormous bear pits, where the Minister was treated like a strange animal in a zoo — to be gazed at, pilloried, baited and in the end to be just plain put up with, until he or she went off to his or her next stop on the Via Dolorosa. Fortunately, I went along knowing that, if I had one strong thing going for me, it was that I had actual teaching experience myself and that I genuinely believed that teachers work hard and contribute much to society by their careful nurturing of a young person — particularly at primary level, I felt (even though my own professional experience had been at secondary level), when one takes over *in loco parentis*, so to speak. Also to my great advantage, I had my valued confidante, Margaret Walsh, who was a secondary school teacher in Dublin and an ex-president of ASTI, and whom, shortly after my appointment as Minister, I had asked to be my Advisor in the Department. To my delight, Margaret had accepted the position and there is no doubt that her presence and wise counsel greatly helped my passage through the ASTI conference and those of the other unions that Easter and in fact throughout my years in Education. Also of huge benefit was the good relationship I had built up during my time as a teacher with my own trade union, the ASTI, and with their then General Secretary, Kieran Mulvey. Kieran, whilst berating me as Minister as good as the next, was always careful to keep things cordial and courteous.

I cannot over-emphasise here the extent to which Ireland was not just in the financial doldrums, but in a financial wasteland. We found ourselves directionless in a vast tundra of national debt, over which the previous government had presided apparently helplessly for more than four-and-a-half years. Alan Dukes and John Bruton, as the two successive Ministers for Finance, had no doubt tried to rein in spending but because of the influence of Labour, were just not able to do so with any kind of effectiveness.

As I have said, the really big cuts Mac the Knife had in mind had not yet been formalised, and so that Easter at the conferences of the teachers' unions, I was given a fool's pardon, so to speak. I distinctly remember going to the INTO's Annual Congress in Ennis that year. As a school principal in a small rural school in County Clare, my paternal grandfather had been a firebrand union adherent, noted for his radical views and his sterling espousal of the INTO. In true Lenihan fashion, he had fallen out with the hierarchy and had had various spats with authority, so there was nothing new in the spark of anti-authoritarianism which was to re-emerge in our family in the following generations. All of this was mentioned in speeches at the conference and I felt a glow of fondness for my grandfather, who had in his own way blazed a trail, allowing me a safe entry to this, my first teachers' union conference. Luckily for me too, the ASTI were hospitable as well and politeness prevailed. The TUI, under the direction of Jim Dorney, were more watchful and wary, but the proceedings at their conference also passed off without difficulty that Easter.

This was all before the really bad news broke, of course. For me, the most painful financial decision endorsed by Cabinet in 1987 to 1988 was the proposal to change the PTR, leaving each teacher responsible for more pupils than heretofore. This proposed measure became known as the infamous '20/87' — a term which has never left my mind and still provokes a degree of dread in me to this day. (Circular number 20 was issued by the Department of Education in 1987, detailing changes in PTR.) It was announced that these strictures were to be imposed at primary, secondary and vocational level, and immediately huge uproar ensued. Of course I could not justify it on educational grounds, only on financial ones and that was proving very difficult. Even now, 25 years later, the present government is finding it difficult to explain to people why there have to be financial cutbacks. It was extremely sore indeed in 1987/88, and there were numerous talks and walks and a huge teacher gathering in Dublin, when the union members and others turned out in force to protest against the proposed change in the PTR.

A more vehement protest against the '20/87' proposals developed back in my home town. One particular Saturday, over 12,000 parents, teachers and children marched up to my very ordinary bungalow on my very ordinary road in Athlone, with banners and shouting and general clamour. As I watched, bemused, I found myself wondering whether this was to become a habitual Saturday occurrence. At one point, Enda and my two sons suggested that they could give expression to their entrepreneurial spirit by setting up a homemade burger bar on the open green opposite the house, but I quickly knocked that idea on the head!

As well as the crowds of protestors, present on that occasion too were the then national reporters on education: Christina Murphy of *The Irish Times*, John Walshe of the *Irish Independent* and Pat Holmes of the *Irish Press* as was. They were three great people on whom I would come to rely more and more, and who had always an unbiased, objective view of all that was going on in the field of education. I remember how, on the evening of that day, when the marchers had dispersed, Enda cooked a big roast of pork with crackling in our house. Christina Murphy and Pat Holmes had gone back to Dublin, but John Walshe was able to stay for a while to partake of the pork. The headline for the piece he ran following the protest was, 'Mary is a *cut* above the rest', which of course was a reference to the cuts in education and to what had gone on under previous Ministers — but I always privately took this too as a sign that John had enjoyed Enda's cooking! The same John Walshe is now Special Advisor to Ruairi Quinn, Minister for Education.

The following week, I got a call from the Chairperson of Athlone Chamber of Commerce, who asked if they could please have another march soon, as the shops had done really well that day. Many of the teachers were women, of course, and what would women do when they are in a strange town but go shopping! On a more serious note, the 12,000-strong crowd which invaded the streets of Athlone that day was an indication of how high feelings were running at the time.

But I held tough, as indeed we all did. I knew that my travails paled beside those of Rory O'Hanlon. Whatever the damage caused by cramming more pupils in under the tutelage of one teacher, it would be an even more serious matter if patients could not get access to hospitals. Yet it was clear that drastic cutbacks were necessary. Of course as time went on and as I got to know the Department better, I began to see where some cutbacks could have been made — not in an easier fashion — no cutback is ever easy — but perhaps more judiciously. Hindsight and experience are great things. But for now, it was the *rí rá*, the *ruaille buaille* and the constant deputations and the continual talks.

Fortunately, fate was to intervene in the shape of a mutual recognition by the unions and the government that the only way out of the dire financial circumstances in which we found ourselves was by working together, rather than against each other. Only through talks and continuing cooperation could a plan be determined, which would put the country on a more even keel financially now and for the future. Luckily, Peter Cassells, who was head of the trade union movement, was a very astute man — and steady, sane and sensible with it. Bertie Ahern was the then Minister for Labour, and he and the Taoiseach and the unions began in a tentative way to talk together to see if they could come up with a plan — a Programme for National Recovery (or PNR). There followed an endless series of talks between the trade unions and the government, known as the Social Partnership Talks. Later, in relation to various programmes, other key players were brought into the talks but in the beginning it was just the trade unions and the government, both sides fully convinced of the need to plan ahead in a realistic, problem-solving way and both going into it wholeheartedly. It was clear to all that there was no way out of the current situation other than a coming together of the various interests, a pay pause and a determination to work together to clear the miasma of Ireland's debt.

And so began the PNR, the first social partnership which highlighted among many other things the importance of Education and Health as the key tenets for a healthy future for the country. Of course, during these talks and consultations, the teaching unions along with all of the other various trade unions of the day seized their opportunity, and put forward that the proposed Pupil/Teacher Ratio cutbacks should not take place. However, Education and I were saved by the bell, so to speak, in that when the school year began that autumn, the cuts were not as first envisaged and gradually the suggested PTR changes fell by the wayside, first in disadvantaged schools and then all over. The main capital cutbacks and all of the other attendant strictures on spending were to be held to, however, and Mac the Knife got ready to introduce a lethal second budget.

It was in the run-up to Easter 1988 that the Taoiseach and the trade unions, along with Padraig O'hUiginn, Secretary General to the Department of An Taoiseach, and Declan Brennan, Secretary to my Department of Education, prepared to finally formalise the various measures to be taken under the PNR, which would relieve a degree of the pressure on many interest groups and introduce a sense of coordination in how the way forward could be charted. After a difficult and at times very fraught week, it was Good Friday before all was signed and sealed.

I was due to embark the following Easter week on my second tour of the teacher conferences. This time, I was to have a far more difficult ride than the previous year. As the details of the new PNR arrangement had not yet been fully worked out, let alone made public, most members at the conferences thought that the changes to the Pupil/ Teacher Ratio, with its draconian effects, were still to be implemented. My first conference was with the INTO on Easter Tuesday in Salthill, and there I got the silent treatment. The INTO Secretary, Joe O'Toole — later Senator Joe O'Toole — was a formidable foe but a decent guy. Prior to the event, he had phoned me and Margaret Walsh, to tell us what kind of reception we should be expecting at the forthcoming meeting — the members had agreed that there was to be no booing, but there would be absolutely no clapping and no welcome either — just total silence.

Nevertheless, I went along as planned. I wasn't particularly upset at the prospect of being greeted by silence — to anyone involved in political life as I was, this can seem like a reprieve: no heckling to be borne, after all! As I mounted the platform and took my place, the room was absolutely quiet. After the president had given his opening address, it was my turn to speak. I stood at the podium. Something which always stood me in great stead in public life was the fact that I have a good, strong voice. This comes mainly, I think, from my teaching days. I was also lucky to never have to rely on a script when speaking: I would read over the text of a speech a couple of times beforehand and then be able to stand up, look out at an audience, and speak fluently and without hesitation. This is a great attribute for a politician and one that is well worth cultivating.

In any case, I stood there in front of the gathered might of the INTO members, said all I had to say and sat down to total silence — but to my mind, that was a relief rather than a penance. Then, as the session was breaking up for lunch, I stood up at the microphone once more and thanked the INTO for their invitation to join them for lunch, saying that I was delighted to accept — which led to a few gasps from the audience. I held my nerve and left the stage, determined not to be shunted out. I made sure to stop and talk to a number of the delegates on the way out. Among these were teachers from Clare and from Westmeath, who broke the taboo and talked to me, shaking my hand and wishing me luck — much to the chagrin of the top platform.

When I got outside that hall, I breathed a huge sigh of relief that I had passed that test! This gave me the strength I needed to go on to attend the conferences of the ASTI and the TUI, and deal head on with the varying degrees of distrust, disbelief and worry with which their members confronted me. In time, as my experience as a Minister grew and the stringency of the financial situation began to ease, I would go on to forge strong working relationships and in some cases bonds of friendship with many of the union members. After all, we were all in the one boat — we all had to work together — and I was a strong believer in keeping relationships vibrant and productive with what could have been warring factions. Fortunately, this turned out not to be the case. I had a strong propensity within me for trade unions, and my ability to relate to them was consolidated by the fantastic work of Margaret Walsh, my Advisor. Margaret was also always adept at buttressing me against bad news, and all in all managed my course in such a terrific way. We became firm friends and have remained such ever since.

The budgets of the late 1980s were truly lethal — spending for every Department was cut back ruthlessly and relentlessly, and as I said earlier, when people talk about the cutbacks being implemented these days, they are nothing to what happened then. And yet, Charlie Haughey's popularity and that of Fianna Fáil continued to rise and rise. How was this possible? How did Charlie do it?

Well, for one thing, as Taoiseach, Haughey was able to distance himself from the austerity measures. They were the cutbacks of his Ministers, not of him: somehow that was the impression which got out and held sway. It was also true that the general population at that time were just plain glad to see *something* being done which might save the country. Everyone was tired of the vacillation and endless feuds between Labour and Fine Gael which had dominated the four-and-half years under the previous government, and it was reassuring to see that finally, action was being taken and decisions were being made. To have someone strong in government raised a beacon of hope for many. In spite of all that has transpired since, it is my belief that in times to come, Charlie Haughey's reputation will be burnished to a degree which is difficult to envisage now. Whatever else might be said, he knew how to lead, he knew how to talk, he knew how to behave in all situations, and you always felt somehow that the country was safe in his hands. It may sound childish to put it like that now, but looking back and analysing my emotions and the zeitgeist of those years, that is how it was.

At that stage of course, I saw Haughey as a distant kind of figure, very much removed from me. By the time I was Minister for Education, I was almost 50 years old, but I still thought of him as a remote guy at the top. In the years that followed, sometimes I was asked, 'Why didn't you question where he got his money from?' But can you honestly see me, as a rookie, a greenhorn in the Cabinet with the great weight of responsibility that was upon me and the huge demands I had to deal with every day, saying, 'Excuse me Mr Haughey, but how did you make your money?' It just wouldn't have happened. Of course, at the time we would have heard gossip about his finances. And we knew that Haughey had a woman friend, a sweetie, who later turned out to be Terry Keane. There wasn't such sense of a shock when it came out.

At the time, I thought Charlie was above all a good leader. He had an air of competence about him, a stately demeanour and a confidence which meant that he was equal to any occasion: you wouldn't have seen him, for example, having his hair ruffled at the Council of Europe, like Enda Kenny. His wife, Maureen Haughey (the daughter of Seán Lemass), was a wonderful wife and mother and hugely respected by the Fianna Fáil electorate. I know Charlie didn't come out smelling of roses. Yet he did give me my first break, and in that sense, I feel that I owe him that recognition.

Chapter 4 ∾

| LIFE AT HOME

I worked too hard, of course. I realise that now. As Education Minister, I was the first person into the Department every morning. There was a lovely man at the gate and he would raise the lever to let me in and say, 'You're the first in again this morning, ma'am.' Yet I loved arriving into the hushed building every day, seeing the place beginning to come to life around me, and everyone coming in for work and knowing that I had the huge privilege of playing such a key role in leading education in Ireland.

However, the downside for me of having such a demanding and all-consuming public role was that I constantly worried about how my family would get on without me being around as much as I would have liked. Was I depriving my children of an essential element of their growing-up years, which would later impact upon their characters and qualities as adults and negatively affect their own future relationships and families? Was I denying my two boys some key ingredient in their upbringing which would leave them inadequate in their later lives? It was a huge dilemma, which many working mothers will identify with, and not one to be discounted easily. Of course you can make arrangements via home help and, if you are very lucky as I was, with the support of a strong and loyal husband or partner — but that doesn't take out of the equation love and worry and care and the need to nurture and to be central to your children's lives.

When I married Enda, he was working for Hanley's the wholesalers in Athlone. After about a year or so, he got an offer to join Jacob's, which was regarded as one of the premier companies in Ireland at the time. They were a Church of Ireland company, which had started as a Quaker company, and Enda was one of the first Catholic representatives to join them, which was a big deal at the time. In the beginning, he was an all-Ireland representative and as such often had to stay away at night. I remember writing him many lovelorn letters, which I found years afterwards when he had passed away — he had kept all those letters for all that time. I would write to him care of whichever hotel he was in staying in. He wouldn't write, but would ring me regularly. I used to pour my heart out to him in my letters: I was very lonely, as we were only just married. When I found the letters after his death, I read them all and I cried, thinking of all the love we had together!

After a while, luckily, Enda got a Midlands region position with Jacob's, which meant he was home at night, as with a regular job. It was wonderful, as he was there for the boys and was a real hands-on dad, great for helping with homework and taking them to sports games and scouts and all the things that children do. I was always regarded as the soft parent — the 'good cop', while Enda was the strict one — the 'bad cop'. Feargal and Aengus would come to me to give out about Dad, and Dad would have to do the giving out and putting the foot down with them.

For the years I was involved with the town council and the county council, I could manage home life very adequately: I knew my days and my working hours and they conformed to a pattern. I was able to combine my work in local politics at this stage very satisfactorily with my teaching job, and the boys' life in primary school, Enda's work and my own commitments could all be programmed together to make a satisfactory whole. I remember very well how, prior to my taking up teaching, my mother had said, 'If you are going to go out to work, two things are important — do not farm out your children, and do get some help at home.' The basis of her belief in not 'farming out' children, i.e. relying on crèches and so on, was founded on the conviction that children are best in their own homes with their own toys and comforters around them, in an environment that they know and love. To this day, I feel very clearly that this is so. Now I know such a thing is not possible for many working mothers, who must bring their children out to be minded and that there are very many childminders and crèche owners who do a wonderful job. I am merely relating here what worked best for me, not demanding or expecting that my approach should be for everyone.

I was very lucky in that early on in my working life, I made the acquaintance of a Mrs Pearl Samuels. She knocked at my door one day shortly after I had taken up my role on the Athlone Town Council, saying, 'You will need some help in your home now.' We hit it off immediately and I engaged Mrs Samuels as a part-time housekeeper. This meant that when the children came in from primary school, she was there until I came home. Enda's shirts and my blouses, instead of being un-ironed and rumpled, were always fresh and pressed, and in a whole lot of other ways, my life became a little easier.

When I went into national life in the early eighties, it was of course much more difficult. I can remember that I had just started on my Dáil career when Enda sat me down one night and said, 'Do you intend to be serious about this business? Do you intend to continue on your political path?' I said that, yes, I did. 'Well then,' he replied, 'there's no point in you racing home every night up and down the Dublin/Athlone road.' This is what I had been doing, driving back from Leinster House every night, so that I would be there for the children and see something of them during the week. Enda continued, 'It is better for you to stay in Dublin. I can be Mum and Dad during the week and then when you come home, you can be Mum again.' I knew it was good advice and we had a full discussion about it. From then on, we agreed that I should stay in Dublin on Monday, Tuesday and Wednesday nights and come home on Thursdays for the weekends. It was easier said than done, of course, in many ways.

In the beginning, I would stay in Buswells Hotel, which was very handy for work: you would land in the Dáil yard, take your hangers and bag out of the car and then go over to book in for the night, and you were all set. At night, however, I got very lonely for Enda and the boys. I could have gone down and sat in the bar, but then I was shy enough about doing such a thing on my own — not now, though. So I would usually just stay late at work. There were four or five of TDs I was particularly friendly with, and I was on good terms with many of the others too.

All the while, Enda provided the steady hand at home and he was the rock to whom we all looked. He and I never had a formal division of labour, so to speak. He knew what I was doing with the children and I knew what he was doing with the children, and in that way we ruled out any reference to any of the developmental child parenting books which had begun to emerge at that time. We managed to forge our way ahead together without them. All the time I was always conscious — again I may seem to be preaching, but I need to say it — that children need a huge amount of love at all stages of their life, into adulthood and beyond. When they are adults, they usually look to someone else to provide that love and reassurance at a certain point, but whilst they are growing and maturing, there can never be enough love and the open *expression* of love between a mother, a father and their family. It needs to be said and done and affirmed and reaffirmed often.

A very interesting development occurred when Aengus was about 14. He went through what I might call a 'bold' phase in his teenage years, wanting to go to discos and staying out a bit, although in a basically harmless way, and at this point, he and Enda were at a particularly spiky stage with each other — you know lads and their dads. I feared that my leaving them to go to Dublin might exacerbate the situation, and that they wouldn't get on at all. But quite the opposite happened! I started to notice when I would come home that the two of them were like allies-in-arms and had become really friendly and matey in my absence. I would have cooked food for them for when I was away, leaving chickens and so on in the fridge for them — but I realised that nothing was being eaten. So one night when I came back from Dublin, I said to Aengus, 'So what were ye doing?' At that point, he told me, 'We actually go out to the Chinese every night you are away, Mum — but Dad told me not to tell you!' In fact, Ken So and his wife Suzie, who owned the Chinese restaurant in question, were to become very good friends of ours over the years, and particularly of Enda. Their delicious food and great company brightened up many a lonely evening for him whenever I was in Dublin or further afield for work!

So my fears about Enda and Aengus falling out in my absence vanished, but there was the ever-present quandary in my mind — was I in fact doing harm to my children and to their childhood? I feel that many women, not just in politics, but indeed in any job that entails being out of the home for a considerable period each day, must share these thoughts and difficulties. In the end, it is up to each individual woman to sort out the bumps and hollows according to their own needs and means. For me, Mrs Samuels, even for a few hours a day, was an essential part of managing our family life. So much so, in fact, that she stayed with us for years after the children had grown up and gone away to their young adult lives — and she sadly passed away while still working for us. The boys grew very fond of her and always called her 'Mrs S.'. God Bless you, Mrs S. and all the many other people like you all over the country who help to oil the wheels of family life! When I read profile pieces on such and such a woman who has made it to the top or who is in a very stressful, demanding job and I see that she has young children, I find myself hoping that she is making it in every sense of the word and that she has worked her own way satisfactorily through her dilemma.

Of course I did my best at all times to be there for my sons as much as I could. I remember clearly one incident with Feargal around 1982, when he had just embarked on his career at UCD to study for a B. COMM. He had a steady girlfriend in Athlone at the time and they were a real item together — very much young love. He was at college in Dublin during the week and came home every weekend. By Halloween he had just been a month in college and was home for a long weekend.

One morning, I was in the kitchen early, ironing. It always seemed that confidences were exchanged between me and my family when I was ironing. I suppose whilst I was physically working, my mind was free and I always enjoyed these interludes when one or other of my sons would come to me with something to say. On this occasion, Feargal came to me and said, 'Ma, I am not going back to college. I hate it. I am really lonely. I don't know anyone. It's huge and I want to be at home!' He was clearly very upset.

For a moment, I was dumbstruck. What should I say? I remembered my own boarding school days when I hated being away, and Feargal and Aengus had been brought up very much in the heart of a hectic but loving family. Somehow, inspiration came, and I said, 'Stay on until Christmas and we'll see what you feel like then. If you still don't like it, then you don't have to go back. We'll find some other way of furthering your career.' I thought perhaps he could go to University College, Galway as a day student, travelling there and back on the train. There was a good rail connection. I said all this to him, and concluded, 'Just stick it out until Christmas and then we'll have a full talk again about it.' He seemed satisfied with this pragmatic suggestion and went back to college happily enough.

Feargal continued to come home every weekend, but he never again mentioned the fact that he wanted to leave. Christmas came and Christmas went, and he began to talk about people he had met, pals he had made, clubs he had joined, and I think the whole of the 14,000-strong student body of UCD lost its strangeness for him and he became attuned, acclimatised and absorbed by being part of that fine institute. In fact, at a certain point during his college days, Feargal and I set up an apartment together in Dublin for a while, as I was based there so much for work. It worked out very well and I was delighted, as I had him for company. Although of course he wasn't wanting to be always sitting in with his Ma! But we got on very well.

I tell the story because so often things are said and done in haste, and bridges are crossed which need not be. I think the Holy Spirit put the idea in my mind of how to meet that little crisis in a young man's mind and in his mum's mind. Feargal's love affair continued, while Aengus was proving to be the typical rebellious teenager. He liked bright lights; he wanted to be in the happening places. He had a number of friends who were calling and ringing and going places all the time, and he provided many a heartache for Enda and me, particularly when he started to go out to teenage parties and dances. I remember waiting up until two and three in the morning, but what parent has not done so? What parent doesn't worry as to the possible outcome for their teenager of that night's festivities?

I cannot emphasise how much Enda contributed to my well-being throughout my career in politics, and especially during my ministerial life, when the pressure was intense. I was able to come home every weekend to him, knowing that he had kept the home fires burning, both literally and metaphorically. He was there for the family and he was there for *me*. What a relief it always was, to come home to him from what was a hectic, overcrowded schedule. For all of us as a family, he was the ballast throughout the years.

There were some very fortuitous developments in Enda's own career, which he took full advantage of to be able to support me in mine. He spent a number of happy years at Jacob's, as I have mentioned. Then, in 1975, he got the opportunity to buy into a local company, Midland Oil, with a man called Don Beddy. Don was offering Enda a managing role but also the chance to be a part-owner of the company. There was much discussion in the family about it. He would be leaving a safe, regular job with Jacob's, who were such good employers: it was clearly a big risk to take.

Midland Oil was a huge decision for Enda, but it paid off and worked out very well, both in terms of his own career and in terms of our family life. Now it's a modern thing that guys are 'house-husbands', but Enda's job meant that he could be at home every evening when the boys needed him — to help them with their night study, to be collected and brought to rugby, GAA, scouts and all the rest. For me, it was a great source of contentment to know that he was at home and the kids were in good hands. At the time and in later years, I still had a lot of angst sometimes, about whether I had neglected the boys. But it seems that I — we — didn't, as they have both turned out fine. The proof of it all, if indeed proof can be taken from it, is that our two sons have grown up to be sensible, well-adjusted young men. They married and have families and appear to be getting on with their lives. I suppose that is the most any parent can work for and hope for at the end of the day.

Chapter 5 ↝

| MY FAVOURITE MINISTRY

It was the late 1980s and I was getting dug in at Education in Marlborough Street. I quickly set myself the task of getting to know all of the main players both internally, in the Department, and externally, in the various teachers' unions, parents' groups, the schools, the lobby groups and the universities. I loved it all and was determined to get ahead, to be progressive, and to make my name — all worthy goals for an ambitious politician. I knew early on in my stint at Marlborough Street that money was going to be very tight and that there would be no let-up in the financial constraints on the Department. Having staved off the threat of a change in the Pupil/Teacher Ratio, I cast about in my mind and spent time talking with all the various officials and interest groups about my wish to move forward in a developmental way which might not necessarily cost money — at least not upfront!

One of the first initiatives I settled upon was the refocusing of the National Council for Curriculum and Assessment (NCCA), which had been set up by my predecessor, Gemma Hussey. Curriculum development is always a worthwhile undertaking in education, and I noted with interest last year that one of the first things Ruairi Quinn, the present Minister for Education, did when he came into office was to take action on the same issue — a wise move. Ably advised by Margaret Walsh, I asked Dr Ed Walsh to remain on as Chairperson of the NCCA, a decision also enthusiastically backed by Charlie Haughey. I was careful to heed as well Margaret's suggestion that it would be a good idea to appoint members of the various teachers' unions to the sub-boards of the NCCA. All of this in place, we set forth on a programme of curriculum reform, firstly at Intermediate level.

There had been for some time a series of examinations at secondary level — the Group Certificate and the Inter Certificate. The proposal was to merge both of these into one examination. I remember well the day Dr Ed Walsh came to see me in Dáil Éireann to discuss what we should call this new intermediate-level examination. Together, we tossed back and forth various suggestions for names and eventually came up with the name 'Junior Cert', which tied in nicely with the Leaving Cert. As we then moved towards formalising this new development, the marvellous Chief Executive of the NCCA, Albert O'Ceallaigh, was immensely helpful. He had a sure and light touch in all of these matters but he was also strongly professional. He guided the NCCA through this process at a very difficult time, and it was a good news story amidst the financial and social gloom and doom which prevailed at the time.

My Opposition Spokesperson was now George Bermingham, a Fine Gael TD for Dublin North-Central, who was thoughtful in his Dáil utterances — far more considered and temperate, I felt, than I had been when in his position a few years back. It is funny how small utterances stick in your mind. George's reaction when I unfolded the NCCA developments and the new plan for the Junior Cert, was 'Two cheers for the NCCA in this regard!' I thought it was a well-judged and generous response. George Bermingham later left parliamentary politics and is now a distinguished and well-respected judge.

Around this time, as well as such formal developments, I was able to bring forward another important measure, which gave me great delight then and continues to do so now when I hear mention of it — the system of the Home–School Liaison Teacher. This marks in my mind a wonderful milestone in my odyssey within the Department of Education and indeed Irish public life.

It all started when a certain Concepta Connaghty came to see me out of the blue in Marlborough Street one day. (This lady has since passed away.) This was a time when all the huge difficulties within the large inner and outer city primary schools were beginning to emerge, due to growing numbers of one-parent families and those living on the breadline. A teacher based in Tallaght, Ms Connaghty had been working with the children in such schools for some time and, as she told me, she saw a great need in these environments for a 'developmental' type of teacher — someone who would be attached to a school but not in a teaching capacity. He or she would be there to liaise between the school and the parent or parents, in situations where a child was not making a fist of school or indeed in some cases not turning up for lessons at all. In other words, to focus on children who might later go on to fail in the system and of whom a high proportion were at risk of ending up as drop-outs and misfits, perhaps joining gangs and turning to criminal activity. I thought the idea was an excellent one. I gave it all some further consideration and I then spoke to Tom Gillen, the then Assistant Secretary in charge of Primary Education. Tom agreed that it would be a very worthwhile initiative to explore, and we prepared a Memorandum for Government.

I must digress here slightly to explain that, if a member of Cabinet has a developmental idea or proposal which he or she wants to bring to Cabinet for consideration, a Memorandum must be prepared and then circulated to each serving Cabinet Member, who will give their own feedback on it at the next Cabinet meeting. Particularly in the strait-ened circumstances of the late 1980s, the proposing Minister would always await these responses with trepidation, especially with regard to the presiding Minister for Finance and his Department. They were always deemed to be the most dangerous ones because they were always against everything! Of course I fully understood that then and I fully understand it now: the job of the Department of Finance is to try to keep the country on an even financial keel, to keep the spending in the various Ministries under control and to put forward their own stringent views. It was ever thus and it will always be thus.

At that time we were in a period in which Memorandums in general were being massively cut back on and so, once I had circulated my proposal to all of my colleagues, I sallied off to Cabinet, armed with my file and all my background information, little expecting that I would find any echoes of approval. Sure enough, when my turn came to bring up the issue, the Taoiseach turned to me and said, 'What is this Memorandum about, Mary? Is it more teachers?'

Ray MacSharry saw his opening, and pounced. 'Yes Taoiseach,' he chimed, 'more teachers and these ones won't even *teach*!'

There was a kind of audible gasp around the table at my sheer effrontery, but that little bold streak in me kept going in spite of it all. I reddened up at all the attention, but I looked at the Taoiseach and caught his eye.

'Let Mary explain, Ray,' he said. 'Let's hear her idea.'

So I ploughed on and explained as best I could: that children in disadvantaged areas would benefit greatly, that this could help to combat some of the difficulties in our troubled urban districts, and so on. Charlie listened carefully, nodded his head once or twice and he then said to me directly, 'Could this be done in a pilot way? Could you introduce these home — whatever you call them — liaison people, let's say, in two urban and rural areas? And if it works, build from there?'

'Yes, yes!' I replied, delighted. Once more, I had followed my 'seize the day' strategy and it had worked. So I went back triumphantly to my Department, and we piloted the scheme in South Dublin, where Concepta Connaghty worked, and in a large rural school too, and ten others besides. We started with these twelve schools, and the initiative grew from there and soon became mainstream.

It almost goes without saying that the INTO were fully in favour. After all, it meant more teachers, albeit not of the teaching kind, but it also meant that their care for disadvantaged pupils would be improved. To give that particular union their due, this was always their aim: to do their very best for the pupils. Of course, they wanted to do their utmost for their trade union members as well, but often, as in this instance, the two aims could overlap and if so, it was always a happy outcome.

After seeing through two budgets, Ray MacSharry was appointed to the post of European Commissioner in Brussels, a job he was happy to accept, while Albert Reynolds would become Minister for Finance.

I would always regard another of my key achievements of my time in Education as the creation of two new universities in Limerick and Dublin City — the first universities to have been set up in Ireland since we became an independent country. Instituting via legislation the University of Limerick and Dublin City University was something of which I was particularly proud, as it was such a positive accomplishment in those very difficult times.

For the four years I had been Shadow Spokesperson for Education opposite Gemma Hussey as Minister for Education, Garret FitzGerald had been pushing forward the idea of conferring full university status on the two National Institutes of Limerick and Glasnevin. When I had first come into office in March 1987, I too had been lobbied — at times mercilessly — by the heads of these two establishments, Dr Ed Walsh in Limerick and Dr Danny O'Hare in Dublin. Initially, the creation of universities did not loom high on my horizon, because there were all those huge, horrendous cuts to be made everywhere, but when 1987 and 1988 came and the financial pressure began to ease slightly, I was keen to pick up the matter again. I went to discuss it with Charlie Haughey, and he too was very much in agreement with the idea, advising me to take the next steps and discuss it with a legal person. We duly did this, after which my Department officials put together a proposal which I was able to bring to Cabinet. Once I had secured general approval there, I went away again to start the task of preparing the legislation, assisted very ably as ever by my Departmental staff.

At the end of May 1989 — just before the one-party Fianna Fáil government fell, in fact — came the day I was to pilot the legislation (the University of Limerick Bill and Dublin City University Bill) through Dáil Éireann. Lo and behold — who was its main adversary that day, but Garret FitzGerald! I was dumbfounded, as he had been so pushy and determined that this should progress when they were in government. Otherwise, our lobbying with the Labour and Fine Gael deputies had worked a treat, and so Garret was the only really adversarial voice.

It was an interesting incident, because Garret was still employed by UCD on a retainer basis as a professor, and he genuinely would have had a strong belief in universities and in the lineage of them and the philosophical merits of their existence. This I fully subscribed to myself, having studied Newman and his ideas of what a university should be. So I was knocked sideways by Garret's onslaught on me that day in the Dáil, when it was clear that he was quite determined to hold sway. In the end, however, his objections petered out — it did not even come to a vote. But to me, the incident showed a side to Garret FitzGerald which was at odds with the kindly, 'wise grandfather' image one had of him. As others have commented in recent years, there is no doubt that he could drive a hard bargain and fight very strongly for something he wanted. I was just surprised that he chose to take issue so strongly with what I was proposing on that particular occasion. That said, in many ways, I admired Garret. I had a high regard for his long

life of political endeavour — in particular, his work on the Anglo-Irish
Agreement and the way he bravely stuck it out in spite of Margaret
Thatcher's infamous 'Out, out, out!' incantations. I well remember
hearing those and my feelings of astonishment at the time that he was
able to pretend she hadn't said such things, or that he didn't understand
her meaning in any case. I greatly respected how he was able to still
plough on, so that some kind of resolution could be reached in the
form of the Anglo-Irish Agreement, which of course laid the foundation for much that followed.

Coming back to the universities, however. I was delighted that the
two men in question — Ed Walsh and Danny O'Hare — quickly
proved to be very able Presidents of their exciting new establishments.
As time goes on, I feel their work will be recognised even more fully. In
later years, I was always very interested to meet graduates from UL and
DCU, and to see how well these two modern universities adapted to the
closing years of the twentieth century and the beginning of a new
millennium. In tandem with the new universities, we managed to
merge Thomond College with Limerick University and St Pat's in
Drumcondra as the educational training arm of Dublin City
University.

In the General Election of June 1989, Fianna Fáil lost seats, and for
the first time we broke the mantra of a one-party government and went
into coalition with Des O'Malley and the Progressive Democrats. All
the manoeuvring that went on at that time has been well depicted by
Albert Reynolds and Bertie Ahern in their books. I remember being at
the Cabinet meeting when the acting Taoiseach, Charlie Haughey, went
around the table, asking us one by one whether we would agree with
the proposal to go in with the Progressive Democrats and if we thought
they should have one or two Cabinet positions — they were pressing
for two, naturally. In the end, Des O'Malley and Bobby Molloy would
take up Cabinet roles. Everyone was amazed that Charlie Haughey
would engage politically with what might have been perceived as the
enemy, but engage he did and with gusto. For Charlie, in politics, as in
many other areas of life, pragmatism held sway and he quite rightly
deduced that the 1989 electorate would not be in favour of an
immediate further General Election — which would have been the
inevitable outcome if he did not form a government this time around.

So, away we all sailed on the good ship Coalition. I don't mean to sound trite here, but for us in Fianna Fáil, the concept of a one-party government had been a key principle for so long. Increasingly now in the twenty-first century, it seems like such an archaic expectation. Already then, in the late 80s and early 90s, a one-party government had ceased to be the norm in many of the other developed European countries, where coalitions of two, three and four parties were in government.

Be that as it may, this new scenario in June 1989 occasioned much angst among Fianna Fáil supporters, angst which was stoked up privately by Albert Reynolds and Pádraig Flynn, who never got over their love of one-party government, or their distaste for coalition. For his pains, Pádraig Flynn as Minister for the Environment was handed a Minister of State by the name of Mary Harney, who was charged with the special task of protection of the environment. There were many in-house tales of how he treated her and how he spoke about her, but Mary was a dogged performer who kept to her brief and brought forward many worthwhile initiatives, including helping to rid Dublin of smog. Publicly, however, Pádraig Flynn treated her courteously and never engaged in any spats.

As for me, fortunately I retained my role as Minister for Education and was assigned an excellent Minister of State in Fianna Fáil's Frank Fahy, who had already been with me for a while before the election. He was in charge of Sport and Youth Affairs and, I feel, has never been given the full acclaim he deserves for the wonderful work he did in both of those sub-portfolios. He was a great colleague and one with whom I very much enjoyed working.

Despite the setback of the 1989 election, economic growth was slowly but surely returning. I embarked on my renewed brief with great gusto, always looking out for what I could do positively, rather than focusing overly on the negative.

I became very interested in the fledgling Educate Together movement, which favoured the setting up of multidenominational schools. The first Educate Together school had been set up in 1978, under the aegis of the then Minister for Education, John Wilson: a hugely influential, learned and witty man. Against much opposition — most of it within his own Department — he facilitated and funded the setting up of the first such school in Dalkey. But the initiative had not been taken much further after that, sadly. My predecessor Gemma Hussey had been in favour of the project also, but due to financial constraints and other pressing issues during her tenure, the matter had been dropped until I decided to take up the ball and run with it.

One of my first objectives was to try to figure out the rationale behind the prevailing hostility within the Department of Education to the rise and spread of multidenominational schools. After all, how could anybody in their right mind be against such a worthy concept, that children of all faiths and none should come together in the primary school their parents wished them to attend, that they should learn to live together, and that their young minds would be opened to influences from all sides, never being required to fix on any particular one — at least, not until they were sufficiently mature to choose for themselves which, if any, to adopt?

I had my own suspicions about why and where resistance to the concept of multidenominational education subsisted. When I talked to various officials in the system, I soon found that my suspicions were not too wide of the mark. The main objector was the established Church, both the Catholic Church — which had of course an almost complete hold on the running of primary schools around the country — and likewise the Church of Ireland. To give those representing the churches their due, there was initially at least no outward animosity towards my ideas, but I knew it was fermenting under the surface. This was the time of Archbishop Connell — later to be Cardinal Connell — and his Education Expert, Father Dan, who was operating out of an office at St Mary's Pro-Cathedral in Marlborough Street, just opposite the Department of Education. Putting the objections of the Church aside, it seemed that there were very few practical obstacles in the way of the implementation of such a worthy project. The initial Educate Together proposals which came in from the various groups were asking for very little in the way of start-up funding; they already had Boards of Management in place, and only wanted to secure the appropriate permission to forge ahead with their ideas.

There were in the Department of Education numerous starter applications on file for primary schools to set up under the Educate Together banner. These were mostly in the Dublin and greater Dublin area; there were also embryonic ones around the country. I made my mind up very swiftly that I would go full steam ahead in fostering and encouraging this flowering of multidenominational education. And so, one by one, I started to give permission for such schemes to be progressed: in Bray and Ranelagh and then Swords, Cork, Sligo, Kilkenny, North Bay Dublin, Limerick and Rathfarnham. Great excitement was generated by the setting up of these experimental schools, and the idea began to grow in popularity. The early pioneering educationalists in the movement would call a public meeting in an area to set out the spirit and ethos of their vision: parents would be invited to come and join in and listen. It became in many ways a stream which led to a deluge, and I moved onwards with the idea all the time.

On a most interesting and more recent note, in the autumn of 2010 Educate Together wrote to me with an invitation to join their National Board of Education. At that time, I had to very reluctantly turn down the opportunity, telling them that whilst I was in full public life, it would be difficult for me to manage the meetings and other commitments the role would involve. As things worked out, however, I lost my seat the following year and when a renewed invitation came in, I accepted with great alacrity. Life is funny, and I am glad that Ruairi Quinn is in charge now of the Department of Education: he will move things along in this area. Our new aim now in Educate Together is to bring the initiative into the secondary sector. After all, it is a natural progression that the parents of children brought up in their primary years in this free, open way with regard to religion and background should wish to keep them on that path of constant renewal and enlightenment. To this day, I regard my championing of Educate Together as one of the highlights of my time within the Department of Education.

All the while throughout my tenure as Minister, I relentlessly kept up a continuing series of meetings with all of the educational interest groups. I was able to give small grants to the National Parents' Council (NPC) at primary level and at secondary level. I also nurtured my strong links with trade union members. I liked to keep up such contacts, off the record. I strongly felt that in this way, I would be in a better position to find out exactly what was happening within the Department and what was emanating from the Department, as distinct from merely relying on the arid, dry files which came to me. As such, I was able to enjoy and benefit from a lively and candid exchange with teachers and other interest groups, and I am sure that our work in the Department was all the more effective because of it. Fortunately for me, Margaret Walsh continued to be my Advisor, my friend and my stalwart companion through all of these efforts, trials, vicissitudes and triumphs.

I believe that it is a given that primary education should be the focus of much of the determination, deliberation and decision-making of any Minister for Education, no matter what his or her financial straitjacket is. After all, primary school is where a child starts learning and first finding their feet in an environment outside the home, and a good experience at this stage will have a lasting impact throughout all of that child's formative years. The most basic requirement is that this environment should be safe and fit for purpose. Yet, because of the dire financial circumstances we found ourselves in in the late 1980s, the Department's capital funding for school buildings was severely curtailed. Huge chunks were chopped off budgets, meaning that plans for improvements and new buildings which had been previously envisaged could not be put into effect as hoped. However, that didn't stop an increasing number of pupils piling into schools with poorly equipped classrooms and prefabs. The plain fact was that I had very little money, there were huge numbers going into the schools and there was a great need for many improvements of school facilities, necessarily of an expensive nature. I began to despair as to whether there was any way out of this financial dilemma concerning our primary schools.

I started to look further into the matter, and whenever a new school was opened — few and far between as these were — I would always read the associated files very carefully. It struck me that there were many teams of consulting architects, of civil engineers, of electrical engineers, and on it went, and so the bills kept mounting up. I was no expert in construction, yet the thought came to me that there must be some way of building what was needed in a more economic fashion, one which related more directly to the circumstances we were now living in.

I enlisted the help of George Rowley, a wonderful person in the Primary Building Unit, and we set to the challenge. When a school deputation came to see me, they would always be fired up with the plan that had been prepared or that was in the process of being drawn up, with its various teams of associated professionals, and so on and so forth. I would say to them, 'What is your greatest need?'

'We need six classrooms, we need a drama room, we need a PE hall and we need and we need and we need . . .' would often be the reply.

And doubtless they did need all of these things — but to make it happen for them, I needed money which I knew I wasn't going to get. So we would say to them, 'We can offer you £100,000.' Now I am talking twenty years ago, when this was a substantial amount of money. And we would propose employing a good Clerk of Works to work with the Office of Public Works who would be able to tell them what they could build for such a sum. 'Oh, no, no, no' would be the schools' first reaction to this offer. They were holding out for the full bells and whistles, of course.

'This is all that is on offer,' I would reply. 'And if you don't accept the £100,000, we will have to give it to the next school in the queue.'

So they would waltz out and the next school would come in, and very quickly the word spread through the primary schools network that you could get funding for your building from the Department, but that you had to take it in a basic fashion. We were not proposing prefabs, however: there would be proper classrooms with all of the necessary modern appliances, but there was not going to be room for sports halls, for assembly rooms, for this room or that room. It wasn't long before the Boards of Management of the schools began to accept what was on offer, and in many cases we were able to reach compromises and away a school would go, to make the best possible use of the money. In due course, I would arrive to open the new building or development and to see the plaque on the wall. I always felt a great pride that in a practical way I was able to move ahead so many schools. It sounds small beer now, but then it was huge. Even today, if I go to a particular part of the country and I see my name on plaque on the wall of a particular school, a surge of pride will come to me.

The presence in Athlone of the then Regional College and my own involvement for many years on the board of this establishment meant that when I was Minister for Education, I was even more intensely interested in that branch of third-level education. Through visits to the various Regional Colleges, through perusing the relevant files and talking to the people involved, I began to realise that the role of the Institutes of Technology was not being fully explored. They had been shoe-horned into being associated with certain disciplines or areas only, and all in all the huge potential they had was not being realised. I thought long and hard about this, and again talked to my officials in the Department. It became clear to me that there was a need for a developmental type of legislation which would give further legs to the existing Regional Colleges, enabling them to develop fully into research, to offer degree-level and postgraduate tuition and, in a general way, to interact more closely and more fruitfully with the wider community.

Now much of this was in practice already being done by the colleges, as they were pushing the boundaries themselves and were taking liberties well beyond their initial remit at the time they had been founded — but all for the good of the furtherance of education, of course. But legislation would put all of this on a more formal footing and enable still more development in a structured way. In due course, my legislative Memorandum went to Cabinet and was approved, and Charlie Haughey was most interested in the idea of RTCS doing more for themselves and for the wider community. I was able to introduce the legislation to the Dáil; although, by the time it had passed through all its stages, I had been moved to another role in government, and it was the very capable Séamus Brennan as Minister for Education who ensured that it came to full fruition.

People have often asked me which of the ministries I presided over was my favourite, and of course it was Education. I often think of what Tony Blair said when he faced into victory with the Labour Party and he was asked by a probing journalist what his main aim would be, if and when he got into government: his unhesitating reply was, 'Education, Education, Education.' How right he was and how right these priorities are. I always believed and will continue to believe that education is and should be the centre of our considerations, both economically and socially.

Chapter 6 ❧

| BRIAN LENIHAN SNR

The drama of the 2011 Irish Presidential campaign brought back very vividly for me the events of 1990 and my brother Brian Lenihan's own bid for the Presidency that year. It was a very difficult time for Brian, coinciding with his unfair sacking from Cabinet by Charlie Haughey and this, as well as other circumstances which conspired against him, resulted in the sabotaging of any Presidential hopes he had. To my mind, Brian Snr should have won that race: he would have made a very good President. The battering he took in his political career at this point was keenly felt by all of us who were close to him.

It is undeniable that the primitive feelings of a family in circumstances such as this are very strong. For good or for ill, I am infused with those primitive feelings as much as the next person — perhaps more, even. Particularly in political situations or in moments of high drama, I do not just get fired up but I become filled with determination and with the intent to kill politically if necessary (in a metaphorical sense. of course) anyone who is trying to thwart what is a very legitimate aim and campaign. With the passing years, that fighting spirit has not left me and I suppose it is above all an instinct — every animal fights for its young. I feel the same in relation my two sons, who are young men in their own right, as I feel and felt for Brian and my two nephews, Brian Jnr and Conor Lenihan.

Let me go back to the beginning of what was happening for my brother Brian in those years. He had been suffering for some time as a result of problems related to his liver. So much so that by the beginning of 1989, his health had deteriorated very badly and he was gravely ill.

The myth went around that the problems with his liver were the result of heavy drinking on his part over the years, but that was simply not the case. In fact, Brian was suffering from haemochromatosis, which is an iron overload in one's system and which can be extremely damaging to the liver. At the time, this disease was practically unheard of in Ireland — although in the UK and the US there was much more medical knowledge about it. In the early stages of the condition, therefore, Brian's doctors hadn't been able to identify the problem and by the time it was finally diagnosed, he was on the verge of liver failure and very seriously ill. He was told that only a liver transplant would give him any chance of survival. This was a highly complex procedure which was not done in Ireland at the time, but it was advised that he could go to the US. The only location where this operation had been carried out successfully was a specialist hospital there — the Mayo Clinic in Rochester, Minnesota. And so in spring 1989, Brian's own hospital, the Mater in Dublin, duly arranged for him to go there and to await a liver transplant.

I often think of those who await transplants of any organ, and how they must feel, especially in the knowledge that they will only have a chance to live if someone else dies. I would strongly urge anyone of a young age to sign up as a donor and carry their card at all times, so that if anything happens to them, such as an accident, the necessary organs can be removed with their prior permission and someone else's life might be saved. (I do not carry such a card myself now, as my own organs are by now well past their sell-by date and would be of no use to anyone, I fear!)

Anyway, off to the Mayo Clinic Brian Snr went with his wife, Ann, to await a suitable donor. There wasn't much time left: complete renal failure and indeed death were imminent. I can only imagine how deeply the poignancy of the whole scenario must have struck him, as he opened his eyes each morning. Brian was to be one of the lucky ones, however, and in May 1989, the call finally came to say that a suitable donor had been found. A young man had, tragically, been killed in a boating accident and his liver was a match for Brian.

The long and complex operation was soon underway and, amazingly, the transplant took hold and the liver was not rejected by Brian's body. Receiving a transplant and having it satisfactorily bedded in are two separate components of a highly complex procedure, and the second does not always automatically follow the first. As an aside to this and very poignantly also, before Brian left the Mayo Clinic, he had the chance to meet the mother and father of the young man whose liver he had inherited. There followed a very emotional and heartfelt exchange. It seemed that the young man had been brought up on the shores of a large lake and that there had been a great similarity between the kind of upbringing he had had and Brian's own early years. Brian was always convinced that this was one of the encounters which the Lord had arranged for him.

As we know, there has since been much discussion around the fact that Charlie Haughey launched a private appeal for funding for Brian to have the operation in the US, which was going to cost a great deal of money. As it turned out, the fund was massively oversubscribed — people were extremely generous. The reproaches levelled at Charlie Haughey in later years in relation to this particular matter centred on allegations that he used some of the money for his own purposes, siphoning it off into his personal bank account. I have always been very clear — Brian got every financial assistance he needed for his trip to the Mayo Clinic, for his stay there and for his aftercare. In that sense, Haughey did not plunder any of the funds which should have gone to my brother. It was the *leftover* money he plundered and, of course, that should have either gone back to the subscribers or perhaps been donated to further research on haemochromatosis. I suppose we took the pragmatic view — Brian got the funding he needed to enable him to have a life-saving operation in the US, and we were extremely grateful to the donors. It could be said that what happened to the leftover money — and whether this was a mortal or a venial sin — is for the historians to establish.

In any case, Brian was returned after the General Election of 15 June 1989. In fact, he topped the polls without ever having canvassed, as he had still been in the US recovering from his operation at the time. On his first day back in Dáil Éireann, he was met with thunderous applause and otherwise was greeted with a rapturous response from his constituency — and from the whole of Ireland, in fact. Subsequently he spoke movingly about his health ordeal on many occasions on radio and TV, and about the condition which is now universally recognised, but was then unknown in Ireland.

Brian Snr was appointed Minister for Defence by Charlie Haughey in the new Cabinet. This was an important position, of course, but also not as onerous for him in his present state of recovery as his Foreign Affairs portfolio had been. He loved working in the Department of Defence, having been reared in Athlone, which is the headquarters of the Western Command.

In his new Cabinet role, Brian was faced straight away with a very difficult situation which needed to be resolved urgently. There had been huge unrest among army wives around that time, which was a reflection of the deep discontent among the members of the defence forces, who, by the nature of their role as professionals, were not able to give expression to it themselves. It was clear that the army had been neglected in a material way and it was Brian's job to build it up again, and to liaise with the newly founded Permanent Defence Force Other Ranks Representative Association (PDFORRA), representing the ranks, and Representative Association of Commissioned Officers (RACO). These were and are quasi-representative bodies — trade unions, in effect, although they cannot be called so.

Brian set to working with these groups and other individuals to address all of the many queries and worries and real shortcomings faced by those working in the army and the navy. He established a wonderful rapport with them. In this work he was greatly helped by Dr Brian Hillery, who was a trained psychologist. Brian did some sterling work and was able to resolve many of the issues and problems very satisfactorily. Towards the end of that year, there was much speculation in the papers regarding the Presidential Election of the following year and which names the parties might put forward as their nominees. Brian's name began to be floated. I still don't really know — none of us do — if Brian was greatly enlivened by the idea, but he went for it anyway and was duly selected by Fianna Fáil as our candidate. All was well, you might think, but there was soon to be trouble in the Garden of Eden.

New Year 1990 came and went, and as the months passed, Brian's campaign for the Presidency gathered pace. Other candidates entered the fray — among these, Mary Robinson, running for Labour, but in an independent way. But Brian Snr was the firm favourite, and regarded by the vast majority as a sure-fire winner. In September 1990, however, on the back of an article in the press, a row arose about who had telephoned the then President, Patrick Hillery in Áras an Uachtaráin in January 1982, asking him to refuse the then Taoiseach Garret FitzGerald's request to dissolve the Dáil. Brian Lenihan became involved in the so-called scandal, when it was alleged that he, on behalf of Charlie Haughey, had made such a call to Hillery in order to persuade or pressurise him into a refusal. To its everlasting shame, *The Irish Times* then printed part of an interview which Brian had given to a young research student from UCD called Jim Duffy. In the interview, Brian admitted he had made the phone call to the President. In his book, *For the Record* (Blackwater Press, 1991), he would later explain fully the exact circumstances of this interview.

Looking back, it's amazing that this action ever achieved any sort of notoriety. But Des O'Malley as leader of the Progressive Democrats, with whom we were in government, demanded that Brian should resign as Tánaiste and Minister, otherwise the PDs would force an immediate General Election. Brian refused to sign a letter of resignation drawn up for him by Charlie Haughey, and the die was cast.

While all of this was brewing, Brian had kicked off his Presidential campaign in earnest in the constituency of Longford–Westmeath. It was already October and the election, which had been set for 7 November, was fast approaching. We all went to Granard, where Brian landed by helicopter. On that cold, early autumn evening, we campaigned through Edgeworthstown, Rathowen, Mullingar, Kinnegad, Tyrellspass, Kilbeggan and Moate. On each stop, people came out to meet him, shake his hand and to pledge their support. It was public knowledge of course that Brian's resignation was being called for. All the world loves a hero, and in the eyes of his loyal supporters, Brian was the hero battling against the might of Charlie Haughey.

I was standing on the step of the campaign bus as we pulled up in Moate. I looked to one side and who did I see, but Pádraig Flynn, getting out of his big Merc with that familiar, grinning face.

'What are you doing here, Minister Flynn?' I said.

'I am here to knock sense into all of you,' he replied.

Of course, he had been sent by Charlie Haughey. I lost the rag completely and, using some very unparliamentary language, told him to get back across the Shannon from whence he had come; that he was not wanted here. It was a raw message and he turned on his heels, got into his car and drove off to Athlone. By the time we arrived there ourselves, Flynn was already at the Prince of Wales Hotel, where our meeting was to be held.

Garda numbers put the crowd that night in Athlone at around 4,000 people. The Prince of Wales Hotel was packed to capacity, as was the main street outside. People milled around, crowding in on Brian, voicing their encouragement and support with low, raucous cries of, 'No resignation, Brian! No resignation Brian!' The issue had clearly formulated itself thus: Brian was battling Charlie Haughey; he was not accepting the call to resign. There followed a tense election meeting in the Prince of Wales ballroom, as more crowds gathered to listen to Brian, who put up a wonderful display. Albert Reynolds was there with us: it was his constituency as it was mine. At one point, Bertie Ahern turned up: he had obviously been sent by Charlie Haughey too. Bertie, however, took one look at the crowds and disappeared back to Dublin — wise man!

A very interesting thing happened around this time, which has never been written about in the media or in any of the books of the period. In the Sunday papers of that Halloween weekend, I happened upon a stray portion of an article, which said that there was to be an urgent Cabinet meeting the following week. Even though I was Minister for Education at the time, I had had no notification of such a meeting. The Bank Holiday Monday dawned and still no word came. I telephoned Teresa O'Hanlon, the wife of Rory O'Hanlon, whom I regarded as a Cabinet friend. Before I even had a chance to broach the matter, Teresa said, 'Mary, are you not gone to Kinsealy? There's a Cabinet meeting in Kinsealy today. Rory got word of it over the last few days.' I knew then that the meeting was about Brian and that I, even as a full Cabinet Minister, had simply not been invited. I was angry on two fronts: furious for Brian, and livid that I had not been informed as was my right!.

It transpired later that the meeting had been called by Charlie and held in his home in Kinsealy, so that he could urge all of the Cabinet members (except for me, of course) to sign a paper calling for my brother's resignation and to support him if necessary in the sacking.

Here I must give credit to Albert Reynolds, who as I have said was my constituency colleague as a TD for Longford–Westmeath. At that surreptitious meeting, Albert simply refused to sign the paper which Charlie had prepared for them all.

Brian was sacked from the Cabinet just a few days later, on 31 October 1990. There was a formal vote in the Dáil, for which I had no choice but to side with the Fianna Fáil Party in a vote of confidence in Charlie as Taoiseach and in the Cabinet. It was a terrible time for us all.

All the while, the Presidential campaign was gaining in momentum and intensity. In spite of everything that had happened, Brian's response was that he would fight on regardless. And he fought like a lion throughout the whole of Ireland, and everywhere crowds and crowds came out to meet him. To this day, I meet people who will say, 'I canvassed with Brian in Listowel'; 'I canvassed with Brian in Limerick'; 'I canvassed with Brian in Carrickmacross.' The party faithful really rallied to him and even after all his recent troubles, it was clear that he still had huge support. As I have said, his main opponent was Mary Robinson. Late in the game, Alan Dukes had put forward the idea that Fine Gael should run a candidate and they nominated Austin Currie, a good guy but one who, realistically, hadn't a chance. Alan Dukes could be very Machiavellian. He wanted Mary Robinson: she was a member of that Davos group of high-flying economists, academics and philosophers. Alan knew perfectly well that Austin Currie hadn't a chance: he was just shoved in at the last moment in order to pump up Mary Robinson with transfers and put Brian Lenihan out.

Although Brian was still riding high in the polls, there was another blow to his campaign, one particular Saturday afternoon, very close to Election Day. As I write this, I can remember that day very well. I was listening to the radio as I was driving to Tyrellspass, where I was going to do some canvassing on my brother's behalf with some local party members. I had tuned in to a lunchtime news programme which included a live political debate featuring Michael McDowell, Pádraig Flynn and some other participants. McDowell was clearly in favour of Mary Robinson. Suddenly Flynn saw fit to interrupt and proceeded to make some highly insulting remarks about Robinson and her 'newfound interest in her family, and in fashion and her hairdo', etc., all of which was grossly untrue. When I heard this interjection, I knew at once that it would have huge repercussions. And, of course, it did. But there is no doubt in my mind, or in the minds of many other commentators at the time, that Flynn sealed Brian's failure on that day. His attack on Robinson had the opposite effect to what he had apparently intended, as women voters in particular suddenly shifted their loyalties and rallied in droves to support the Robinson campaign. This was very difficult for Brian to overcome and for us to quantify now just how damaging that interview and Flynn's comments were.

When the vote came around, Brian still came out top, as the number one first preference. As a family, we always felt a certain delight in the fact that he was the first choice of the people of Ireland. To my mind, since the Presidency was for one job, the voting should never have been done under the 'PR' voting system anyway: it should have been a case of 'first past the post'. Of course, what happened was that when Austin Currie went out as expected, he gave the vote to Mary Robinson. So in that sense, Alan Dukes's dream was realised. Brian went along to the count at the RDS and when the final announcement came, he took it so manfully and in such valiant spirit that you couldn't but be enriched by his demeanour and by his courage. I cannot leave any account of the battle for this particular Presidency without saying that during her term as President, Mary Robinson appointed me to the Council of State. It was a great honour to be so invited and I very much enjoyed my time in that service, which gave another enriching dimension to my life at that period.

To my mind, there is no doubt that Charlie Haughey did Brian a great wrong in having him sacked from Cabinet. Of course, Haughey would say afterwards that it was through loyalty to the party that he had taken that course of action; that he had no other choice because the PDS were calling the shots, and so on. It wasn't the case, however, that Brian and Charlie Haughey were ever very close friends, because they weren't — they were political allies. Some may say that Brian lost face at a certain point, with his 'on mature reflection' remarks (when he appeared to contradict what he had said earlier about having made the calls to President Hillery). But in my view, he was done for by that stage anyway: someone had it in for him, and wanted him to go. Jim Duffy, the researcher in question, was sent out to get Brian. In any case, even if he had made the calls, would it have really been so wrong? It wasn't such a big deal, but it was purposely blown up into something extraordinary.

In the final event, Brian was able to overcome all the terrible experiences he went through during those two years, and in the 1992 General Election he was triumphant once more. He died in 1995, having had the extra five years of life which his surgeon had promised him following the transplant — and one bonus year besides. To his immediate and wider Lenihan family and indeed to the Fianna Fáil Party, Brian will always represent our Camelot. He was the shining one whose lustre had never dimmed; the man who survived all of the years of politics without ever being tainted with having done anything underhand or smacking of a venal transaction — unlike so many of the others of his time. I will always be proud of him, as will all of our family.

Chapter 7 ✌

⎸ EUROPE AND EDUCATION

The early 1990s was a wonderful time to be involved in Europe. Walls were coming down (literally!); everything was opening up; spring was flowering. As Education Minister for Ireland, I remember well a visit to my Hungarian counterpart in Budapest. He had recently broken free of communist shackles and his party were in government but he was still filled with a huge sense of paranoia, that elements of the previous regime were spying on him. I remember how I went up in an old-fashioned lift in a beautiful old building in Budapest to meet him. He brought me into his inner office, closed the door, checked all the windows, looked behind the pictures and said, 'I have to be very careful. The communist spies are watching us all.' Now I didn't know if they were or not — how would I? But I felt greatly enriched by the whole meeting between us. He was a wonderful person: a professor of history with huge, terrific ideas on education, and I very much enjoyed working with him.

In 1990, Ireland held the Presidency of the European Council of Ministers for six months, and I can remember the great leadership Charlie Haughey gave in this context. For me as Minister for Education, it meant that each time in the course of those six months that the Council of Ministers for Education met in Brussels, I would chair the meeting and preside over the discussion of the issues on the agenda. It was during this period I met and had a very fruitful relationship with Kenneth Clarke, who was then Minister for Education in the UK. When I see him now on TV as a serving Minister in David Cameron's government, I think to myself, 'Well, you really lasted the course, Kenneth.' He was quirky then, as he is quirky now, but also very intelligent and astute.

In this period in Europe, the Erasmus scheme for third-level education was bedded down. The seed for the scheme, which provided grants for third-level students to travel and spend time at universities in the cities of other member countries, had been sown in Gemma Hussey's time, but now it was flowering and I was able to fully nurture its growth. Fortunately for me, of course, I did not have to take the money from my budget to do so, as the programme was fully funded by Europe. Whenever now I meet a young person and they say, 'I have been on Erasmus for a year in Turin' — or in Paris, in Budapest, in Vienna — I am always so pleased, and I think back to the day I chaired the meeting in Brussels of all the European Education Ministers, at which we firmly set the full financial parameters and targets of student numbers of the Programme. It was and is and will always be a wonderful scheme and it gave full expression to the European ideal.

I remember coming back on the flight from Brussels that day, very excited about what we had achieved. I was aware too that the path we had set ourselves was in fact nothing new. I thought of Clonmacnoise, so close to my home town of Athlone, just twelve miles up the road in County Offaly — Clonmacnoise, the place to which, centuries ago, scholars from all over Europe flocked for reflection, for learning, for study. I found myself reflecting that the students of now, by going to these foreign cities, these other centres of learning in Europe, were replicating the paths of the scholars who came to us then. I remembered also the students of eighteenth-century Ireland who, because of the penal laws which forbade the education of Catholics, flocked to France and to Italy to enrol in the great halls of learning there, to bring back in turn their new knowledge to Ireland.

Travel broadens the mind, as they say, and there is many a man and woman in Ireland now or across the world who can look back to the Erasmus scheme and what it gave them. Of course, I am not dwelling on this here in order to say how wonderful I was — after all, the scheme had already started and I was just fortunate enough to be in charge of the European Education seat when it reached its full flowering. Rather, I am telling the story to highlight the great remit and range of European policies on education, and what these meant for a small country in the Atlantic Ocean off the coast of Britain. Europe saw how education could help and, as full members of the European project, we were able to benefit wholly from this wonderful vision.

As well as the Erasmus scheme, a huge range of other literacy projects and various other measures were introduced, in which Ireland was keen to participate. Initially, we would receive full funding for such schemes, as the Vocational Training Opportunities Scheme (VTOS), which enabled those who had opted out earlier a wonderful re-entry into education. As time went on and as we grew comparatively richer, we would have to make our contribution to it, but all in all, the early 1990s was a wonderful period for the flourishing of education in Ireland. I was so much aware at the time of the extent to which the good reputation and renown of Irish education had spread, and Ministers from other countries would always show a great appreciation of the role Ireland had played throughout the centuries. In fact, long after I had left Education, I remember meeting in Clonmacnoise the then Austrian Minister for Education: she had come to visit the site with a group of her friends, not as part of her parliamentarian duties, but purely out of interest and a desire to see that ancient seat of learning. I thought to myself how wonderful it was, that we had been able to build on those foundations.

Of the latter years of my tenure at the Department of Education, there is one episode in particular which gives a sense of the flavour of life back then in the early 1990s and still has resonance today. Sometime in the late summer of 1991, I was contacted by Joe O'Toole, then General Secretary of the INTO, along with two educational professionals from North County Dublin, Dr Deirdre McIntyre and Dr Maria Lawlor. These two women had been involved in a particular school project about which they wanted to tell me. I was always very easy to meet. I do not regard this as a fault — in fact, I always regarded it as a positive thing in any Minister, that he or she should not think themselves so important that they are not prepared to meet, on the spot, people who have something to tell them.

It was the month of August, and we had arranged a meeting in my Department for 2 p.m. It was a beautiful sunny afternoon. Joe O'Toole and the two women came in and the tale they had to tell was a good one, which I was very glad to hear. At a primary school in North County Dublin, Dr McIntyre and Dr Lawlor — an educational psychologist and an educational psychiatrist respectively — had initiated a project they were calling 'Stay Safe'. The aim of this initiative was to highlight the importance of assuring the safety of young children in their journeys to and from school. They had devised a very simple programme which outlined for young pupils the rules of the road — not just in a traffic way but in a 'human traffic' way too. It also emphasised in particular the importance of never getting into a stranger's car, and so on. I think at that time there had been a spate of incidents whereby total strangers had been pulling up in their cars and saying to a little boy or girl walking home, 'Your mammy sent me to pick you up . . .' Fortunately in each case, another adult had spotted what was happening before the child in question could get into the car. My memory is that it was these incidents which had sparked this initiative on the part of these two professionals.

I felt it was a very worthy scheme and set about looking into it further. We called in Tony O'Gorman, Head Psychologist at the time in the Department of Education, and Tom Gillen, Head of Primary Education. After a long discussion with them, I made an on-the-spot ministerial decision. Now, for those who are not political anoraks, ministerial decisions made on-the-spot are relatively rare: things are not often done this way and sometimes such an approach can go awry. But my instincts as a parent told me that this particular measure would not go wrong — in fact, all it could do was go right.

Tony O'Gorman and Tom Gillen consulted with their teams and each other, and came back with a circular for the primary schools — all 3,250 of them throughout the country — asking them to implement, or to consider implementing the Stay Safe Programme. We couldn't order anyone to do this — only the Chairperson of each of their Boards of Management would have had such authority — but we indicated that the Department of Education was giving the scheme their strong stamp of approval, and that the Minister — i.e. myself — was very much behind such a move. Most of the schools reacted enthusiastically and began to take steps to implement the programme.

A very curious matter developed on the back of this initiative, however. As I had done for many years, at the time I would hold a public clinic each Saturday in an office at my home. This was basically for my constituents, but anyone in Ireland was welcome to come to see and talk to me. On two successive Saturdays after the unveiling of the

Stay Safe Programme, I found my clinic being visited by busloads of parents from Cork, there to protest against the Stay Safe Programme. Put down in cold print and plain English like this, I know it sounds dotty — but that is what they were about. They couldn't all come in — because they wouldn't all have fitted into my office — but they sent in their spokespersons as they waited outside. Their point of view, they explained, was that it was solely up to parents to ensure the safety of their children going to and from school. It had nothing to do with, as they saw it, interfering teachers and interfering Ministers and interfering officials from the Department of Education, who had no business coming in and trying to lay down the law about what a child could and couldn't do.

I was baffled, horrified and completely unable to understand their point of view, and as I tried to do so, echoes kept coming back to me of what had happened four decades earlier with Noël Browne and the Bishops, and how they and the Church had been so vehemently opposed to his proposed measures to ensure good healthcare for expectant mothers, insisting that doing so was solely the job of the husband and not the Irish State!

Many years later, when I was in the Dáil between 2007 and 2011, I put forward a question in the House as to what percentage of the country's primary schools had implemented the Stay Safe Programme — an echo in fact of an earlier question I had put down in an Adjournment Debate in the Seanad. Interestingly, the percentage of schools not participating in the scheme — which had as its only purpose to try to ensure the safety of young children — remained stubbornly high, at over 25 per cent. Most of these non-participating schools were in the Munster region. I puzzled over this for a short time, but soon the reason became obvious. It was not that the roads were safer in Munster than anywhere else. It was not that Munster did not have its fair share of lone drivers with bad thoughts cruising the roads. No — it was, in my opinion, the wide prevalence in that part of the country of a typically strong, far-right Catholic ethos which determined that people there were going to steadfastly resist the Stay Safe Programme.

Of course, time has moved on and, sadly, recent revelations about the terribly damaging effects some elements in the Church have had on the lives of children and young people have made it clear that it is not always the stranger a child must fear, but sometimes a person within their own community circle. As was brought home to me in later years when I was Chairperson of the All-Party Joint Committee on the Constitutional Amendment on Children, there is a strong underlying attitude in Irish national life of, 'My child is *my* child, and hands off anyone who seeks to interfere.' The vast majority of Irish parents will send their child to school because they need education, but as regards many other needs, the overriding feeling is that the mother and father know best, and that is that. Of course, most often, they *do* know best, but surely matters of child safety are of huge importance and any way in which the State can assist in this area should be welcomed with open arms by any reasonable and caring parent?

One very important task which I undertook in the latter years of my time in the Department of Education was the preparation and drafting of a Green Paper — later to become a White Paper — on Education Development. Just to clarify these terms, if a Minister in any Department wants to set out key policy ideas for eventual implementation, the way he or she must go about it is to firstly produce a Green Paper, which will lead to a White Paper, which will ultimately be translated into the formal legislation. The Green Paper with which I was associated, *Education for a Changing World*, would be published in 1992, shortly after my departure as Minister, to be succeeded in due course by the publication of a White Paper, *Charting Our Education Future*, in 1995. John Walshe, who was then Education Editor for the *Irish Independent*, later wrote an invaluable book in relation to this type of legislative process: *Partnership in Education: From Consultation to Legislation in the Nineties* (published by the Institute of Public Administration in 1999). This key initiative — the preparation of the Green Paper — was, I always felt, a very satisfactory way of rounding off the happy and productive four-and-three-quarter years I spent in my favourite ministry.

I suppose the genesis of the idea for the Green Paper came about in many ways as a spin-off from my very cordial and productive relationships with the various education correspondents in the media. As I have said earlier, I maintained good professional friendships with Pat Holmes of the *Irish Press*, John Walshe of the *Irish Independent* and the late and much lamented Christina Murphy of *The Irish Times*.

From time to time I would meet with each of them separately, either in my Department or for lunch somewhere nearby, and in that way I was able to exchange views and ideas about very many worthwhile advances in the field, or discuss shortcomings in the current system, etc. These meetings were, I felt, always very useful, both for me and for the journalists in question. It is from that period, in fact, that I date my ease with the media, because it became clear to me then how much can be achieved by an elected Minister through building and maintaining good journalistic contacts. I felt that such relationships also helped both parties to gain a good sense of what the boundaries should be, of what could be released into the public domain and what could not.

Towards the end of 1989, *The Irish Times* ran a major piece on education, of which the main gist was, 'Yes, a lot is happening in the field, but there is a real need for a shape to be put on all of it'. The tone was mildly castigatory, while noting some positives here and there. I confronted Christina Murphy about it and out of the ensuing discussions, an idea grew in my mind — that perhaps it was time to do a Green Paper/White Paper on education. After all, apart from the Vocational Education Acts of the early 1930s and, further back than that, Stanley's Education Letter and Stanley's Education Act in the nineteenth century, there had since been no educational legislation which would frame progress in the field or chart the way forward.

I shared my thoughts with Christina Murphy and, in a general way, started to talk publicly about the idea in newspapers and on radio and on TV. It wasn't long, however, before I got a call from Padraig O'hUiginn, the then Secretary General to the Department of An Taoiseach. He said that this idea of mine was a very good one, but that I should stop talking about it all the time! 'Why?' I asked him. He explained that the Department of An Taoiseach wanted to make some sort of pacifying gesture to the teachers' trade unions following the whole debacle of the Pupil/Teacher Ratio, and they wanted the idea of some kind of new policy legislation to come from the Taoiseach, so to speak.

Very quickly, meetings were set up between our Department and the trade unions and the Department of An Taoiseach, and from these came the formal announcement that the Department of Education and Minister Mary O'Rourke would be embarking on the writing of a Green Paper on Education. Of course, it would be the late Séamus

Brennan, in his brief 12-month tenure as Minister for Education, who actually oversaw the publication of this Green Paper in 1992, and Niamh Bhreathnach as Minister in 1995 who would be responsible for the publication of the White Paper and later the implementation of the legislation. But, as history and the paper trail will show, the idea had come from me.

Noel Lindsay was the Secretary General for Education when the work on the Green Paper began. A highly intelligent and effective person, he had been for many years at the World Bank in the US working on educational matters, before returning to the Department of Education in Dublin. He had succeeded Declan Brennan, another fine Secretary General who had been heading up things when I was first appointed Minister in 1987. Declan Brennan himself was a talented administrator and a pleasure to work with. When things got rough, he would keep the head down and keep his composure too. When things were looking up, he would become more buoyant. All in all, he had a wonderful command of his Department and was very well liked and respected.

When the time came for Declan to retire and we were looking to find his successor, there were a few very experienced people vying for the top job. I had my eye particularly on Noel Lindsay, who, I felt, was progressive and forward-looking, as well as very competent. When the matter came to Cabinet, it was he whom I espoused. In the end the collective Cabinet decision was for Noel Lindsay, albeit with my strong support. Noel took up his job with relish and set about his new role as the talented civil servant that he was.

There were many key people involved in the drafting of the Green Paper. These included the various Assistant Secretaries in the Department — the wonderful Tom Gillen, then Assistant Secretary for Primary Education; the Secretary for Second Level; the Secretary for Third Level; and the Secretary for Continuing Education. They each took a hand in the writing; and under them, the various Principal Officers, Assistant Principal Officers and Executive Officers all threw in their tuppence-ha'penny-worth, as the magnum opus began.

Early in the summer of 1991, Noel Lindsay delivered the draft content and format of the Green Paper to me. I remember bringing this long-awaited document home to Athlone to read, and I also recall being utterly, utterly dismayed and shocked. Why? Well, it was a load of civil service twaddle and I clearly recall saying to *Irish Independent* education specialist John Walshe, 'I feel like throwing it in the River Shannon, I am so upset!' In fact all of this, along with many other of my comments during this period of compilation, is recorded in John's book.

As soon as possible, I confronted Noel Lindsay about the disastrous draft document, telling him that it wouldn't and couldn't and shouldn't do. It was simply not worthy of the Department: it was nothing but civil service droning, and would have to be changed. There followed a great scurrying around in the Department. What was to be done? How would they get over this? In other words, how would they pacify the Minister, who was enraged? And enraged I was indeed!

Finally, a name surfaced: that of John Coolahan, the then Professor of Education at Maynooth College. The same man, I was told, had been the saviour of the Department in earlier times and he was a gifted writer. Professor Coolahan was duly drafted in and presented to me as the guy who would put a human face and a more palatable shape on the Green Paper. The Department commissioned him straight away and he set to the job with gusto. Having spent the day in the Department, going over the raw material and labouring to put a shape on it, he would come into my office every evening between 5 and 5.30 p.m. before he set off home. He would discuss with me various issues that had been raised in his work that day and I would have my say in his ongoing dialogue with my staff.

Professor Coolahan's contribution was invaluable, not only in terms of the new clarity he brought to the wording of the Paper, but also in terms of the fresh ideas and perspectives he was able to offer. One of his great ideas, for example, related to teacher training. In the barren years for education of the late 1980s, the teacher training budget had been brutally slashed, and Professor Coolahan now felt that it was time to reinstate its central role in education. And, of course, he was right. How could a young man or woman aged 20 or 21 be expected to go into a classroom, armed only with their degrees and their ideas from those degree and post-degree years, and remain at the top of their game for the rest of their careers, if they are never again to be challenged or trained in fresh approaches, ideas or new ways forward? And so teacher

Left to right: Brian, Anne, Paddy and Aunt Chris — I hadn't arrived!

Captain of the Bray Loreto netball team, 1953–54.

Spiddal beach, 1958.

Shamrock Lodge Hotel,
1 January 1959

Enda and I, 14 September 1960.

Hodson Bay Hotel,
14 September 1960.

My father, P.J. Lenihan (*right*), 1964.

My mother, Annie Lenihan (*right*).

Left to right: Ethna Madigan, Michael Madigan (RIP), myself, Enda (RIP), Ann Lenihan, Brian Lenihan (RIP), 1962.

Éamon de Valera and Brian Lenihan.

Enda and I in Sitges, Spain, 1966.

Christmas 1969.

Mid 1970s, boarding the glass-bottomed boat, Palma de Mallorca.

Athlone, 1975, down by the Shannon.

Chairman of Athlone Town Council, 1976.

J. Crehan, Patrick Cooney, myself and Seán Fallon at an official opening, 1976.

Brian and Ann with Breen, Conor and Mark.

1980: Glasson Cumann, Co. Westmeath.

Brian, Ray MacSharry, myself and Charlie Haughey.

My first day in Dáil Éireann. *Left to right*: Aengus, myself, Enda and Feargal.

1984: Myself and Nora Owen.

Charlie Haughey and I at a Fianna Fáil function in Athlone, 1985.

Myself with P.J. Coghill and Máire Geoghegan-Quinn.

Fianna Fáil Government, 1987–89: the last single-party government.

Late 1980s: Albert Reynolds and myself.

1987: Athlone Fianna Fáil women's group.

Brian and I, March 1987, both appointed Ministers for Education and Foreign Affairs: the first brother and sister in the Cabinet together. (*Courtesy of* The Irish Times)

FATAL STABBING AFFRAY.

Bernard Scanlan, the young farmer who had, as alleged, been stabbed by a neighbour, named James Nicholson, on Saturday night last, succumbed to his injuries yesterday evening. The deceased was a member of the North Sligo Executive of the United Irish League, and was well known throughout the district.

A press cutting recording the death of my maternal grandfather, Bernard (Brian) Scanlan. Note that no mention is made of my bereaved grandmother and the six — soon to be seven — young children left without a father.

education became central to the tenets of the Green Paper.

Slowly but surely, the Green Paper began to take the shape I felt it should have — lively, accessible and informative, instead of sterile and stylised. By the end of the process, it was truly what in my view a Green Paper should be: full of historical facts, yes, but also packed with fertile, creative ideas about the way forward.

As regards the key issue of teacher education, it was during this last year of my tenure in the Department of Education that we were able to get some funding — both from the national exchequer and also from Europe — to go towards setting up a network of Teacher Training Colleges around the country. There had earlier been some, but not nearly enough of them and, with the new European and national focus on training, it became a very logical step to take and I was glad to take it. To this day, I continue from time to time to meet at various events the personnel who are running these Teacher Training Colleges, and they always remind me of how the inception of their various establishments came about. I am so glad that this is something we were able to facilitate during my time in the Department.

When, in November of 1991, there was a Cabinet shake-up and Charlie Haughey asked me to take on the Department of Health, I realised with some sadness that I would not be about for the launch of the Green Paper in which I had been so much involved for so many months. I felt pleased, however, that I had conducted thus far the whole process thoroughly and in such a collaborative way. I was very glad to have had the opportunity to engage in such a fruitful way with so many of the various interests in education: the parents' groups, the teachers' groups, the students' and managerial groups, and so on. In this respect, one person stands out with great vividness in my mind: Sister Eileen Randles — a fine, wonderful woman with terrific ideas, who was working with such commitment in the voluntary secondary sector.

I still recall so clearly the night in November 1991 that I finally left the Department of Education. The Assistant Secretaries and many others gathered in my office and we had a few informal words together. I remember how I stood up and said to them that, in all of my life to date — apart of course from having and rearing my children — there had been no more productive or enjoyable time for me than the days, weeks, months and indeed years I had spent in the Department of

Education, and in such good company. I totally and genuinely felt like that, and still do. To this day, the things which interest me most in the media and in current affairs are matters of educational interest and I am always so thankful that I was given that time in the Department and was allowed in many ways to give full rein to the creativity within me in that regard, and to pass on my ideas and vision to its various branches and activities. Charlie Haughey gave me that opportunity from which so much flowed in my life and I will always be grateful to him for this. Of course, this did not and does not blind me to the venality of some of his later actions, but I do think it is only right to give proper recognition where it is due.

| YES, MINISTER

When I had entered my fifth year in the Department of Education, I had been very much aware that mine had been one of the longest tenures of any Minister there, and that the time would surely come for me to be moved somewhere else. That time came more quickly than many of us had expected, however. In the autumn of 1991, there was another heave against Charlie Haughey as Taoiseach and leader, which he managed to quell, for the time being. The expression of no confidence in Haughey had been strongly championed by Albert Reynolds and Pádraig Flynn, and so it was not a surprise that, when Charlie subsequently reshuffled his Cabinet, these two men were relieved of their ministerial responsibilities, which was Finance for Albert and Environment for Flynn.

As I mentioned previously, during this time of regrouping, Charlie Haughey had called me into his office and said, 'Well, what about the Department of Health? Would you take that?'

'An Taoiseach,' I replied, 'I will be going from one Department in which I had battled for five years against spending cuts — am I now to go to another one, where there will be even more radical cuts?'

He came back with, 'Mary, I think you would be good in Health, and we won't be too hard on you for your first budget, anyway!'

And so like that, it was decided that I would become Minister for Health.

The truth is, I was terrified of going. I had become so familiar with and attached to the Department of Education — not in terms of the grandeur and all of the titles associated with the Office, but with the civil servants and all of my advisors and staff, as they had come to know

me. I felt I had mastered Education and that it had not mastered me
and that, by virtue of my teaching career, I had come into that
Department with the right background knowledge. And I had loved
every minute of working there. Now I was only too aware that I knew
not a whit about health beyond what any adult knows about his or own
health and what I would read about the subject in the newspapers, out
of a genuine but a layperson's interest in the topic.

However, off to the Department of Health in Hawkins House I had
to go, my heart full of trepidation. My great colleague-in-arms and now
predecessor, Dr Rory O'Hanlon was meanwhile to take over in the
Department of the Environment. One thing which I knew would make
my new challenge much easier to contemplate was to be able to bring
with me my invaluable Private Secretary, David Gordon, and indeed I
insisted on doing so. I have not mentioned David Gordon up to this
point, but I simply must give full flight to him now. David had become
my Private Secretary two weeks after I went into the Department of
Education in 1987. He had been recommended to me by Peter Baldwin,
who had been Private Secretary in the Department to Gemma Hussey
and indeed her predecessor, Patrick Cooney. I had initially asked Peter
to stay on because I knew him and he was a sound guy whom I thought
I would enjoy working with, but he had been very keen at the time to
get back into the mainstream civil service. However, he put forward
David Gordon's name, as a young man he thought would be very
suitable for the post. David and I established an immediate rapport
within the Department and, from that point, went on to work very
happily together.

The whole species of the Private Secretary in politics is a very
interesting one, in fact, which I will say a little more about here so that
those readers not intimately acquainted with the ins and outs of the
civil service will get a greater sense of some of its machinations.

Every Minister and Minister of State in the Dáil has a Private
Secretary, who will act as the bridge between that Minister and his or
her Office, and the wider civil service. Those who are picked for such
roles are usually very bright, and very competent: generally, they will
have already been working in the civil service and will have made a
name for themselves, albeit perhaps a small one, in some area of work
in which they have been involved. They need to be quick, sharp,

confident and effective, and they need to be able to keep simult-
aneously to the forefront of their minds at all times the needs of their
Minister and the needs of the Department. A Private Secretary is after
all the conduit to the other officials in that Department, and these other
officials will come to know very quickly if he or she has the ear of the
Minister, and if he or she is in tune with him or her. You may remember
the hugely successful television series, *Yes, Minister* (now defunct, but
re-runs of which can still be seen from time to time)? Well, it is often
exactly like that in real life — the Private Secretary and the Permanent
Secretary encircling the hapless Minister; the Private Secretary wanting
to do the right thing by his Minister; the Permanent Secretary wanting
to have *his* say too — and so the battle goes on and on!

Once initial trust has been established, a smart Minister learns to
rely more and more on the word of his or her Private Secretary and
indeed on the actions of this individual. I know that I could not have
wished for a better civil servant to be in this key position than David
Gordon, and many a dilemma with which I was confronted was solved
by the courage and the sheer smartness of this young man. Later in my
career and his, on the day we parted, I said to David by way of a
prediction, 'Some day you will be Secretary General to the Department
of Education', and I am awaiting that day with anticipation.

When talking of Private Secretaries, I am anxious not to overlook
the great importance of civil servants in general and the huge — and
often unsung — contribution which is made by those who work within
Departments. I never forgot that in his earlier days, my father had been
a civil servant and he would often speak of what can be achieved where
there is a good working relationship between the civil service and a
Minister. Each party has a powerful dynamic which, if used correctly
and in tandem, can lead to great momentum within a Department and
very fruitful outcomes. As a Minister myself, I was always mindful of
that and tried to manage this dynamic to its fullest ability, and in turn,
the civil servants I worked with responded with me and to me.

To my mind, however, there has always been a lacuna in that
relationship and that lies in the question: who is ultimately responsible?
The files on a particular issue come up to a Minister and then the
Minister has discussions with various civil servants — and I always
believed in having these discussions down as well as up the lines of

authority. Then a final summation is presented to the Minister for approval or disapproval. I would always read these files with great enthusiasm, working through the wordy sentences in order to grasp what they really meant in practical terms. Finally my decision would have to be taken. In that sense, the decision is taken on the advice of the civil servant.

So who then is really responsible? Of course, in the final analysis, one will say, it is the Minister — it is he or she who is in charge. But there has been a huge reluctance in Ireland for any degree of blame to ever be attributed to a civil servant, either to a top civil servant or someone further down the line. Yet how many incorrect and uninformed summations will have been put forward to a Minister for approval? I was always very much aware of this danger: that is why on so many occasions, I added questions to a final document, asking for the whys and the wherefores of how a particular conclusion or recommendation had been arrived at. It does seem lopsided in some ways to me that the Minister is always held responsible, regardless of what decisions have been put to him or her, and their accuracy. It is an unsatisfactory state of affairs, I feel, and legally and legislatively, there does not seem ever to be a proper way of resolving the issue. But there should, I believe, be greater accountability within the ranks of the civil service.

Anyway, back to November 1991. After my conversation with Charlie Haughey about my new position in Cabinet, I duly went back to David Gordon in the Department of Education with the news. 'Heigh-ho, David,' I said, 'we are going to the Department of Health!' We soon learned that we would meet there the new Secretary General, John Hurley (who was later to become Governor of the Central Bank). John would be pivotal to much that unfolded in my new post.

Although Charlie Haughey had for the present won the day and succeeded in quashing his detractors, things were far from harmonious, and once the new Cabinet was in place, we settled back to work in an uneasy run-up to Christmas 1991. Albert Reynolds was now very much the focus for those in the Fianna Fáil parliamentary party who wished to topple Charlie, particularly those led by what I referred to as the 'Gang of Four' — Noel Dempsey, Liam Fitzgerald, Seán Power and M.J. Nolan. Other key figures were Noel Treacy, Máire Geoghegan-

Quinn and Pádraig Flynn. At the same time Albert Reynolds was much preoccupied with his own domestic troubles, as his wife Kathleen had been diagnosed with breast cancer. Christmas came and went, and Charlie was still at the helm — but many of us had the sense that the current situation was a precarious one.

Regardless of all this, I was determined to make the most of the challenges of my new posting in Health. To that end, every night I would trawl through the huge files — related to various aspects of health — which had come up to me for signature. Some of these dealt with very specialised issues, but which I was determined to master in a factual, knowledgeable way. I had got into the habit in the Department of Education of reading as many of the back files as possible, and I continued to do so now. But in an area I knew so little about, I had to work much harder than previously. Nevertheless, I would bring the biggest dossiers home with me at night and read as if I was preparing to give a lecture or go to a lecture. I was thankful once more for my ability to absorb new information like a sponge.

As it transpired, I would only be in Health for three short months, but some significant episodes from that brief period have stayed in my mind. The first of these was that, within a few days of my having been appointed, I was contacted by Gemma Hussey, who had been my predecessor as Minister for Education. Gemma had since left politics and was now Chairperson of the Dublin Rape Crisis Centre, and she was seeking, with a small delegation from this organisation, to meet with me. I readily agreed. The purpose of their visit to my Dáil office was simple — they were looking for more finance for the running of their Dublin operation. Fortunately, we were able to accommodate this. It is a very good cause, and the women who started the centre were brave in the extreme, to take on what was at that time a taboo subject, even for discussion purposes, let alone in terms of funding. The Eastern Health Board, under whose auspices the Leeson Street Dublin Rape Crisis Centre fell, had been sparse in their funding and indeed had not been very open-hearted about the matter in general. But we changed that, I am glad to say, and set an example which has been followed by subsequent Ministers, luckily. Ever since then, I have kept up great contact with the Dublin Rape Crisis Centre. In the interim, Gemma Hussey has moved on and they have had a succession of Chairpersons there, with all of whom I have been able to maintain very good relationships.

Another very interesting development during my short tenure in Health was in relation to the distressing phenomenon of cot death — such a sad thing for any family. A mother and father will go to sleep with their lovely bonny baby in the cot beside them and wake up in the morning to find the baby still and lifeless, or a baby will be put down for a nap during the day, only to be found lifeless in the cot when the time comes to wake the child. Numerous studies had shown that there was no predisposition in these infants to such an event, which could happen any time from the age of two months to twelve months: there appeared to be no underlying medical cause as to why. Numerous theories were being advanced at the time as to the whys and wherefores, and research efforts were beginning to focus on the physical position in which the child was laid down for its sleep.

At that time I had been following with interest the endeavours of Anne Diamond, the ITV presenter, who had tragically lost a child to cot death and who had taken up the cause. Anne came to Dublin and met with me and we had a very good exchange. It seemed clear to me that, in the end, all of the studies pointed to the fact that when putting a baby in its cot, it was better to lie the child on his or her back. It doesn't sound like much now, but this realisation then was momentous and hugely significant. Soon we got to work on a circular, which was sent out by the Department of Health to all the health boards and hospitals, maternity homes, nurseries, mothers, and to public health nurses in particular. The main message was that the Minister and the Department were of the belief that, when being put down to sleep, a child was best positioned on his or her back. The following year there was in fact a reduction in cot deaths and this continued to be the case in the years which followed.

Now, why did I make up my mind so readily on this? Well, apart from looking at all the many studies, I also thought back to my time of rearing my own two sons. I had never laid them on their tummies. This practice, of putting a child face-down in his or her cot, had been a new-fangled idea which swept Europe and the world at the time. It was thought to be best then, but it was, tragically, proved not to be so. I know that the anguish continues and that there still are cot deaths. I often think of bonny children who would have grown up to be fine adults.

In my time in Health I also undertook to play a prominent role regarding the AIDS issue, in which I had a huge interest. As we know, in the mid- to late 1980s, there was a massive AIDS scare on an international scale, and a belief that it could become a worldwide epidemic, mowing down all in its path. At that time we truly thought that AIDS was going to overwhelm the world.

Rory O'Hanlon, my predecessor in Health, had started the government's AIDS campaign, and I took it up in a very upfront, in-your-face way. We put out the big ads, hosted seminars and talks, and so on. While everyone was very worried about AIDS, there was also a really unhelpful attitude prevailing at the time — a 'don't-talk-about-it-because-it-has-to-do-with-sex' approach. Working in close conjunction with the new Minister for Education, I aimed in my own way to play a role in the demystification of the disease, trying to dispel the attitude of horror people had, and the hysterical feeling that it was going to sweep the world. I went out and met people with HIV/AIDS; I also did my best to encourage and foster the various support organisations which were being set up. I remember in particular making a valuable contact with a very good guy in Dublin — Ger Philpott, who wrote a book about his partner who had died from AIDS. Ger ran a Trust that had been set up to combat and raise awareness about the illness, and he and I became very friendly. In all the work that I've done, I've always had a habit of cultivating and working with people I like, and I have always followed my instincts with such people, even if they might be regarded by others as a bit 'out there'. I was definitely a bit like that in Education too, and also later in Public Enterprise, particularly in relation to the trade unions, in which I was always a believer.

It seemed to me that in that period of the early 1990s, we were living through terrific technological advancements in all aspects of life, and particularly so in the realm of health. Wonderful new drugs were being developed, which promised to prolong life or stave off debilitating diseases. Consequently, the world's population was getting older, propped up mostly by these technological advances in medicine.

All of this led to a review of health spending. I noticed then — and it continues to be the case — that in the UK, under their National

Health Service, such wondrous life-enhancing drugs were rationed. In other words, not every wonderful new drug which might have afforded an extra lease of life to patients was to be dispensed and paid for by the NHS. There were and are no such limitations here — as yet, anyway. If a drug had passed all the national drug tests and was proved to be safe to administer, well then, it was widely made available, either completely free of charge to those on medical cards or, for those on the long-term medical scheme, for a monthly payment which represented a very small fraction of what the over-the-counter costs would have been. I know that we constantly moan about the health system in Ireland, and yet, as I say, just look at the UK's NHS as regards newly-developed drugs. It is wonderful what research, development and technology has done in the area of life-affirming medicines and I have always felt it is important to pay full tribute to all those involved in that often thankless task.

Equally, while the capital cost of medical practice in Ireland was and is huge, even back in the early 1990s, we in Ireland were able to continue to sustain a variety of hospitals throughout the country — from small cottage hospitals in remote western areas, to wonderful, state-of-the-art places like St James's, Beaumont, the Mater and St Vincent's. It was clearly not possible to do all that ad infinitum, and yet any nod towards rationalisation in the hospital facilities on offer led to endless marches, protests and deputations. This was understandable: a hospital means so much to a town. It is a safeguard to the people, a reassuring place to which they can get their loved ones quickly and easily in times of illness and emergency. When cutbacks had to be made, and it was my job as Minister to set them in motion, the rational part of my brain always recognised quite clearly that the right course was being taken. Needless to say, I could fully identify too with the very strong feelings behind the public's protestations.

I continued to try to learn all I could about health while I was in the Department, even though I had, as others did, the sense that our days were numbered. Many macro health ideas have stayed with me since then and I have a huge and an abiding interest in the big, general issues of health, and its related spending and consumption in the world. I served happily and I hope fruitfully in my short time as Minister in that field.

Over the period of Christmas 1991, rumblings of discontent against

Charlie Haughey continued unabated. By this stage Albert Reynolds and Pádraig Flynn — along with Máire Geoghegan-Quinn and Noel Treacy, who had also recently left Cabinet or junior Cabinet positions — were openly speaking against the Taoiseach. Christmas came and went, and when we arrived back in early January, it seemed as if Charlie Haughey might yet be unassailable — but of course this was not to be the case. Leinster House at this time was a hotbed of gossip. Far worse than women hanging over half-doors blethering, men were in corners plotting, their embittered faces and tongues willing on the demise of their wounded leader. Something was going to happen soon.

Quite early on in the New Year, in mid- to late January, I heard that Dr John O'Connell, who had at one time been Ceann Comhairle, had his sights set on the Department of Health and the Minister's job. This I could understand, I suppose. O'Connell had aligned himself quite firmly with Albert Reynolds and was viewing him as the putative Taoiseach. It was a weird feeling, however, to know that, whilst you were serving and acting as Minister for Health, there was in fact an aspirant for your post waiting in the wings, preparing to jump into Hawkins House and take over your work.

All at once, political turmoil was unleashed, in relation to events which dated back to more than a decade earlier, and would in turn lead to a debacle which was the undoing of Charlie Haughey. The late Seán Doherty TD had been Minister for Justice under Haughey in the early 1980s, and it was he who had taken the rap for a scandal which had emerged over the nefarious practice of phone-tapping, when phones belonging to Geraldine Kennedy (later to be a PD deputy and then Editor of *The Irish Times*) and political writer Bruce Arnold had been tapped. There had been huge uproar about it all at that stage, with Garda investigations and so on. There the matter had rested until now, in early 1992, when Seán Doherty appeared on a late-night TV programme during which he said that, although at the time he had insisted that Haughey had known nothing about his actions, it had been the Taoiseach himself who had ordered him to tap the phones. Charlie was adamant in his denial. Yet again, uproar ensued and our leader was left with no choice but to resign, paving the way for Albert Reynolds and his cohorts to come onto the political scene.

In the wake of Charlie's departure, several of us put forward our names for the leadership, but in a half-hearted way only. There was never any real debate as to who should be the next leader: there was only to be acceptance of this wonderful person who had already come along. We had *had* Charlie and now we *were having* Albert; later on, we *would have* Bertie and after Bertie, we *were to have* Brian Cowen. I think the party has most definitely been too loyal to the leaders who were ushered in. Of course, in organisations that have hierarchies, you have to have a sense of loyalty, but in ours, in terms of the next-in-line, it always seemed that it was loyalty *über alles*.

And so, even though in February 1992, there was a too easy assumption within Fianna Fáil as to who would be the next leader and it was all laid out that Albert Reynolds was to be Charlie's successor, I threw my hat into the ring anyway, as did Michael Woods. I suppose from my point of view, it was partly because I thought there should be a woman in the race for the party leadership. It was such a male-dominated environment then, as in many ways it still is — Fianna Fáil was male, male, male! There was a lot of sexism, of which I certainly faced my fair share over the years: 'Didn't you do well to get here?'; 'You should know your place!' and so on. But my bid for the leadership was never really very serious: I didn't go all out, lobbying people for support or anything. Apart from the fact that I knew Albert had it sewn up anyway, I felt strongly that, in the end, Charlie had been treated shabbily. Beyond this, I knew deep down that I wouldn't have liked to have been leader — I would never have had the heart for it. Which is just as well, because in the end both Michael Woods and I got miserable votes: I got six and Michael got ten. It was kind of a non-event, as I had very much anticipated. It would later come to light that, during the two weeks when leadership bids — such as they were — were being accepted, Bertie Ahern too had flirted strongly with the idea of putting himself forward. But he quickly realised that at that stage, the parliamentary party was bound hand and foot to Albert Reynolds and had no notion of being driven off course.

So the Dáil approved of Albert Reynolds and he duly assumed the role of Taoiseach as expected. Then followed the notorious 'St Valentine's Day Massacre', as it would become known in party circles, when Albert proceeded to axe Chief Whip Dermot Ahern, eight Ministers — Gerry Collins, Michael O'Kennedy, Ray Burke, Noel

Davern, Rory O'Hanlon, Brendan Daly, Vincent Brady and myself —
and ten Ministers of State. Looking back on it now, it was almost
comical, the way we were all ordered to line up outside Albert's office,
so that we would be called in one by one to be told our fate.

My own encounter with the new Taoiseach that day still comes so
vividly to mind. Albert was standing by his desk, on which was sitting
a tray with tea and sandwiches. He was eating the sandwiches because
it was all very rushed and he was expected to appear in the Dáil shortly
after. I was the last to see him, and it seemed that each Minister who
had been in before me had just accepted their fate and bowed out
without protest. Now that it was my turn, however, that bold streak in
me which comes out from time to time suddenly surfaced again.

'Why are you sacking me?' I said. 'I *demand* to know the reason why
I am getting the sack! Did I not do my job properly? What did I not do
right? I'm entitled to know under labour law!' Now, this last part wasn't
true, but I was livid and I continued to push for an explanation. Albert
started to expostulate and argue with me and, as he did, bits of the
sandwich he was eating flew all around the room. I couldn't help it, but
at that, a small part of me enjoyed an inner smile and I thought to
myself, 'Ah, you never heeded your mother's lesson, that you shouldn't
talk with your mouth full!' I know it sounds caustic now, but it was
funny at the time.

Also comical in retrospect was how, at a certain point in the
proceedings, history began to repeat itself. As Albert remonstrated —
spitting his sandwich around him all the while — he suddenly blurted
out, 'Well, would you like to be Minister for Women's Affairs?' Clearly
there was some civil servant in an advisory capacity still floating
around, who wanted me to be Minister for Women's Affairs!

'No, thank you,' I said. 'I refused it in '87 and I am refusing it now!'
And with that, I flounced out of the room. I know 'flouncing' is one of
those words always associated with women, but that is exactly what I did!

It was funny too, when, later on, after Albert had finished with us, all
of us — the massacred ones — had to file into Dáil Éireann — one by
one, in a long line — just before the new Taoiseach walked in with his
new gang. Among them was Bertie Ahern, who was to be Minister for
Finance, Máire Geoghegan-Quinn as Minister for Justice and, as was
loudly proclaimed beforehand, Dr John O'Connell as Minister for

Health. Later that evening, I met up with Enda, who was up in Dublin to be with me for what we knew was going to be a difficult time. We went out for dinner and commiserations with a few friends, and then Enda drove home to Athlone, while I had to go back to my rented flat in Dublin. After a few stiff gins, I cried into my duvet cover for quite a considerable time.

I was awoken the next morning by my telephone ringing. It was Dr Martin Mansergh — who had been invited by Albert Reynolds to stay on as his advisor on the North — saying that the Taoiseach was going to telephone me later that morning. It appeared there had been a huge flood of telephone calls into Albert's office since the day before, protesting about me being flung out with the rest of them, and demanding that I be reinstated in a decent government job. Later that morning, I did indeed receive a call from Albert's office. I was asked to come over and meet him, which I did.

So, for the second time within that 24 hours, I was in front of the Taoiseach. 'Look, you refused Women's Affairs,' he said, 'what about Junior Minister in the Department of Industry and Commerce — Des O'Malley will be your Senior Minister?' I thought that sounded interesting and so I agreed, and left his office somewhat pacified. Later that day I went over to meet Des O'Malley, who said, 'Look Mary, I know this isn't pleasant for you, so I am going to give you free rein. You will have your own office space in a separate office block quite near the Dáil and I will be asking you to take on the business of Consumer Affairs. There is a major piece of legislation, the Consumer Credit Bill, which has to be put together and brought through the Dáil, and I want you to take charge of that.' I have always had an interest in consumer matters and what he was offering was something useful I felt I could do well. So I accepted at once and I went off to my office, mollified and happy. Now, as we know, a Minister of State's position is not the same as being in Cabinet, and that was a blow to me, of course. I do take these things to heart, but I was quite lucky in this instance because I came back from it and recovered pretty quickly.

That afternoon, Albert had a press conference at which he said that he would have two main aims during his time in office. One would be to achieve lasting peace in the North, and the second would be to bring about economic recovery in Ireland. To give credit where credit is due,

Albert really worked at the North. He made it his own; he went where nobody else would go; he met people nobody else would meet. I really feel that under his time as Taoiseach, matters in the North began to move at last, and in a very positive direction. And, of course, I never had any lasting animosity towards him. Why would I? He was my boss: he gave me a job, and I worked hard at it. I brought the Consumer Credit Bill to the Dáil and Des O'Malley was great to work for. He appreciated my situation and gave me free rein. All in all, I was to enjoy that brief sojourn as Minister for Consumer Affairs in the government of Albert Reynolds and the Progressive Democrats.

Chapter 9

MANAGING THE SMALL JUMPS

Initially Albert Reynolds was very popular as Taoiseach and the new leader of the party, and internally, people responded well to what was a much more open style of leadership than heretofore. But then, very early on in his tenure, the curse of the knotty and difficult issue of abortion struck, in the form of a very high-profile and controversial court case, and Albert was left floundering in an awful mess which was not at all of his own making.

The 'X case' of 1992 (*Attorney General v. X*), which had become the subject of a major public controversy, concerned a 14-year-old girl who had become pregnant as a result of being raped by a neighbour and wished to leave the country in order to have an abortion — something which is illegal in Ireland, except in very specific, legally defined situations. The girl's predicament had rendered her a significant suicide threat. The then AG, Harry Whelehan, took a stance on the matter, seeking an injunction to prevent the girl from having the procedure carried out. It looked like there was going to be a stand-off. An appeal to the courts ultimately led to the girl receiving permission to travel, but all in all, it was a very fraught time. There were many TV and newspaper interviews, in which Albert Reynolds increasingly called on me to participate.

My position then regarding abortion, which remains the same today, is that once there has been a conception, well then, there is a life and there is another person involved. The decision to abort that life is not something that can be taken as lightly as the 'pro-choice' people seem to think. Pro-choice for what, anyway? Of course the real crux of the dilemma lies in the question: when does life begin? Do you consider this to be the moment that conception has occurred, or is it 10 or 12 days later, when the impregnated egg clings to the wall of the womb, or is it at a specific phase in the development of the foetus? This issue poses a conundrum to this day and was to come forward quite a few years later in my career — in 2002, when Micheál Martin was Minister for Health and I was also in the Cabinet and he attempted to put forward to the people a further constitutional amendment, which among other things would have removed the threat of suicide as a grounds for legal abortion where the health of the mother was at risk (but which was decided against in a referendum at that stage).

Finally, we were able to put the dilemma of the 'X case' behind us, but it was not long before the next difficulty for Reynolds presented itself. In autumn 1992 the Beef Tribunal — a public investigation which had been set up to look into allegations of widespread fraud and other irregularities in our meat industry at the time — started to gather its main witnesses to give testimony. One of these was Des O'Malley and another was Albert Reynolds, who had been Minister for Industry and Commerce during part of the period under scrutiny. In 1992, O'Malley was the Minister for Industry and Commerce and he gave evidence about certain information he said he had found in various documents in the Departmental records. When Albert took the stand, he said O'Malley had told untruths and, predictably, all hell broke loose. Albert refused to apologise for his remarks and things reached breaking point. There is no need for me to go into great detail concerning matters which have been so successfully dealt with in other autobiographies — suffice it to say, the PDS pulled out of the coalition and a General Election was called, for November 1992. It looked as if King Albert's reign would soon be coming to a choppy end.

We had a dreadful campaign in the run-up to that election: it rained morning, noon and night, and the response to Albert was very poor. The key reasons for this were no doubt that progress in the Northern Peace Process had badly stalled, and also that a gloomy feeling generally abounded, that Fianna Fáil was going to do badly in this election. The final result in November 1992 was not so bad for Fianna Fáil in percentage terms, in fact, but in terms of seats lost, it was not good news at all. With the loss of nine seats in total, for the first time we had become a transfer-unfriendly party. I was glad to have retained my seat, as had Albert Reynolds, but the general result was a bitter disappointment for him. He had clearly hoped that the PDS would be eliminated from the field altogether, while in fact the reverse happened, as they increased their seats from four to ten.

It seemed that Fianna Fáil was out of the political picture in terms of the forming of a government, but over the Christmas period, matters would change. Attempts were made to start coalition talks between John Bruton of Fine Gael, Proinsias De Rossa of the Democratic Left and Dick Spring of the Labour Party. These proved abortive quite early on and there was a clear animosity between John Bruton and the Democratic Left. While this had been ongoing, Albert Reynolds, who was still acting Taoiseach, went to a European meeting in Edinburgh, at which Ireland was to gain a large slice of the European Social Fund. Before too much of a lacuna could develop, Martin Mansergh had our manifesto ready and informal talks were begun between the Labour Party and Fianna Fáil.

There were many of us in the party, myself included, who were extremely partial to the idea of an alliance with Labour — and this was ultimately agreed upon. Yet it was clear throughout the tenure of this new Fianna Fáil/Labour government that it irked Albert Reynolds to have to consult widely with Dick Spring, just as it irked him that the office of An Tánaiste was occupied by Dick. You see, Reynolds had always belonged to the school of thought that a one-party government was the ideal and that Fianna Fáil should as such have sole tenure.

However, the new coalition worked quite satisfactorily as it turned out, and the two parties pulled together in government well enough. On a more individual level, I found this to be the case too, and as Minister of State for Labour with responsibility for Consumer Affairs to Ruairi Quinn as Minister for Employment and Enterprise, I was able to enjoy a close and fruitful working relationship with my senior counterpart. There was never conflict between us and he gave me space on many issues. In relation to this, in fact, I learned from contacts I had within the parliamentary Labour Party that at party meetings of that period, Ruairi was quite frequently upbraided by members who were saying such things to him as, 'Mary O'Rourke is here, she's there, she's everywhere — you are giving her far too much leeway and allowing her too much free rein!' But fortunately Ruairi Quinn is a wise person and he knew that only by the two of us working together like this would we best be able to serve the country — and so this is what we did.

One area which Ruairi put me in charge of was FÁS. The scheme was then in its heyday, and together we worked out a new community employment programme which would give a boost to FÁS projects all around the country. It was I, in fact, who came up with the slogan — 'FÁS has changed the face of Ireland' — and indeed it did during that period of 1993 to 1994 also. Quinn was very worried about long-term unemployment and this was the impetus for the whole Community Employment Project for which I was given full responsibility.

Looking back now, I so enjoyed that period of my involvement with the Community Employment Project and FÁS. I worked hard at it and I saw Ireland at its best. All over the country, community groups conceived their project — which could be anything from, say, tidy town initiatives to local historical research to architectural development — got their applications together and submitted them to FÁS, where they would go through a vetting procedure. Then, if a project was given the go ahead, a number of people were approved to work on it: they would be taken mostly from the long-term unemployed register. Both Ruairi Quinn and I insisted on rigorous and in-depth training for those who were to be involved in this way and so, many unemployed people got new skills and a renewed sense of purpose in their lives. Whilst the employees' payments were small, they were regular, the jobs were structured and the contracts could be for up to three years' duration. There were county exhibits, which we visited. There were prize-giving ceremonies in various areas and there was constant encouragement for the groups to come together and keep in contact. In turn, these projects gave way to a huge flowering in the communities of pride in one's village or town or area. I feel there is sorely a need for a decent social history of that period and of the close interaction between FÁS and the community groups all over Ireland. The scheme really did change the face of Ireland, and I was so fulfilled and happy to be part of it. And no better comrades in work could be found than Ruairi Quinn and myself. Years later, FÁS was to 'lose its way', and now it is broken into different sections, each under the auspices of different Departments.

I cannot leave this subject without mentioning Dr John Lynch, the then Chairperson and Chief Executive of FÁS, whom I would in fact in later years appoint as Chairperson of CIÉ. John is one of those public servants to whom not enough credit has been given, in relation to the magnificent work he did during his very productive time at FÁS, and certainly in the two years during which I had responsibility for it. A fine, clever, hardworking man, he always sought only to work towards enriching and improving the country, and creating as many opportunities as possible for employment and community pride.

As well as Ruairi Quinn, there were other Cabinet Ministers in that government with whom I was very impressed. Among these was our own Fianna Fáil Minister for Justice, Máire Geoghegan-Quinn. She had been in Albert's corner in the previous years when they had flounced out of Charlie Haughey's Cabinet. When Labour were making the arrangements to go into government with us in 1992, they had said they would not do so if Pádraig Flynn was in Cabinet, hence he was happy to accept the generous offer to become Ireland's Commissioner for Social Affairs in Europe, and he sailed off to pastures new. Subsequently, Máire Geoghegan-Quinn became Minister for Justice and proved to be more than capable in the post.

Early on in that two-year Fianna Fáil/Labour regime, Máire brought forward the Bill which finally gave homosexuals their rightful place in society, and which abolished an archaic law dating back to the nineteenth century. It must be pointed out of course that the government was under duress to make this issue a priority. Senator David Norris had brought his case to Europe and won, and there was now an onus upon the government to ensure that the 'crime' of homosexuality was wiped from the statute books. Máire moved swiftly and clearly and it is to her credit and the credit of that government that this grossly unfair legislation was made obsolete, and that proper, legal recognition of homosexuality was at last granted.

Mervyn Taylor was the then Minister for Equality and Law Reform and it fell to him to ensure that all instances of discrimination against gay people in the workplace should be erased. As the Minister of State for Labour Affairs, I was responsible for bringing that piece of legislation through the Seanad and in my own way, I felt very proud to do so and to know that I had contributed in that sense to a wonderful, modern step forward for Ireland. To this day I still meet or hear from people who were helped by that legislation and who are glad of it. I was delighted to make great friends within the Gay and Lesbian Equality Network (GLEN), an organisation which was and is strongly committed to equality in the workplace in all these matters.

In the summer of 1994, however, relations worsened between Dick Spring and Albert Reynolds. An edginess had begun to creep in to their dealings with each other — there was resentment over the determination of the Labour leader and his party to frequently assert their differences of opinion with their Fianna Fáil colleagues in government, and there was a prickliness on various other things also. Yet it all ostensibly came to a head over the publication of the Beef Tribunal Report.

There had been an arrangement in place whereby Dick Spring would get a copy of the findings as soon as they were available, and at the same time as Albert. But Albert managed to get them first and holed himself up in the office with his Press Secretary at the time, Seán Duignan — and neither man would come out or answer the phone to Spring. Meanwhile Dick and his advisors had to sit outside, waiting until the Taoiseach had finished with the report. It was only once Albert had been through every line with a fine-tooth comb and had ascertained that he had been found innocent of any misdemeanour that he finally handed the document over to Dick Spring, who was by this time seething, of course. The episode only served to further heighten the tension which already existed between the two men and which would give way to the full-blown discord which ultimately caused a final split in the coalition. All of this began to seep into the newspapers, via 'authorised sources', and one way or another, it was not a pretty scene. There was at one point an effort at rapprochement, and apparently when Albert's and Dick's paths crossed in a hangar of Casement Airport around that time, it was all sweetness and light between them. But not long after that the Brendan Smyth affair broke, which would put the final nail in the coffin of the coalition.

There is really no need to go into the Smyth case here, I feel, because it has been so well documented elsewhere. Suffice it to say that the blame began to be laid firmly on the shoulders of the then AG, Harry Whelehan. Now Whelehan had baggage, of course — right-wing baggage. The Labour Party essentially distrusted him because of what they saw as his very conservative disposition and they felt that in some way, he had sought to hide the Brendan Smyth matter and not bring it to the attention of Cabinet or into public view — which, I should stress, was absolutely untrue.

In the meantime, Albert Reynolds as Taoiseach had proposed making Whelehan the President of the High Court: this was approved at a Cabinet meeting from which Dick Spring and the Labour Ministers had felt they had no option but to withdraw. Nevertheless, Albert now had the bit between his teeth and up he sailed to Mary Robinson, the then President, to have Harry Whelehan ratified. The Labour Party kicked up, but to no avail. The pictures of that visit to Áras an Uachtaráin tell their own story: a stony-faced Mary Robinson, a grim Máire Geoghegan-Quinn as Minister for Justice and a dour Albert Reynolds stand uneasily side-by-side as the necessary documents for the controversial appointment are signed. In the final event, as we know, Whelehan would serve in his new role for only six days.

It was hardly a surprise when, in the autumn of 1994, Labour decided they wanted out of the coalition. There were frantic efforts between Charlie McCreevy as Minister for Social Welfare, and Ministers Máire Geoghegan-Quinn and Michael Smith to sort out the matter, but these were all in vain. The problematic issues at hand were so petty that to any external observer they did not in themselves warrant a break-up — but of course the cited reasons for break-up were merely symptomatic of a much greater malaise between the two parties. The bottom line, as I have previously indicated, was that Albert did not want to be in a government with any party other than his own, Fianna Fáil, and he greatly resented what I always thought were the proper concerns of a Labour Party determined that they were not going to be done down by the larger party. Seán Duignan (ex-RTÉ), Government Press Secretary at the time, has written of this period in great detail and in an amusing yet thorough fashion in his book, *One More Spin on the Merry-Go-Round* (Blackwater Press, 1996), which is worth reading for these episodes alone!

Anyway, there were many discussions and last-ditch efforts to resolve things, and out of these came a new development which seemed to offer hopes for a future between Fianna Fáil and Labour after all. Formal soundings were sent out between Fianna Fáil and Labour, and it appeared that Labour might be willing to stay in government if there was a new leader in Fianna Fáil — Bertie Ahern. We all perked up, particularly those of us in the lower ranks, some of whom had worked hard and got on well with our Labour bosses and counterparts, as was the case with Ruairi Quinn and myself.

The atmosphere of that tense, uncertain time comes back so clearly to me now. There were meetings, sub-meetings and interviews outside government buildings; endless comings and goings. In the end, it crystallised in Albert Reynolds coming to a Fianna Fáil parliamentary party meeting and resigning as president of the party, ostensibly over the Brendan Smyth affair and what to my mind was the trumped-up story of a cover-up of what Labour insisted would have been important information for them at Cabinet. In hindsight, this was the beginning of the whole process of the clerical abuse of children being brought to light, and as such, it was a hugely important episode. Albert went to the Dáil the next day and resigned in a very emotional speech. His wife Kathleen and some of her family were in the distinguished visitors' gallery that day, and of course Albert's voice cracked. One phrase he said was so true and stays with me: 'You will manage all the big jumps, but when it comes to the small ones, they're the ones that catch you.' And so it was with this. Labour sat well away from Fianna Fáil in the Dáil chamber, and the whole thing seemed surreal and uncertain.

In the few days which followed, it seemed as if the Bertie Ahern/Dick Spring axis would be consummated and that we would stay in government. We had even been given our portfolios by Bertie: I had been told I would be Minister for Environment. I was pleased. I liked to be active and to work hard, and it seemed that this appointment would meet those criteria. That is how certain Bertie was that we would be in government with Labour: he had already prepared the files for each Cabinet member and decided who he was going to appoint in the key positions.

But it was not to be. We all went to bed on the night of 4 December 1994 and woke up the next day to the *Morning Ireland* headlines: 'A new development has cast doubt on the Dick Spring/Bertie Ahern burgeoning alliance.' *The Irish Times* carried a similar lead story by Geraldine Kennedy, which seemed to hint at some big new revelation in relation to Harry Whelehan, although also in very vague terms, but which led to a scattergun reaction among the Labour Party members. Bertie Ahern was in Brussels in his role as Minister for Finance when this 'story' broke. While to us, it seemed that it was all most likely nothing more than smoke and mirrors, that night, when Bertie had returned from his trip and was crashed out asleep at home, he was woken at 2 a.m. by a telephone call from Dick Spring. Dick's message was clear: 'I'm sorry, Bertie, it's all too much — our deal is off.'

Even in time, none of us ever got to the bottom of the reason for that call to Bertie. It would later transpire that Dick Spring himself had got a call that night, and I wonder now if it had anything to do with some of the things which have since come out in the Mahon Report? Perhaps this is what gave Dick Spring such cold feet. For us at the time, it was a huge mystery — and it remains so today, in fact.

While I fear it would be tiresome of me to recount in detail what has already been recounted in so many books, suffice it to say that during the 24 hours that followed, Labour agonised as only Labour could, before making an announcement that they would pull out to Opposition. In fact, they had already begun talks with Fine Gael and the Democratic Left. Some years earlier, of course, when offered such an opportunity, John Bruton of Fine Gael had been stiff and awkward and really hadn't wanted to engage. But on this occasion, the then AG Dermot Gleeson made sure that a welcoming venue was found and the initial signals were good. And so for the first time in the history of Ireland, there was a break-up in government but no General Election. Instead, the Labour Party simply glided seamlessly over to what had been the Opposition benches and formed a new coalition government with Fine Gael.

It was surreal, in many ways. The night before the formal announcement of the crossover, I had been on RTÉ's *Questions and Answers*, and had had a rousing good night which had all felt so positive. But we all knew the signs. In the next General Election in May 1997, Labour would insist that the losses they suffered could largely be put down to their time in government with Fianna Fáil. It has always been my belief, however, that it was not the link with us that caused the electoral damage to them, but rather the fact that they had been able, in 1994, to so casually ditch us and move over to a new partnership so seamlessly.

Chapter 10 ❧

| LIFE IN OPPOSITION

New Year 1995 dawned chilly and unfriendly for Fianna Fáil, in political terms anyway. Bertie Ahern moved into his role as leader of the Opposition. I was to be Shadow Minister for Employment and Enterprise opposite Richard Bruton, and Bertie had also offered me the role of deputy leader, which I was delighted to accept. I suppose his thinking was perhaps that it would be a good idea to have a male/female team, and he knew too that I was a hard worker. I don't think he realised until later on that I was also a bit of a wild card.

We took over the fifth floor of the old Leinster House building. The big parliamentary party room was given a makeover, as was Bertie's office adjoining it. I remember very well coming upon him one day, standing among the debris and the chaos of the workmen measuring and sorting out that fifth floor. Despair was deeply etched on his face. Of course, I played my cheerleader's role and did my best to jolly him out of it. At the beginning of that time, Bertie was very disgruntled and down-at-mouth, and it was easy to understand why. He had been so close to becoming Taoiseach, with Dick Spring as Tánaiste — it had been within his grasp, but then had all simply dissolved into fairy dust.

Meanwhile, I was quite happy to take up the mantle of Opposition. After seven long years of government, I felt it was time for a thorough appraisal of our time in government and for us to regroup and plan our way forward as a party now in Opposition, but with hopes of looking to government again when the time was right. I was also enjoying the simple, practical ways in which life was less fraught than before. I was delighted, for example, to be driving myself around again after many years of being taken up and down to Dublin by my trusty and

dedicated Garda drivers. Of course, sometimes it was good to be
dashed around, but I had always done my own driving at weekends at
home or had been driven by Enda, and therefore had never been
completely reliant on Garda drivers. By contrast, I knew some of my
Cabinet or junior Cabinet colleagues were now finding being driven
everywhere something very difficult to forgo!

To me then and now, the freedom of the road was and is wonderful.
With the wheel of the car in my hand, the tank full of juice and a good
engine under me (something which Enda always looked after for me), I
was a free spirit and could go wherever I wanted to go. Back then there
weren't the motorways that there are now between Dublin and Athlone,
and yet, when I drove myself to work during those two-and-a-half years,
the winding road and the endless recitation of the successive villages
would form a reassuring background pattern to my life. Athlone–Moate
–Horseleap–Kilbeggan–Tyrrellspass–Rochfortbridge–Milltownpass–
Kinnegad–Enfield–Kilcock–Maynooth–Leixlip–Lucan and then Dublin:
it was a rite-of-passage for me every Monday or Tuesday as I made my
way up to Dublin, and every Thursday or Friday as I went home to
Athlone. I can remember a motoring correspondent asking me at that
time, 'What is your favourite drive in Ireland?' and, without any
hesitation, I said, 'The drive between Dublin and Athlone — because it
means I am going home.'

All in all, during those years, life was good for me. We were in
Opposition, and I had a useful role to play. Home life was harmonious
too: Enda's health was good and our two sons were both working and
happily married by this time. I was lucky in that phase of my public life,
as indeed I was in so many others, that Enda was there for me always
and that no matter what were the ups and downs, he was my full
partner and my full supporter in them. Looking back now, I know I was
very fortunate to have such a wonderful, loving person with whom to
share my life. I knew, and know, that there were many who could not
count on such happy circumstances. Enda and I supplied to each other
what we wanted and needed, and I suppose all successful marriages
must have that generosity of spirit and above all, that physical love
which was the bedrock of our own relationship.

Before we worked together as leader and deputy leader in those
Opposition years, Bertie and I had already been well acquainted with

one another as colleagues, having worked side-by-side for many years previously. Initially, when I first entered the Dáil, I had been a bit in awe of him, I suppose — although he was not senior in years, he was senior to me in experience, having first got in as a TD in 1977. Bertie had subsequently sat beside me both at Shadow Cabinet (1983 to 1987) and Cabinet (1987 to 1992). He always had a habit of cracking his knuckles when he was speaking. In fact, from sitting beside him for five years at a stretch at one point, I can tell you that he cracked his knuckles incessantly, and I would always be asking him to stop it! I think it was a kind of nervous habit, for which he would always apologise. He certainly had bad dress sense too, and would often wear an old anorak that you really wouldn't have worn — but maybe it was all part of his image as a man of the people? Anyway, the mid-1990s was not a time for bling. Haughey had had bling of course, but somehow in those days, we expected him to have it!

In spite of his initial low spirits, Bertie was gradually able to take to his new role of Opposition leader, and began to make his mark in the Dáil and around the wider countryside. He had a job to do and, to give him his due, he did it magnificently, whether it was travelling to each constituency, speaking to local organisations, speaking at their social functions or whatever other events they had mustered up for his visits. And so it was that week-by-week, he mastered his role and week-by-week, he became very well-known and liked — and, in time, loved.

As deputy leader I did a lot of travelling too: visiting constituencies, and mopping up if there were signs of unrest within particular areas, and there were always a lot of those, as with all parties. My new role also involved a good deal of TV and radio work. Then, as now, I found that type of exposure easy, although I know many people have difficulty in these situations. My trick when I was on the TV or radio was to always imagine I was just talking to Enda at home in Athlone, or the person immediately in front of me, rather than thinking that I was talking to the world at large. Also, I never went in for meaningless economic phrases or difficult words which no one understood, least of all me! I felt that, if you could talk normally in a normal tone and if you were open about your life, both public and private, it would ensure that people would listen and want to hear what you had to say. I found that approach very useful throughout my public life, and I am still using it now.

Meanwhile, back at frontbench, Bertie was running a good ship. Early on, he determined that he wanted to preside over a party free from internal wrangling and rancour, and in the main, he succeeded in this. He always said that in Charlie's time, there had been far too many divisions, leaks and backbiting. I didn't subscribe fully to the view that under his benign influence, we could reach that heavenly place of no political divisions: I always felt, and still do, that where there is politics, there will be rows, and where there are rows, there will be divisions. I had experienced enough of it in my own constituency of Longford–Westmeath to know that this was the mainstay of constituencies all over the country.

In November 1995, as I recounted earlier, my brother Brian Lenihan sadly succumbed to haemochromatosis. It was a hugely difficult time for everyone in our family. Brian had been our shining star. He was a good man in every sense of the word, and bright and intelligent as well. Throughout all of his long years in Fianna Fáil, as Tánaiste, as deputy leader and in various Ministries, he had never fallen into the dark ways of politicians who could be swayed by cash. In that, he was like my father and the rest of us who undertook a life in politics. You can say what you like about the Lenihans, but none of us as politicians has ever been involved in shady dealings — these would have been anathema to every one of us. With Brian's death, I felt as though a part of me was gone, never to be recovered. He left us too soon but with such grace and such elegance in the face of his illness — the same as would be shown by his son, Brian, when he too departed this life.

The by-election to fill Brian's seat in Dublin West was to be held in April 1996. His son and my nephew, Brian Jnr, who had followed the usual processes to put himself forward, was nominated as the Fianna Fáil candidate. When young Brian had been christened, in fact, he was given the Irish name 'Breen', but once Brian Snr passed away and Brian Jnr became the candidate, he was just known as 'Brian Lenihan'. It made things easier for everyone all round.

It would be both a difficult and an interesting by-election. I was placed in charge of Laurel Lodge, a large urban area in the Dublin West constituency, and I worked very hard there. Many of the Fianna Fáil personnel based in Athlone and elsewhere in Westmeath joined me in the evenings as I went out with the Cumann in Laurel Lodge to canvass, and we covered the area twice over. I had fantastic support too from my very good friends, Kathryn Byrne and Margaret Walsh. Aside from my sadness at having lost my brother, I have some happy memories of that campaign, when I made some great friends in that area.

Brian Jnr was a great candidate: a young man of 37, he was good-looking, strong and intelligent, and at the height of his energies. He had been responsible for all of the canvassing in the previous election in which his father had fought and, indeed, had often represented him at constituency functions and at organisation level. So it was hardly surprising that the members of the party wanted him to be their candidate now. There was no dissent or discussion about it. They went to the convention and they voted more or less en masse for Brian Jnr.

Of course Brian himself canvassed far and wide and with great support. The Fianna Fáil Party were terrific and all the members of the frontbench came out and willingly did their bit for him. The day of the count dawned and we all assembled in the centre. In the beginning, the results were not too enthusiastic. Brian had polled well, but had he polled well enough? I was there from 9 a.m., and as the day went on and the preferences started to be divided out, Brian continued to gain more and more. By eight o'clock that night, it seemed clear that he was going to be elected.

Bertie Ahern was also very committed to Brian Jnr getting the seat but, oddly enough, on the day of the count, he didn't turn up until late in the day when it seemed that victory was already assured, and he arrived into the count centre to wild joy and enthusiasm. I have always felt a bit edgy about that — not for Bertie the heat of the day, in that respect. But in the end, what did it matter? Brian got elected and became a member of the Dáil and I was so happy to have him there. I remember saying afterwards, 'It wasn't Brian Jnr who won that election, but Brian Snr,' and in some senses that was true, because loyalty for my brother was still very strong and his constituents wanted to ensure that his son got in. It was not very long before Brian Jnr would forge his own path and more than justify the faith everyone had shown in him.

And what of the government itself during this period? Well, it was proving, under John Bruton, to be the opposite of what people had expected. Bruton was able to tame his impatience and learned to live with good grace with Proinsias De Rossa and Dick Spring. In turn, the various Ministers seemed to be attending to their jobs with great dedication and by and large, the country was beginning to gradually move out of the economic decline of the early 1990s. In fact, my feeling was then, and still is, that if that Fine Gael/Labour coalition had been able to hold on until the full five years were up, they would have won through the next time too. By 1997, however, the momentum was building generally towards a General Election that summer. This was indeed to be the case and soon we were all caught up in the fray of fighting for our constituencies. As for the Progressive Democrats at that time, they had a new leader in Mary Harney and during our two-and-a-half years in Opposition, she and Bertie Ahern had worked together very well in putting forward policies and in flailing the government on a daily basis, as was their role. Mary was quite a star, in fact, and led many Opposition campaigns with great vigour and success.

Meanwhile, we at Fianna Fáil ploughed on and it was good to see cordial relations gradually being re-established within the party, and a more even, more harmonious mood take hold. In theory, the next General Election was not due until November or December of 1997. But then, who wanted a December election? And so gradually, it became the accepted wisdom that the General Election would be held in early June of that year. We were soon working towards that and ensuring that throughout the country the Fianna Fáil organisation was primed and in good working order. Constituency conventions were held and the usual wars broke out between factions, but it wasn't too long before the candidates were in place.

It was sunny weather as our campaign gathered momentum, and Bertie sailed around the country like a blessed icon. The girls kissed him and he kissed them, from Galway to Kerry and Dublin to Donegal. He was a beaming, affable hero and hailed as such. It was as if the country was ready to be entertained again, and Bertie showed every evidence of being the one to do that. Perhaps he was helped in this by the fact that the three amigos, John Bruton, Proinsias De Rossa and Dick Spring, seemed to form a very stern triumvirate as they gave their governmental press conferences and as they moved about their various campaigns. Jollity did not seem to be the order of the day with them, that seemed certain!

On the eve of the General Election, I can remember doing an interview for RTÉ's *Six O'Clock News*, in which I said it had been a sunny and happy election campaign. So indeed it proved for me and for many other candidates in the party throughout the country. Fianna Fáil won handsomely, with 77 seats, and decided to go ahead and form a government with a small number of PDs. Here Bertie showed his distinguishing skill as a political diplomat and facilitator between different parties with separate agendas, and sought to bring on board the Independents as well, so that he and we would have an extra cushion as a bulwark for government. These were skills he had been able to hone during his time as Minister for Labour in the late 1980s, when a key part of his role was to bring together groups with opposing interests into a workable and mutually beneficial cooperation.

Labour had not had a good election, and it remains my belief that it was because they had 'crossed the floor', so to speak, in the way that they had. Fine Gael had had a so-so result but it was Fianna Fáil who triumphed. In forming his Cabinet, Bertie invited me to take on the role of Minister for Public Enterprise, in relation to which many of the state agencies were amalgamated into one government portfolio. Mary Harney of the PDs was offered the position of Minister for Private Enterprise. We were both to have offices in Kildare Street: Mary would be in charge of nurturing and encouraging employment growth in all of the private businesses in Ireland; I would be responsible for all the state businesses, including CIÉ, An Post, ESB, Bord Gáis, Aer Lingus and many more. I was very happy to accept the honour given to me, and so, from their bases in Kildare Street, the two Marys would become the new tsars of business in Ireland.

Chapter 11 ∾

| PUBLIC ENTERPRISE

I approached my new role as Minister for Public Enterprise in a way
which for the most part was very much in line with my own
instincts — which were and have always been inclined in favour of
the interests of the workers and the unemployed, as opposed to those
of big business. I suppose these were values I had inherited from my
father, whose own thinking, as I have recounted earlier in this book,
was greatly influenced by the ideals of socialism — even though he ran
Gentex very successfully for 20 years, employing at times well over a
thousand people. For these reasons too, I had always been keen at
various stages in my career to consolidate the strong links I had with
the various trade unions — this was certainly the case during my time
as Minister for Education, as Minister of State for Labour Affairs and
indeed later in Opposition, as Shadow Minister for Employment and
Enterprise.

I remember well my first day in the Department in Kildare Street in
June 1997. The Secretary General for Public Enterprise at that time was
John Loughrey, and he met me on arrival. Then there was the usual
drill when a new Minister arrives in office, by now familiar to me —
meeting the various Assistant Secretaries throughout the Department
and their key staff; the handover of the files for me to peruse, and so on.
This time, there was a very crowded agenda indeed and I made it my
first priority to set about meeting the boards of all the 'semi-states' (i.e.
the state-sponsored companies and businesses). In the days which
followed, I would go to meet with them at their various HQS and I was
able to engage in some good initial discussions.

It seemed to me quite early on that one of the most immediate causes for concern was the CIÉ group of public transport companies, and in particular, Iarnród Éireann — CIÉ rail. When I first met with their board and the then Chief Executive, I was party to a number of complaints — justified, it seemed — about the lack of finance being made available by government for the essential repair work needing to be done as a matter of urgency on railways throughout Ireland. I became very worried about this because I had the example before me of a number of years earlier when, in August 1980 and during a time when Albert Reynolds was Minister for Transport, there had been a terrible rail crash at Buttevant. On that occasion, 18 people lost their lives and 62 were injured. And yet for many years, nothing had been done to invest money in maintaining and updating our railway tracks or systems.

It seemed that some of my worst fears had been confirmed when, on Saturday 8 November 1997, I got word at home that there had been a rail crash at Knockcroghery, a village about 12 miles away from Athlone, on the way to Roscommon. I went straight there, to find a scene of chaos. Thankfully no one had been injured severely, and there were just a few minor casualties. But it was clear that that rail crash could easily have been a rail disaster. The train had just come out of a level crossing when it came off the rails. Luckily it had been flanked by two high grass sidings, with the result that, even though it had been derailed, it had just come to rest against one of these. The train had been quite full with students and civil servants heading back from Dublin to the various towns in Mayo for the weekend. As I said, there were no serious injuries — some passengers were brought to Roscommon hospital, but by the next day they had all been released.

The crash and the later findings troubled me greatly. It seemed that the cause of the accident was a faulty track which had given way, and that the track in question had been laid well over a hundred years earlier. The following Tuesday, I went to Cabinet to give a full account of the accident and I sought permission to employ outside engineering experts to investigate fully the precise detail of what had happened and what should consequently now be done to render our trains safe.

A team of engineers, headed by a very competent Scotsman, was duly recruited via a tendering process, and they spent some weeks carrying out a very thorough investigation. Once this was completed, they came to visit me in my office, laid out the results and issued a very stark and comprehensive warning. They had done spot checks throughout Ireland and had concluded that there could at any time be a similar crash on any of our main track lines — and further, that if this should happen, the likelihood was that the result would be a deadly one. It seemed clear that the previous government would have been aware of the extent of the danger too, but in the straitened economic circumstances in which they found themselves, they had not been able to take any action. The ominous feeling I had had in relation to CIÉ was justified indeed, and now it fell to me to do something about it.

I quickly brought a detailed Memorandum to Cabinet and said quite clearly that if money to do full remedial work on all the rail tracks of Ireland was not forthcoming, then I could not stay on as Minister in charge. What had always amazed me, in fact, was the very grudging support that railways got in Ireland, as compared to the situation in the UK and even more so in relation to countries such as France, Germany and Belgium, where the railway systems had always been hugely financed. But of course, as Minister I knew that the difficulty for Ireland was we had neither the long distances nor the large population needed for a railway transport system to be a success. However, whether they were used by one person or a thousand, it was also clear that many of our railway tracks were well over a hundred years old and needed massive remedial work, as confirmed by the Scottish engineer's report.

Cabinet was quickly persuaded that the job should be done, and we set up a Railway Safety Committee in the Department, with Pat Mangan, the then Assistant Secretary, being put in charge. I had and retain a great respect for Pat: he was one of those civil servants who worked at his job morning, noon and night and was full of integrity and sound advice. All of the staff in the Department took to this work with energy and enthusiasm: I think they had a sense that for the first time in many years, there was someone in charge who was at last going to do something for the railways of Ireland.

We soon had a detailed proposal which I could put forward to Cabinet for approval, and for which funding was then agreed in principle. The Railway Safety Programme was conceived as having three distinct phases and would run over a total of 12 years. The first programme would be implemented from 1999 to 2003, and require a budget of €661 million; the second programme, with a projected budget of €512 million, would run from 2004 to 2008; the final phase was to be put into effect between 2009 and 2013 and would require a spend of €268 million.

And so we embarked straight away on the first phase, and a four-year programme of remedial work on the rail tracks throughout the entire country began. I retained the services of the fine Scottish engineer who had advised us initially and he proved invaluable. But of course it was a thankless task in many ways. Yes, all of the country agreed it should be done and it was done, painstakingly and properly and safely — but to the external observer, what was to be seen in terms of tangible results? There were no shiny new trains. There were no sleek new railway stations. There were no new advances as such, because all the money was ploughed directly into the ground and into the essential repair work on the tracks. My satisfaction, however, lay in the knowledge that we were making the railways safe. Safety in matters of transport was my guiding star and I never made any excuse for that. Why should I? If you are offering a public service which involves transport, well then, safety above everything else should be your motto.

On a personal note, having been brought up right alongside the CIÉ station in Athlone, the railway had been central to my childhood in many senses. The railway station was exactly opposite the Gentex complex of buildings among which we lived, and indeed it became part of my playground. It was the playground too of the children of the Lally family. Martin Lally Snr was the Station Master and I can picture him standing on the platform station in his pristine uniform, raising his hat to every woman passenger. Old-fashioned maybe, but he was the salt of the earth and took such pride in his job, a pride which came across in the respect he gave to his workers and to all the passengers who travelled in and out of Athlone. My home town was quite a railway hub, as you can imagine, and it was pivotal in railway transport terms. Incidentally, my bridesmaid on my wedding day was Nuala Lally, the mother of the new Director of Public Prosecutions, Claire Loftus.

Early in my tenure in the Department of Public Enterprise, in the summer months of 1997, the Mary McAleese saga began to unfold. The next Irish Presidential Election had been set for 30 October that year, and there had been one or two vague murmurings in the press that

Mary was considering running for the Presidency, but nothing definite. For us in the Fianna Fáil Party at that time, the only person who looked to be shaping up as a possible candidate was the ex-Taoiseach, Albert Reynolds. But it was still early days.

The Saturday in question had passed for me in a flurry of clinic work: having recently been re-elected, I was particularly busy in this regard at the time. Enda was a huge help to me in my clinic work, which I did each Saturday from home. During the week, he would have arranged by telephone those who wanted to come and he would then be there on the day itself, to show them in and move them up the line. All of this he did on a completely voluntary basis — remember, in 1997 we were still in a more innocent era, when personal assistants and such sophistications were relatively unknown in the lives of elected people.

Anyway, earlier that week, I had had a telephone call from Mary McAleese, asking if she could call to see me that Saturday after my clinic. Enda and I had a habit of sitting down on a Saturday evening when the crowds were gone and having a drink and a chat together. It was a moment of relaxation, and we would then decide if we would go out to eat or have dinner at home. On this occasion, we were mulling over such trivial matters when the doorbell rang. Enda went to answer it, and there was Mary McAleese with her husband, Martin.

I knew Mary at this time — I knew her quite well, in fact. Years ago in my early days as a TD — from 1982 to 1987, when Fianna Fáil were in Opposition — Eileen Lemass and myself, with the benign approval of Charlie Haughey, had set up a women's group for the party. We ran a series of conferences around the country, each one a big success, and the group quickly grew in stature and in renown. Soon we had an executive group of women running the conferences from the Fianna Fáil HQ: there was Eileen Lemass, myself and a number of others, including Noreen Butler, Kathryn Byrne, Betty Coffey, Sadie Jordan and, of course, Mary McAleese. Mary was spirited, talkative, determined and knowledgeable. At that time she was living in County Meath with her husband and her very young family, which included twins. Our women's events continued to meet with a great response, and good friendships developed between members.

Time went on and by 1987 we were in government again. The women's group changed as other women took centre stage, and from time to time I would hear of Mary McAleese, or I would hear from her. She had become a very busy person: a practising barrister, a professor at Trinity College and a presenter on RTÉ's *Prime Time*. And I too was increasingly busy. So life moved on, but our paths would cross fleetingly from time to time and we kept in touch whenever we could.

On that warm mid-summer day (now fifteen years ago) when Mary and Martin called to see us, we had tea and talk and no, they wouldn't take a drink. As has remained her wont, Mary very quickly came to the point: she wanted to run for the Presidency and had come to ask my advice. True to form also, it soon became clear that she was very serious about this idea, and she proceeded to tell me how she intended to set about her task — she had already some very firm ideas in that regard. Crucially, Martin was in full agreement with her. We talked and we planned and I very quickly felt that they had a good chance of success. During the course of our conversation, I also incidentally discovered that it was Mary Leneghan (now McAleese) who was now talking with Mary Lenihan (now O'Rourke) — a quirky and odd coincidence indeed!

Before Mary and Martin McAleese left Enda and me that evening in Athlone, I had pledged her my troth and promised her my support. She hadn't asked me to, but it was something I wanted to do. I felt she would be a great candidate for our party and a more than worthy successor to Mary Robinson, who had blazed a trail for Ireland in her Presidency. Of course, the whole exchange of that evening was bitter-sweet for me, as I kept thinking back to the time seven years previously when I had been so involved in my brother Brian's campaign for the Presidency, and had lived through the highs and lows of those exhilarating months with him.

As also discussed that evening, Mary set about her strategy with intent, and next went to see Rory O'Hanlon. Then she followed through with all of the other approaches she had planned, culminating with an early visit to the Taoiseach, Bertie Ahern. Time went on and soon her bid to be the Fianna Fáil representative for the Presidency began to gain momentum. At that time however, the sure-fire bet in our party seemed to be Albert Reynolds, who had embarked on his own separate campaign, although soon another very renowned figure within Fianna Fáil — Michael O' Kennedy — would declare his candidacy too. As well as Mary, there was at one point great talk of another Northern figure, John Hume being put forward — but that dissipated quickly.

The parliamentary party meeting early that autumn was to be the decisive day for the Fianna Fáil candidate for the Presidency to be finally chosen. An amusing aside here is that three Lenihan votes were submitted on that occasion, and that each of us would back a different candidate! Brian Lenihan voted for Michael O'Kennedy, whom he knew through the Law Library and through legal work; Conor Lenihan voted for Albert Reynolds, who had always been a pal of his in the party; and I voted for Mary McAleese. So there was certainly not a combined vote from the Lenihan family for anyone in particular!

The most interesting aspect of that party meeting for the vote was the role played by the Taoiseach, Bertie Ahern. Earlier in the summer, Bertie had taken Albert out to lunch and reassured him that he was going to be in his corner and that he would be supporting him all the way as the Presidential candidate. And so, Albert had gone into the vote that day, thinking that the Taoiseach was on his side — although a part of him must surely have been aware of just how cunning and devious Bertie could be. There had been a Cabinet meeting the day before the party meeting, and after the business part of the meeting was concluded, the Taoiseach had turned to the Cabinet Secretary to say that he wanted to talk political strategy with us. As soon as the Secretary withdrew from the room, Bertie began to talk about the forthcoming Presidential campaign. He left us in no doubt whatsoever that Mary McAleese was the candidate we should support, and when I spoke afterwards to fellow Cabinet members, they would confirm having had the same impression. That night, there was another meeting in Fianna Fáil HQ, at which the message was again repeated, albeit in various degrees of intensity, depending upon who was being addressed.

The day of the parliamentary party meeting dawned bright and clear. I know from subsequent conversations that both Albert and Michael O'Kennedy had been told there would be no need to have a prepared speech — that there would, in fact, be no speeches. However, as it transpired, there were, and Mary McAleese was the only person to have done any preparation. Accordingly, she spoke fluently and very well, and left the other two far behind in her wake. At one particular point later in the meeting, and in a gesture which would go down in party folklore, Bertie Ahern held up his voting card to Albert Reynolds to show that he had indeed voted for him. However, as many of us knew then and as all of us would know later, what Bertie held up to Albert may well have been his *first* vote but where did his *final* vote go?

Mary McAleese won by a street and went on to be our very successful candidate in that campaign, and our President for 14 years. Obviously, when Mary McAleese became President, she represented at that point all of the people of Ireland and not any one party — but we in Fianna Fáil were always proud of the fact that she had been chosen by our party to be the standard bearer that autumn of 1997.

Mary's Presidency was, as we know, hugely successful. Right through her 14 years in office, she remained buoyant, warm, thoughtful and reflective: all of the things needed in a Head of State. Even in May 2011, each time I saw her on television with the Queen, I felt that whatever visit they were making would be a success with Mary in charge. She always exuded that reassuring air of confidence and capability. For me, it was an unfailing pleasure to meet her at the numerous official functions where our paths would cross. Whenever we saw each other, I was always warmed through by her enthusiasm and friendship, and she would always ask about Enda. Indeed, she would do our family the great honour of travelling down to be present in person at Enda's funeral when he died in late January 2001.

Back at the coalface of the Department, the next challenge up for me was Luas and how this huge public project could be advanced. Luas was to be an urban transport network for the city of Dublin, much along the lines of those which had been set up some decades earlier in various forms in most of the other European capitals — as always in these matters, we in Ireland had been slow to catch up. There was the DART, of course, which had been set up in the early 1980s and was a huge success, but since then, there had been nothing new in terms of public transport for the city, except for more buses and even those had always been dragged unwillingly from successive Finance Ministers. Luas as an idea had been knocking around since Brian Cowen's time as Minister for Transport in 1993 to 1994, and when Labour crossed over and went into coalition with Fine Gael, it had become the remit of Michael Lowry and then of his successor, Alan Dukes. Luas was a big, big project and the provision of it could draw down some much needed European funds.

When I in my turn took over the Luas portfolio, I discovered that the previous Cabinet had been very divided over the way forward. Fundamental questions still remained unanswered. Was it to be over ground; was it to be underground; should it be a combination of both? The debate had raged internally and in the media, while resentment bubbled within CIÉ at the idea of huge sums of money being pumped into an alternative transport system. At this stage, Donal Mangan was the CIÉ Project Director of Luas.

When I initially perused the files, it became clear that, yes, there had also been bad feeling high up in CIÉ decades earlier, when DART was mooted. So what's new, I thought? Seán O'Connor, a young man who was in the Dublin branch of Fianna Fáil and a grand-nephew of Seán Lemass, suggested that I set up a kind of 'Shadow' Committee within the Department but with my own nominees on it, who would ensure that the work was done. I thought it a very good idea and asked Pádraic White — the then CEO of the Industrial Development Authority (IDA) — if he would chair it, and luckily he was happy to do so. This new committee was an entirely voluntary one with no payment for those involved in it, but all of its members, who were very experienced people — like Pádraic White and Pat Mangan, the Assistant Secretary of the Department of Transport — had huge records in the field, and took to their task with energy and enthusiasm.

Meanwhile, both at Cabinet and in the papers, the debate over the way forward for Luas grew ever louder and more declamatory. I found very quickly that when you are going to embark on a mammoth project such as this one was, everybody is an expert — or thinks they are. Cabinet, it seemed, could be divided in three camps: those who thought it should be on the ground; those thought it should be under the ground; and those who thought it shouldn't go ahead at all. As for me, I kept my ears primed and my eyes open and absorbed everything I could. I knew that public expectation was high. On one of his radio programmes at the time, Tom McGurk christened me 'Mama Luas'!

Finally, I was ready to bring my proposal to Cabinet. The day in that summer of 1998 when the scheme for Luas — which was to be over ground — was approved and finally given the go ahead was an exciting and very satisfying one for me and all those who had helped me along the way. At that point, the work had only just begun in real terms, as there was the funding and European drawdown to be sought and countless other matters to be attended to, all of which made for a busy, busy time for me. The Taoiseach dug the sod for the first Luas line and Dublin was at last to get the urban transport network which had been so long in the planning. To this day, whenever I see the Luas gliding along the streets of Dublin, I genuinely feel a sense that I was part of the history of Irish transport.

On the home front, in 1999 Enda had a serious health scare and had to be hospitalised in the Mater in Dublin. Fortunately I was able to go to see him there frequently. He was really quite ill but proved very resilient both physically and mentally, and was able to rally through and in time come home, under a very strict regime of rest and medication. I will be forever indebted to one of my sisters-in-law, Maureen O'Rourke, for the help she was able to give us at this difficult time. An ex-theatre sister at Sir Patrick Dun's Hospital in Dublin and now retired, Maureen took wonderful care of Enda when he came home. Although it had been recommended by his medical team in the Mater that he should recuperate in a nursing home for some time after his discharge from hospital, Enda was adamant that all he wanted to do was to come home as soon as possible, and I was with him on that. After all, when you are bruised, hurt and shaken, what more do you want than to get back to your own bed, among your own familiar surroundings? Of course, work dictated that I had to be away during the week, but Maureen moved in for two weeks and stayed overnight with Enda on week nights until I came home each weekend. She shopped and cooked and made him exercise and take his tablets, and in general, it was as if he was in the best nursing home in the world: he had the care of his own private nurse in his own comfortable home. The fact that Maureen was able to do this gave me much peace of mind while I was away. I was most appreciative of her efforts then and remain very grateful for her generosity of spirit. Enda's two other sisters, Eithne and Gertie (who has since passed away) were always so kind to me, Enda and my extended family too.

The next semi-state up for our attention in the Department was Telecom, which later became called Eircom. The issue at hand, which had been on the cards for several years previously, was the proposed flotation of this state-owned company. Two key decisions needed to be taken: firstly, whether the flotation should happen at all and secondly, if so, what the opening share price should be. We were aware that these were hugely important, momentous decisions, but no one could have predicted what the outcome would be — that the sale of Eircom would become a saga almost biblical in its implications, soon to be referred to by the critics as 'the Eircom debacle'. However, those of us who inhabit the grown-up world know that shares go up and shares go down, and that there is absolutely no guarantee ever that their value will hold or stay consistent.

Throughout 1999, we had numerous meetings on the matter, with Bertie Ahern, Mary Harney, Charlie McCreevy and myself, together with each of our civil service advisors. Finally, after much debate and toing and froing, the decision was taken at a full Cabinet meeting that Eircom would be floated. I strongly felt it was the correct thing to do. Even once this decision was formally made, there were many more deliberations before the final steps to put things in motion could be taken.

A very important side issue related to the flotation of the company involved a prior arrangement with the trade unions, which went back some years. In the Fianna Fáil Party manifesto of 1997, we had pledged that if Eircom went to flotation, the unions would be given 14.9 per cent of the share value. Mary Harney of the PDS had also been party to this pledge to the unions. Early on in my time in Public Enterprise, I had been visited in Kildare Street by David Begg, heading up a trade union delegation of the Communication Workers' Union (CWU), along with their then General Secretary, Con Scanlon. They were very clear that, if the flotation were to go ahead, they were going to call in the government's promise. I consulted with Bertie Ahern and Mary Harney, and they confirmed that both Fianna Fáil and the Progressive Democrats were inextricably bound to this earlier commitment.

After numerous further meetings, the only question remaining was what the share price offering should be at flotation. Too high, and the shares wouldn't sell. Too low, and they would be given away. This led to many more arguments, debates and another series of discussions. Although this is not generally known even now, it transpired that at one of the last tense meetings on this issue of thrashing out an equitable, middle-of-the-road price for Eircom, Charlie McCreevy said that his Secretary General would resign if such and such a price was not achieved — and this would be the price at which we eventually floated. Charlie was quite determined on it because, quite rightly, he did not want to see the government and the country deprived of a fair price. Ultimately, the billions earned through the sale would go into the National Pension Reserve Fund and so, in an odd way, it is that fund which is now helping to get Ireland out of some of the banking and financial difficulties in which we find ourselves. What goes around comes around, indeed.

While we at Cabinet debated as to the price, Con Scanlon and his team of advisors for the trade unions in Eircom were busy negotiating the terms and conditions of their 14.9 per cent. Even now, I recall distinctly the long night when the government vacillated at the very eleventh hour, wondering whether it would go ahead with the flotation at all and what should happen about the union stake, and so on. David Begg assumed a pivotal role in these discussions, demanding that the promise be fulfilled, and on the night in question, he and his fellow union members did not leave the government buildings until midnight and they had secured the final guarantee on their 14.9 per cent.

Eircom was floated on the New York Stock Exchange on 8 July 1999. We went there for the flotation and visited the Stock Exchange. I stayed one day and one night, during which time I also had a meeting with some industrialists who were interested in coming to Ireland. Then I came straight home.

As the months passed, myths grew up and criticism of our handling of the Eircom sale became a very popular bandwagon to be jumped upon. As the figures showed, the share price initially held up well above the flotation price for over twelve months. When, however, the share value began to fluctuate, as all share prices do, it seemed that 'the Eircom debacle' was born. Of course, as I have since said and will continue to say, it was up to any individual to cash in their shares at any time during the first twelve months if they wished to make a profit. Many people did, in fact, and made quite a handsome little profit. But for some reason, others thought that they should hold on to their shares and that the price should keep going up and up — and of course that was never to be. When I now hear David Begg, inter alia, saying from time to time that Eircom should never have been floated, I smile and remember. This is not in any way meant to be castigatory of David Begg, but I cannot help but recall how hard he pushed for that 14.9 per cent for the trade unions.

By May 2000, condemnation far and wide of the course of action taken by us on Eircom had reached a kind of fever pitch, and so I was in fact very glad when Fine Gael's Ivan Yates put down an Adjournment Motion in the Dáil. The request for an Adjournment Motion is a measure which, if agreed, leads to the immediate interruption of normal business by the House for the discussion of a matter or issue deemed to be of urgent public importance. This gave me a much-needed chance to go to the Dáil and to set out the situation exactly. What follows here is a verbatim copy of my statement of 24 May 2000, in which the importance of the detail can be appreciated.

Adjournment Debate
24 May 2000
Ms Mary O'Rourke, TD, Minister for Public Enterprise

A Ceann Comhairle

As you know I am always very happy to come into the House, to debate issues and to share information on matters for which I have direct political responsibility.

On this occasion, however, I would like to ask my colleagues in the House to exercise great prudence in refraining from say anything under privilege which might give rise to erroneous investor perceptions of Eircom.

As the Deputy is aware, Eircom is now a private company and I have no responsibility in relation to either its commercial operations or its capital structure.

The Prospectus and the price range set prior to the flotation were agreed by both Government and the Company. The final price of £3.07 was within this price range and just above the mid-point of the range.

The balance sheet of the Company at the time of the flotation was very strong. The price set by the Government for Eircom at the flotation date was set on the basis of what the market was prepared to pay.

The strategic partners in Eircom, KPN and Telia, were prevented from selling their stakes in the Company for up to six months. This position was made clear in both the main Prospectus and the mini-Prospectus. The mini-Prospectus was distributed to all of the 1.2 million people who registered their interest in purchasing shares.

The pricing of the shares in July 1999 was a delicate one of balancing the need for a fair price for taxpayers and the need for a fair return for retail and institutional investors. Criticism was expressed in the immediate aftermath of the flotation from certain quarters, that the price of the Eircom shares was in fact set too low by the Government.

The Government could have chosen to float the Company at a higher price than it did, but chose not to do so. The Government received advice from one of the Joint Global Co-ordinators, Merrill Lynch, to the offering (sic) to float the shares at £3.27. Merrill Lynch are now advising the Company.

As the House knows, the launch price was £3.07 (Euro 3.90). In the immediate aftermath of the flotation, the share rose in price by 20%. The share has traded well above flotation price most of the time since the-flotation. The share price has been below the issue price on 35 days out of 230 days since the launch.

In the first three months of this year, the share price was never below the issue price and reached a high of £3.78 on a number of occasions in that period, a premium of 23% on the flotation price.

The potential returns to Eircom investors have been available against the background of a market which has been, at best, sluggish or in decline since the flotation.

Bonus shares of one for every 25 shares held will issue to people who retain their shares up to 7 July 2000, which is equivalent to 4% interest.

An interim dividend of 1.26p (1.6 Euro, cents) per share was paid on 14 January 2000. A further dividend of 2.4p (3.0 Euro, cents) per share will be paid shortly. The two dividend payments are equivalent to over 1% interest.

Deputy Yates has suggested that I should apologise to the people who bought shares in Eircom. I would like to say to him that I was very careful throughout the process to stress that the price of shares can and does fluctuate. Contrast with this Deputy Yates' statements on *Morning Ireland* on 22 April last year. He stated that 'this is not a risky investment; this is a sure bet' and went on to say, 'I'm telling people, this is money for old rope'. The interviewer, Richard Crowley, even suggested to Deputy Yates that he was 'doing a great sales pitch, they [Eircom] don't need to spend £3 million if they had you working for them'.

As I have said, I was grateful to have the occasion of the Adjournment debate to be able to face down some of my critics at the time. I cannot say there was no satisfaction for me in being able quote back to Ivan Yates those infamous words of his on *Morning Ireland*: that an Eircom share was 'money for old rope'. I have often thought about the matter since, and how much he must have regretted that early morning interview! It would not be until some years later that it became quite clear, as evidenced by well-known economic commentators, that the Eircom flotation was not a 'debacle'. A good price was achieved for the government and the punters had a chance to make their money over the share price for quite a while afterwards. I would have been devastated if we had priced too low and by so doing, we had denied a fair price to the government and to the country.

As can be imagined, it wasn't easy being under such intense public scrutiny at times, and sometimes the only way through was to see the funny side. It was, of course, during my time as Minister for Public Enterprise that the then Chairperson of CIÉ, Brian Joyce, resigned. Asked in a live media interview at the time what I had been doing when I had heard of the resignation, I had replied, perhaps a little too spontaneously, that I had been in the bath listening to the radio when I had first learned the news. Lo and behold, the cover of the next issue of *The Phoenix* was an image depicting Bertie Ahern and me in a bubble bath together when we got the news of Joyce's departure!

With the year 2000 fast approaching, Ireland was in the grip of millennium fever. Séamus Brennan, our Chief Whip, was appointed Minister for the Millennium and he set about putting together an inspiring programme to mark the new century, pivotal to which was a small sum from our Lotto which he made available to communities throughout the country to apply for a particular commemorative statute or event or memorial. Each project of this kind would be vetted rigorously by a very competent committee before any money was awarded.

One of my own favourite initiatives relating to the millennium celebrations came from An Post, in fact. As well as issuing a magnificent special issue of their wonderful commemorative stamps, they set themselves the goal of giving a 'millennium tree' to everyone in Ireland. Each person was to receive a certificate bearing the 'address' of their tree — i.e. details of the place where it had been planted. The idea was that they could go to visit it to see how it was doing. The project quickly caught the public's imagination. Just the other day I came across my own certificate and, poignantly, a certificate for Enda. Our trees were planted out beyond Glasson, but I have friends whose trees are in Kilkenny, in County Dublin, and so on. I don't know if people have kept up the viewing of their trees. The last time I went to see mine was about two years ago, and it was growing tall and strong. I think this was one of the more fanciful ideas for the celebration year, but one which took root (if you will pardon the pun!), and was a real success.

I remember now so well New Year's Eve 1999, when churches all over Ireland held commemorative ceremonies. I can still recall how Enda and I went to St Peter's in Athlone that evening at 7 p.m., and how everyone held hands and sang hymns and ushered in the year 2000. With a new century in the offing, it seemed that perhaps a new Ireland with new hopes lay ahead of us too. If only it was so easy to erase the hurts, the bitterness and the difficulties of the past, and to dress in shining new clothes.

Just as I was, Enda was very enthused about the year 2000 — we often talked together about the new century, about new lives and fresh hopes. It seemed as if he had forgotten his illness of the previous year, had risen above it and was determined to go forward with new energy and health. And so he would do for a good number of months until the day in late January 2001 which, all these years later, is still so difficult for me to contemplate.

| THE LOSS OF ENDA

Enda died on 30 January 2001. On that winter afternoon I had been out with my dear friend Celine Campbell at a mutual friend's house for Sunday lunch. All was well when I had left Enda at about two o'clock, and when I came home at around five o'clock, he was still in great form. It was a bright and sunny, cloudless January day. We don't get many of these, but when they do come, it is exciting, because they hold a promise — early and tentative as it may be — of spring and summer yet to come. I can still remember so well Enda's words, 'I can already see the stretch in the evenings.' It would have been five weeks since the shortest day, and yes, a stretch was clearly discernible.

As we looked out the living room window together, Enda relayed to me details of the telephone calls there had been and the fact that he had brought in the line of clothes I had hung out to dry earlier. He also noted with great love a telephone call he had had that afternoon from Feargal, who was in Limerick at a rugby match. We then sat down companionably and I said, 'I'll get the dinner on now,' and got up to go into the kitchen. When I said I was doing roast chicken, he said, 'Would you do some of your own stuffing?' And I replied, 'Of course I will.' He loved the stuffing done in a separate dish, not in with the chicken. It was just a quirk he had and one I was always glad to indulge. Then he said to me, 'Before you go out to the kitchen, let's look at the news together.' And so we did and watched as opening credits and headlines came up for RTÉ's six o'clock news programme. The leading item was a story about some political row between John Bruton and Michael Noonan over a speech Noonan had given. Enda and I discussed it with great interest and then he said, 'I'll go up to The Green Olive [his local pub] and I'll have a pint, and by the time I get back, we can sit down to dinner together.'

I went into the kitchen to turn on the oven, put in the chicken and make the stuffing. All at once, I heard a muffled cry from the living room. Our living room opens off onto our kitchen, but it is around a corner. So, while I could hear everything, I couldn't see Enda. As soon as I heard the muffled cry, I came out to find him slumped in the armchair, but still coherent and talking to me. 'I don't feel well,' he said, so I rang two friends of ours, Mícheál Ó'Faoláin and Jack Lally; and I rang Dr Maurice Collins, who was an Army medical doctor, but was on call for that weekend in Athlone.

By the time Dr Collins arrived, and he came very quickly, Enda was slumped further down in his chair but when we straightened him more comfortably, he was able to talk to both Dr Collins and myself. When Dr Collins gave his opinion — that he should immediately go to hospital — Enda said quite firmly, 'No, I won't go to Ballinasloe.' Then I too insisted, 'We'll bring him to the Mater.' I knew that Enda had always felt happier there, even though he had often been very sick during the two long stays he had had: he just somehow felt more comforted and cared for there. We didn't call for an ambulance. Instead, my two friends and I got Enda into the back seat of the car and I sat with him as we set off. Dr Collins had rung the Mater and they were expecting us. I cradled Enda's head on my breast as we drove.

I always thought afterwards, what a comforting way for anyone to die, cared for in the arms of one who loves you, speeding along in the dark night. We somehow knew. Certainly I knew that the end was coming for Enda. He was coherent and still talked from time to time as we drove. From Enfield on, a Garda escort took us right to the door of the Mater, where they had a stretcher and a crew waiting. Whenever now I read of paramedics and particular types of ambulances, I find myself wondering if Enda should have gone to the Mater in one of those? But he went in the way that suited him best at the time, in the way that he wanted to go.

Our two sons had been awaiting him, and he was soon settled in bed with all of the medical paraphernalia around him. I remember saying to one of the medics, 'There is no hope.' 'You are right,' he replied, 'but we will do our best.' Tests were done and examinations carried out by the medical experts who were brought in, but the damage to the brain was huge. Enda never came out of the coma he had fallen into. But when we went in to see him in his bed, he looked so peaceful, just as if he was sleeping. He was kept alive for a certain length of time. We would talk to him and sit with him, but I have always been relatively serene in my own mind that Enda's last memories and thoughts were that I had my arms around him and that together we were speeding to somewhere where he would be comforted. Yes, of course: he was speeding to death and to his God.

Enda was brought home to Athlone and there followed all the business with John McNeill, the undertakers, and the priests, and the Mass. And of course there was his family to be comforted: his three sisters who loved him dearly, as did all his friends. Enda had a terrific gift for friendship, which he shared with so many. On the day of his funeral, I remember with great clarity how, as the hearse went by The Green Olive on the way to the church at Coosan, we paused and all of Enda's regular friends came out. The pub was closed and dark, and they stood in silence as he went by and then they all began to clap.

The Mass was huge because of the presence of all his friends and relatives, as well as all of the Fianna Fáil supporters in Westmeath and all over the country. All my friends and relatives came out in force too. Enda was greatly loved. For many people, he had been the face of Mary O'Rourke, the voice of Mary O'Rourke and the mainstay of Mary O'Rourke — all of which he so undoubtedly was. Most of the day was a blur. After the Mass, we brought everyone who wanted to come to the Hodson Bay Hotel for a luncheon. My two sons were strong and stalwart beside me.

I have never forgotten my debt of honour to Enda and my sense of obligation to him. It was he who put me on the political path; it was he who was steadfast for me and with me. It was he who gave me courage when times were bleak; it was he who rejoiced with me when times were good. He was my lover, my husband and the father of my two sons. And now I was bereft and alone. Widows are a lonely, often unacknowledged section of society and I have always thought that their plight and their sorrow are not fully recognised. Later it was confirmed to us that the cause of Enda's death had been a massive brain haemorrhage from which there was no hope of salvation. He was a very spiritual man, in the proper sense of having one's religion, and in the end he faced death with much courage.

When Enda died, I tortured myself for some time with thoughts of how I had perhaps sold him short during those frantic, frenetic years. As I have related in an earlier chapter, this was something which had much preoccupied me over the years — the dilemma of how to achieve a happy home life while fulfilling all the many commitments which come with being in public life. But for me, the quandary came to the fore again so strongly following Enda's death. Should I have been with him more? Had I sold him short on that day in September 1960 when, aged 22 and 24, we had taken our first steps together into the unknown? Had Enda envisaged then a happy-ever-after scenario in the traditional scene, where I would be there every night when he came home — which was how it had been in the very early years of our marriage, but which was later to change so radically into such a very modern set-up? Could I have been more of a soul mate to him?

But then I am comforted by the thought that Enda had always wanted and pushed me to go forward. From the time I entered the political field as an elected member of the town council back in 1974, when we had two very young children, he was the person who prodded, pushed, supported and stood by me — as he would do right throughout my political odyssey. In fact I would never have embarked on it all, only for him: I would, I feel, have quite happily continued my career as a secondary school teacher. You see, Enda believed in me and in what I could do for people then and in the future. He also realised early on that, to bring that about, he would have to play the huge part he played in our home activities. And so he did. Yes, we had rows, as every married couple has. What relationship is utterly harmonious 100 per cent of the time? Find me the couple who makes this claim and I can tell you, I don't believe their story! In the end, I know that Enda and I worked things out to the best of our abilities and we built an enduring, satisfactory and very happy relationship. For that, I will always be immensely grateful.

Chapter 13

⎮ 11 SEPTEMBER 2001

W e can all remember where we were when the terrible events of 11 September 2001 happened in the US. In 2011, the tenth anniversary commemorations of such a hugely significant and dreadful occurrence in American history brought back some of the intensity of the horror we had all felt. Like many of those I know, I found the images and words of the various documentaries and programmes of remembrance from RTÉ, BBC and other stations so moving, so real and so full of personal sorrow. Particularly poignant was the footage of some of the friends, companions or close relatives of those who were killed in the attack on the Twin Towers, as, ten years later, they visited the memorial at the site to find the names of their loved ones on the cold bronze slabs. I can only imagine the havoc in the stomachs and in the minds of those people as they kissed the inscriptions of the names of their lost loved ones.

To pinpoint where we were and what we felt on that day now more than a decade ago seems somehow poignant and fitting. In fact I was in the US on that morning of 11 September 2001, on holiday on Cape Cod with two good friends, Ailish O'Donoghue and Kathryn Byrne. It was the first holiday I had had in the nine months since Enda died, and I had been looking forward to the break. A Boston College colleague of Seán Rowland, another close friend of mine, had offered us, through Seán, his house in Falmouth, Cape Cod for a week and we had gladly seized the opportunity. I had been several times to the US but mostly for work-related business functions and for a short period each time, so the prospect of the week on Cape Cod was an exciting and welcome one.

Ailish, Kathyrn and I had landed at Boston Airport, which is the nearest major landing point for that part of the US. Before we left we had made arrangements to hire a self-drive car and Ailish took the wheel when we duly collected it at the airport. Ailish is my Valentia Island friend whose husband Tadhg had been in Revenue and stationed in Athlone, which is where we met them. Tadhg is from Valentia; Ailish herself is the daughter of a lighthouse keeper and as such, can be said to be from many parts of Ireland, including Donegal, Blacksod and Valentia. It was when her father was stationed on the island that she had met Tadhg and they married. During their time in Athlone, they lived two doors up from us on The One Mile in Arcadia and we very quickly made friends with them and their increasing brood of lovely children. For a few years before I went into national politics, Tadgh and I played bridge together, even representing Ireland at National Junior level at one stage. I can always remember how, just a few days after having twin boys, Ailish was out playing bridge herself, and that is the way she is — perky and plucky and ready to take on life's challenges. In later years, Enda and I had gone on several very memorable holidays to Valentia to Ailish and Tadhg, and later to Portmagee, a lovely spot in South Kerry.

And so, off we friends went on the highway from Boston to Cape Cod, passing through those beautiful little towns — Hyannis, Provincetown, Chatham, Plymouth, Barnstable — until we finally arrived in Falmouth. Picking up the key as arranged, we then went to our lovely beachside house. A short hop down the back garden led to the ocean's edge. We were delighted with our good fortune and began to settle in, choosing our bedrooms.

Kathryn Byrne is a friend of mine from long-ago Fianna Fáil days. She had been working in the Fianna Fáil head office during the period when, under the auspices of Charlie Haughey, we set up the women's group I have referred to earlier. Kathryn did much of the adminis-trative, organisational work for us all back at head office. We had shared a lively working relationship together and we have remained friends ever since.

Once we had stocked up on provisions in nearby Falmouth, a lovely town straight out of an American novel, our first few days on Cape Cod quickly settled into a relaxed routine. We would get up in the morning and, after a leisurely breakfast, amble down to the little beach behind the house and swim in the ocean. We just adored it. Ailish didn't like swimming so she would come down to join us around noon or one o'clock. And the three of us would sit on the beach, looking out to the ocean and thinking, 'This is the life!' We then went on different drives to various towns, coming back to the house each evening and going out again to eat in one of the nearby restaurants, which were very reasonable with delicious food, particularly fish. Fortunately, Ailish was well-versed in American restaurants, and explained how we should behave and all about the tipping protocol there! We soon understood that the staff were paid very little but that they expected — and in many cases, demanded — a decent tip. We were happy to comply with this.

We were about four days into our week-long stay. On the morning of Tuesday, 11 September, we were up early, having breakfast and planning our drive for that day to Hyannis Port. I was in the kitchen with Ailish, while Kathryn was in the breakfast-cum-living room with the TV on. She suddenly shouted out, and when both Ailish and I ran in to join her, she was pointing at the TV screen, exclaiming, 'Look!' There was the picture of the first plane slicing right through that New York skyscraper. All three of us decided it was some sort of spoof film, and we continued to drink our coffee and munch our toast there in the living room. Suddenly, however, we heard a terrible note of alarm in the voice of the announcer on CNN and as we looked at the screen again, we saw a second plane crash into the Twin Towers. This was for real! Immediately I knew in that lovely little seaside house in Falmouth that this was a huge, awesome, awful moment in American history, and indeed in world history.

We immediately tried the telephone but all the lines were down. Eventually, we did manage to get through and quickly let our loved ones back in Ireland know that, as far as we could tell, it was safe where we were — but that we were obviously part of the American scene. The rest of that day was numbing. We went into Falmouth: half of the shops were closed, half were open; there were terrified, worried and distraught people on the streets. Everyone seemed to have someone or know of someone in the World Trade Center and we wandered aimlessly, trying in our own way to give comfort to those we met. Back at the house, we continued to watch television throughout the day. It wasn't long before I got word from Ireland that there was to be a special meeting in Brussels of all of the European Ministers for Transport, so that they could form some response to the atrocities and try to plan forward. Obviously we didn't know what was going to happen next. The Pentagon strike had followed close on the heels of the attacks in Manhattan, and it was as if the whole of the US was gripped by a miasma of fear.

For us now, the main question was, how were we going to get out of the US? From the bulletins and updates on the TV stations — CNN, Fox, and so on — we were doing our best to keep informed about what was happening. There was a complete closure on all skies over the US. The only thing which was really clear to us was that nobody knew what was going to happen next. No one knew if there was going to be more devastation from the skies, and people all over the country were, like us, literally cowering in their houses, waiting for the next newsflash to tell them what was coming.

Meanwhile the Department of Public Enterprise back in Dublin was trying to make arrangements — via the American Embassy in Dublin and then the Irish Ambassador in Washington — to get me out of the US, so that I could go to the Brussels Transport meeting within the following 24 hours. It was extremely important, it seemed, that Ireland be represented there. I fully understood the situation and was as determined as the Department that I would get out of the US. Anyway, as you can imagine, by then that was all that any of the three of us wanted — to get back home. Much as we sympathised with all that had happened in the US, all we wanted was out, out, out.

The calls about possible transportation arrangements, when they came, were spasmodic and attempting to be informative, but not always succeeding in that. Finally, late that afternoon, we were told that, as early as possible the following morning, we should travel to a small airport which was nearby, and that from there, we would be told of our next steps. Our mood was sombre and anxious that evening, as we gathered together our stuff and made ready for our departure at dawn the next morning. As you can imagine, we all got very little sleep that night.

The small airport to which we travelled the next day was in fact a defence air base. When we got there, I was interviewed and required to produce my passport and other official documentation. I was informed that a private plane would coming to take me to Brussels, and that this would be one of the very few flights in the air that day. The sheer terror of that would not strike me until later. We were told that there would be no room for Kathryn and Ailish: it would be a small, small plane. The US Foreign Affairs Information Department told them that if they could get whatever coach they could to New York and stay there overnight, they would be able to take their places alongside those seeking to leave the US within the following few days. Of course, Kathryn and Ailish were disappointed that they could not get away as quickly as I could, but they understood the protocol of the situation. Leaving me at the defence airport, they set out on their long journey back to New York.

After several hours waiting at the small defence airport, I saw a plane arrive. It was tiny, and I felt cold dread at the thought of it up in the skies over the US, where those who had carried out the terror attacks might be waiting, primed to seek anything at which they could strike. However, I swallowed hard and got on board. Other than me, the passenger list consisted of the pilot and one female cabin attendant. That girl and I huddled together in the two seats, and away we went.

Looking back on it now, I marvel at the lack of fear which allowed me to take that flight. Oddly enough, once in the air, I felt secure. I quickly decided that the only thing I could do was to go to sleep, which I did. I woke up within two hours of Brussels and was elated to know that we were now so close to the security and safety of Europe. As soon as we landed, I got off the plane and made my way to the government buildings, where I had a shower, washed my hair and was ready for business. Luckily I had heeded a key piece of advice one is always given when in a government job: to bring a dark jacket with you whenever you are travelling, even if you are going on a holiday, as you never know if you might be called to a funeral or a state occasion. I had such a dark jacket with me, which I had brought in my overnight bag from Falmouth and so from the waist up at least, I was able to portray a business-like appearance.

When I arrived at the Transport meeting, I was, as you can imagine, the talk of my colleagues and had to tell all about my escape from the US — all marvelled at how I had managed to do this. There was important business done that day at the Brussels meeting and for

Ireland as an island nation it was, I think, vital that I should be there, so that I would be party to the new strategy which was being worked out for airport procedures, such as security, vetting, the checking in of luggage, etc., and which was to be adopted at all airports in Europe. It was a busy but fruitful day, and I was able to give all these matters my full attention.

When we got back to Ireland that night, as you can imagine, I was wrung out and exhausted. I spoke by mobile phone to Kathryn and Ailish, who were staying in New York as planned. I was happy to learn that they had just heard that within 48 hours, they would be able to get a flight from Newark airport to Dublin with many, many others whose travel plans had been completely disrupted by the terrible events of the previous day.

I was back in Dublin for the day of mourning for America. Ireland was the only country who undertook such a day of mourning — and why not, given all the links we share and the 84 million direct and indirect descendants of Irish people who live in the US, as well as all of those who had been lost in the Twin Towers? In the long and tragic catalogue of victims, there are many Irish names, which raises a chill of recognition and an awareness of the extent of the evil which was perpetrated on the American people on that awful day.

Of course, we know the aftermath — Bush's 'War on Terror', the enlistment of Tony Blair to his cause, the utter disregard for the resistance of the UN who had not approved of all-out war, and the gung-ho behaviour of Bush, which ensured that war there was to be, a war which has never ceased to this day.

I think it was difficult for us then and it is still difficult now to comprehend the sheer terror that Americans felt and the deep, deep anger at having war perpetrated in their own homeland by this unknown, elusive and evil figure, Osama bin Laden. A sheer terror evoked in George W. Bush a primitive urge to destroy and wipe out this evil. And in that sense, it was hard to fault him at the time. He had the full support of the American people in the immediate aftermath of 9/11 and it was only much, much later that the full repercussions of this sheer atavistic response would begin to emerge.

When Kathryn and Ailish got back home, we met up soon

afterwards to talk it all over at some length. I related to my friends and others at Cabinet the whole tale of my escape to Brussels and, of course, this was a foolish thing to do. Within ten days, there were front page headlines in a certain Sunday paper, talking of the extravagance of Mary O'Rourke and the privately commissioned flight out of Cape Cod. The story failed to mention that I had gone into the skies that day in sheer terror so that I could do my job in Brussels. That never emerged, naturally, and it took the publication of a strong and accurate, fact-filled letter from the Press Office of the Department of Public Enterprise to put things in perspective. I didn't want to cost anyone anything, but I got the call that I had to go to Brussels and my feelings didn't come into it. It was a matter of doing my job.

I have been back to Boston since, but I have never again been to the Cape Cod coastline. What we saw of it during our short stay was beautiful, but it will be meshed forever in our minds with the terror unleashed on the people of America that day, the stark horror which struck us in that small beach house in Falmouth, and the way we clung together — three Irish women on an innocent holiday, caught up in the maelstrom of those terrible events.

Chapter 14 ∽

LIFE IN THE UPPER CHAMBER

For a while after Enda died, I thought that life was over for me and in a way, it was. There was never again to be the surety and serenity of love, of comfort, of sustenance and of support which he gave to me so freely and generously for all of the years we were together. I was bereft. I was back at Cabinet within four or five days of him passing away and back in the Dáil within a week, but nevertheless, I thought for a while of resigning completely from public life and devoting myself to misery, so to speak. But then I rallied, and friends and family around me urged me to get back up and get going, and I did, sustained by the belief that this is what Enda would have wanted me to do. I had great friends — Hugh and Celine Campbell, Mícheál and Maura Ó'Faoláin, Niall and Angela McCormack, Seán Rowland, and so many others — who kept me going in those darkest of days.

On 17 May 2002, barely 18 months after Enda's death, there was to be a General Election. From the outset of that election period, I was very doubtful of the outcome. It seemed that Fianna Fáil, in the guise of P.J. Mara and Bertie Ahern, wanted to get three seats out of four in Longford–Westmeath. Or this is what Bertie and P.J. Mara told me, at any rate. Peter Kelly had emerged as the replacement for Albert Reynolds. There was myself in Athlone; and Bertie and Mara were, they said, keen to push Senator Donie Cassidy to become the standard-bearer in the Mullingar end. The night that Donie won that convention and became the approved candidate for that area, I knew that it was a bad omen for me.

Why so? It wasn't that Donie Cassidy was any bright, young, shining star — far from it. But I knew that there was an agenda to put me out and put him in. It was a political agenda, activated by P.J. Mara and by Bertie. It was being done under the pretext that they wanted three seats in my part of the country, and that they could get three seats. But I knew there were never to be three seats and there never could be. There had perhaps been a time, some fifteen years earlier, when this might have been feasible but we were now in very different times.

I rang Bertie Ahern and arranged to see him in his office in St Luke's in Drumcondra one morning. Now remember, at this point, I was deputy leader of Fianna Fáil and I was one of his Ministers at the Cabinet table. And I just couldn't believe how the political ground was shifting beneath me and shifting me decisively *away* from him. When I met Bertie that day face-to-face, he was what I can only describe as evasive. Shifty would be too strong a word, but evasive is about right. 'Oh no,' he assured me, 'that is not my agenda and never would be.' He went on to say that of course I had 'a great reputation as a high-profile Minister', that of course I would 'sweep the county', and so on and so forth.

But not so long after that, I saw the dirty work begin to operate. Fianna Fáil voters in Westmeath were told to vote 'number one Donie Cassidy; number two Mary O'Rourke', and that this would be the best way for us to get two seats in Westmeath, plus the seat in Longford. It was all so absurd and yet it happened anyway. Donie started to swagger, saying he would 'drive Mary O'Rourke back to the bridge and the walls of Athlone'. When he started his canvassing in earnest, he began to put up posters in Moate and Kilbeggan and Tyrellspass — all my strongholds. 'No holds barred' — that seemed to be the mantra.

So, why did I not, as a feisty person, put up a feisty response? Looking back now, it is clear that, in terms of my career, this was where the loss of Enda really began to manifest itself. He would have been up in his local, The Green Olive; he would have been around and about the town and would have had the ears and confidences of many; he would have been able to suss out what plots were going on. But Enda was gone and I was alone. Yes, of course I had my friends and my family and their great love and support, but I was alone as I never had been before, and, in a political sense, I had no one to watch out and be vigilant for me in the way that Enda always had.

I did my best, however, to put up a good campaign and I canvassed as always, and my faithful rallied round me. But I had a leaden weight in my heart each night, when I came home to the house alone, knowing what awaited me. Added to that was the residual physical discomfort of having broken my left ankle some months earlier. Of course, it had been expertly fixed with five pins in the Mater Hospital, but it caused me discomfort and pain from time to time, particularly when I was tired. Add it all up, and I had a dispiriting campaign. When I went to Kenagh on the day of the count, it was as I had anticipated: I had lost my seat. In Mullingar they were rampant and, boy, were they rampant: 'Back to Athlone with you, Madam', was more or less what I was told, and the Cheshire cat grin on the face of P.J. Mara when he was asked the following day, in an RTÉ review of the election, what he thought of the result — well, that said it all, really!

I was on RTÉ myself that night, beamed in from the Athlone studio to join Charlie McCreevy (our then Minister for Finance) and the commentator in a discussion. At one point the presenter said, 'Well, is it back to the knitting for you now, Mary?' I was indignant at this, and when I replied, 'I never knitted and I don't intend to start now', McCreevy chipped in and said, 'No, I can't imagine Mary either knitting or being quiet . . .' Anyway I went home after that, and I was fuming, absolutely fuming!

I was angry about the subterranean campaign which had been waged against me and annoyed with myself too, for not putting up more of a fight in the face of it. As well as the loss of Enda, I suppose one other reason for this was that, as deputy leader of the party, I had felt that I should set a good example to other candidates throughout the country, go with party strategy and not be seen to get involved in internal wrangling. Apart from my own instincts about it all, I had had an early warning about what was to happen, and I should have heeded it. John O'Donoghue, my colleague and dear friend from Kerry, had telephoned me one day some time before the election and said, 'Beef up, Mary! I have been told to give territory to [whichever candidate was running with him], and I said "Oh sure, yes, that's what I'll do", and off I went. But I have no intention of doing what they've told me, of course!' But John's patch in south Kerry was a long, long way from Dublin, whereas I was right in the line of fire. Anyway, be that as it may, I suppose in the end we have to take fate as it comes. I tried to keep thinking of Enda and what he would be saying to me, now that I had lost my seat. But, of course, none of it would have happened if he had been alive.

There was to be a further development, however: a positive adjunct to that defeat. Later on, when I got home that night to my house in Athlone, all of my friends and my political colleagues came round, and we drank and talked and moaned for a number of hours. I suppose I didn't get to bed until about two o'clock in the morning, in fact. Before I went to bed, Feargal — who was down from Dublin and staying overnight — and Aengus and I came up with a plan. They bolstered me up and egged me on, saying, 'You'll ring Bertie tomorrow [which was a Sunday], and you'll tell him what you want!'

I finally went to bed. At five o'clock in the morning, I got a call from Senator Terry Leyden, a good friend whom I had always held close, from the time when he was a young man, aged 21 and Deputy Director of Elections for my brother Brian, and later as a family friend. Terry commiserated with me and then said, 'By the way, there is an immediate vacancy in the Seanad now.' It seemed that Senator Tom Fitzgerald had decided just a few days earlier to retire because of ill-health. Terry was insistent, saying, 'Get in touch with Bertie Ahern immediately, and say you want to be given this.'

With Terry's words and the urging of my sons the night before still ringing in my ears, when I got up a few hours later, I was more or less decided that I would ring Bertie. I can still remember how determined I felt that I would do now what I had not done throughout the whole campaign: stand up on my feet and demand! Interestingly but not surprisingly, I suppose, was the fact that the night before, and with all the otherwise good news for Fianna Fáil, Bertie Ahern had not once thought to telephone me in Westmeath to commiserate with me — and I was his deputy leader, after all. But that was Bertie. No doubt he knew that I would begin to berate him and probably he thought, 'Let's put it off for a while.' The night before, in fact, Mandy Johnston — who was Communications Director of Fianna Fáil at the time, and a very fine one too — had telephoned me to say that she was prevailing on Bertie to call me.

Mandy rang again that Sunday morning to say that I should be expecting a call from Bertie soon and so I held myself in readiness.

When he rang, I took the call in the room I use as my office, and Feargal and Aengus came in to stand beside me. The Taoiseach offered his commiserations in that nice, soft voice and, do you know, I very nearly weakened. But I had a son on either side of me, prodding me and spurring me on. I told Bertie I wanted the vacant Seanad seat and that I wanted to be Leader of the Seanad too, which was also in the gift of the Taoiseach. I said this was the least I was owed for the way I had been 'done' — and many more strong words besides. It was as if suddenly I got my voice and spirit back and was determined to see this through. Finally he agreed to my request, telling me too that he would as leader put forward my nomination when the time came, so I would not have to go around the country myself, seeking the votes of the Fianna Fáil county councillors and borough councillors.

I had at least taken something from the ashes and I began to feel more mollified and settled. There was a further little twist to this tale, which is illustrative, I suppose, of my nature and my approach, and indeed of Bertie's nature too. It happened after he had been proclaimed Taoiseach once more, with the Progressive Democrats as his partners. Some of the Independents were being kept on board also: Bertie always clung to them as a kind of comfort blanket to ensure that he would have a fall-back position if need be, and how wise he was in that. There is no doubt in my mind that he was 'the most cunning, the most devious', as Charlie Haughey famously said.

Anyway, in the time immediately after his reinstatement as Taoiseach, Bertie said he wanted to meet with me. I duly went over to his office — down that beautiful, long, blue-carpeted corridor and into his inner sanctum, with the portrait of Pádraig Pearse on the wall. There he was waiting for me, with his gentle, limpid eyes. He proceeded to ask if I would not go around the country after all, to get the votes of the councils, as he felt sure that if I did so, I would be returned to Seanad Éireann without any difficulty. I just looked at him, horrified. It was not that I was afraid of the hard work which would be involved, but that he had *promised* me that I would be one of his eleven (by law, the Taoiseach is entitled to appoint eleven members of his own choosing to the Seanad)!

When I said as much to him, Bertie backed down quite quickly, saying, 'Oh, okay, okay, alright, alright, Mary! You will be appointed.' Yet

Presentation to me when I was appointed Minister for Education, March 1987. *Left to right*: Paddy Cooney, Councillor Breffni Rowan, TD, Chairman of the Town Council, and John Walshe, Town Clerk.

At the Town Council presentation, with Feargal, Breffni Rowan and Enda.

Feargal, Stephen Roche and myself, 1987.

Meeting with Dr Hilde Hawlicek, Austrian Minister for Education, 1988.

Dr Ed Walsh, President of the University of Limerick and Chairman of the NCCA.

Jack Daly, Chairman of the Board of Directors of NIHE (Limerick) — soon to become the University of Limerick — and Dr Ed Walsh, President of NIHE, 1989.

Stirring the pot, flanked by Mary Hanafin and Pat Carey, 1989.

Visiting a Dublin primary school with Pat Ingoldsby, 1990.

As Minister for Education in Marlborough Street in Dublin, 1990. (*Courtesy of* The Irish Times)

Feargal, Séamus Browne, Paddy Foley and Senator Seán Fallon, during Brian's presidential campaign, 1990.

Female TDS and Senators, 1996.

Bertie Ahern and myself canvassing in Battery Heights in Athlone, with Senator Camillus Glynn in the background.

May 1997: Feargal, Enda, myself and Aengus in the back garden at home.

At the White House with Bertie Ahern and Hillary Clinton, 1997.

May 1999: Taoiseach Bertie Ahern, TD, and myself as Minister for Public Enterprise at the launch of the Fianna Fáil Local Elections Manifesto at the National Concert Hall, Dublin. (© *Photocall Ireland*)

July 1999: At the launch of the Telecom Éireann share offer price in St Stephen's Green, Dublin with Charlie McCreevy, Minister for Finance, Taoiseach Bertie Ahern, myself as Minister for Public Enterprise, Chairman of Telecom Éireann, Ray MacSharry and Chief Executive of Telecom, Alfie Kane. (© *Photocall Ireland*)

July 2000: as Minister for Public Enterprise with the Right Honourable Lord Mayor of Dublin, Alderman Maurice Ahern, pictured at the formal launch of the Finglas Quality Bus Corridor in Dublin. (© *Photocall Ireland*)

August 2000: launching an appeal as Minister for Public Enterprise, with Paul Byrne (left), member of the Chernobyl Children's Appeal, and David Byrne, Managing Director of TNT, on behalf of the Chernobyl Children's Appeal to assist four projects in the Mozyr region of Belarus. (© *Photocall Ireland*)

Aengus and I at the 2002 General Election Court in Kenagh, Co. Longford.

Brian Lenihan Jnr and myself at Athlone Institute of Technology, 29 March 2011. Brian died 10 June 2011 — this was his last public occasion and his last visit to Athlone. The College were hugely honoured that he came, and gave him a full welcome.

21 May 2012: photographed by *The Irish Times* at the Radisson Hotel, Athlone. (*Courtesy of* The Irish Times)

he had tried the trick to see if I would go for it, because he would have preferred to have had another Seanad seat to give away to someone else. But I was fired up by the thought that I was well due this kind of recognition at the very least, for all the time I had worked for the party, right from my very early days and including my years as a Minister and as deputy leader. In addition to this, Bertie had already promised to grant my request, so there was no way I was going to let him away with anything else! In many ways, this encounter spoke volumes about my modus operandi — and his.

Anne Garland was very good to me. Anne — who has since retired — was in charge of looking after the Fianna Fáil TDs and Senators with regards to office arrangements, equipment, staffing, and so on. She was excellent at her job and was in fact an office manager, a housekeeper and a fairy godmother all rolled into one! Anne and I had always been friends and got along very well, and she was very sympathetic when she heard I had now lost my seat, as well as very annoyed at the way the campaign had been played out. After my conversation with Bertie that day, I sought her out, saying, 'I have no office, Anne — so where should I go?' I told her confidentially that Bertie Ahern was going to make me Leader of the Seanad, although it was yet to be announced and that she should not mention it to anyone for the time being. Anne immediately offered to try to help, saying, 'I'll find you an office, not to worry!' And she did.

When he stood down as Taoiseach, Albert Reynolds had been given an office at the top of the Ministers of State corridor. It was a big, lofty, cold office, but it was an office nonetheless and had an adjoining office with two places for staff. So Anne said to me, 'Why don't you move in there, Mary, and for the time being, I'll put a notice on the door saying "Reserved".' And so this is what she did and I did. I would spend the rest of the summer in that office, mopping up the correspondence left over from the General Election, feeling weepy and emotional at times and feeling generally that life had passed me by.

In due course, Bertie officially announced his eleven nominations, as well as my new position as Leader of the Seanad. Then followed the election of the Cathaoirleach (Chairperson) of the Seanad by the Senators. When the first day of the assembly of the new Seanad dawned, we were all formally inaugurated. My son Feargal came to see the ceremony. After the formalities were over, I stood up and gave the Order of Business for the day, and so my life as a Senator began. To be truthful, I had absolutely no idea how one acted as Leader of this House, but there was, and is, a very supportive, professional and talented office team attached to the Seanad, headed by Deirdre Lane as Clerk of the Seanad and Jody Blake as Clerk Assistant. Of course Deirdre and Jody gave full respect to the Cathaoirleach and to the Leader of the Seanad, but they were also very helpful in filling me in on what my duties would be and how it would all would operate.

And so I was able to settle in to the routine of political life again. Yes, of course, I felt diminished not to be within the Dáil at that time, but after all, I reminded myself, the Seanad is called 'the Upper Chamber', and I resolved that I would use my five years there productively, and that I would make something of the position, as I had done in every other posting with which I had been honoured in my political career. It was never my intention to stay on in the Seanad, but I did intend to use it as a stepping stone back into the Dáil. Of course, I was no stranger to that beautiful chamber with its magnificently carved ceiling; early on in my public life at the beginning of the 1980s, I had spent two six-month periods in the Seanad, and had relished it then as a discussion forum and debating chamber, where I was able to get used to speaking, standing up and contributing to political debate. Lo and behold, now in 2002, I was about to embark on a most productive phase in my working life. Little did I think it at the start, but this would turn out to be the case.

Very early on, I had a huge stroke of luck, when it was confirmed that Eamonn McCormack had been approached to take up the role as PA to the Leader of the Seanad, and that he had happily accepted. A young civil servant, Eamonn had worked with me when I was Minister of State for Labour Affairs. Then, when I became Minister for Public Enterprise, he came back to work in my private office in the Department as my personal assistant, still in his civil service status. I had quickly come to rely more and more on him: it was not just that he was a meticulous civil servant and administrator, but he was also a very valued confidante. Now, as my PA in the Seanad, Eamonn would occupy the adjacent office to mine. As soon as he too had undertaken his tutorial at the hands of Deirdre and Jody, he and I settled in harmoniously enough. We were lucky that, after some skirmishing with different staff, Lisa Foran, who had also been in the Transport section of the Department of Public Enterprise, agreed to move over as Eamonn's assistant. So there were the three of us, all workers and all determined to do the best we could during our time in the Seanad.

When I became a Senator in 2002, I was very much aware that down through the years there had been numerous reports on possible ways of reforming the Seanad, as well as a constant refrain from many quarters to the effect of, 'Is it really needed anyway?' Accordingly, one of my first initiatives as leader was to set up a debate on reform in the House and then to form a sub-committee which would review the workings of the Seanad and look in to how they could be revised and improved. This sub-committee was headed up by myself and included Brian Hayes as Opposition leader in the Seanad, Joe O'Toole as head of the Independents, John Dardis as leader of the Progressive Democrats, and Brendan Ryan as leader of the Labour Party. Peter Finnegan was appointed as Secretary to our group, and we set to work straight away.

We put extensive advertisements in the daily papers both North and South of the border, seeking submissions from anyone who wanted to contribute to the ideas for the reform of the Seanad. We duly set ourselves up then for a week in the Seanad Chamber to hear those submissions orally. It was a terrific exercise, and the people and groups who came to us were full of good ideas. Interestingly, not one individual or group put forward the proposal of the abolition of the Seanad. It was recognised generally by many as a useful chamber, not just for debating purposes but as a safeguard for legislation and a very useful tool in the whole democratic process.

There were many enjoyable aspects to my new role as a Senator and to my working life in the Seanad during those five years, but one of the things I remember mostly fondly is that it was a period when I had the opportunity to grow much closer to my nephew, Brian Lenihan: our already strong bond as aunt and nephew would deepen and intensify into a friendship between colleagues and comrades-in-arms, so to speak. Brian Jnr and his brother Conor had in fact been serving along-side me in the Dáil since the late 1990s — Brian since 1996 and Conor since 1997 — and I always enjoyed the company of my two nephews, although our paths did not necessarily cross very frequently in the work environment in the early years. I always found Conor to be a good and lively companion (and to this day, I enjoy keeping in touch with him on a regular basis, generally by e-mail, since his working life is now based full-time in Russia).

Brian Jnr had been appointed Minister of State for Children by Bertie Ahern in 2002, of which he had made a great success. It was a period when there was money available for the setting up of crèches, children's playgrounds and many other valuable facilities, and Brian played a key part in ensuring that the full potential of these resources was realised. Although as Minister of State for Children he was at the time not a member of Cabinet as such, he was entitled to participate in Cabinet meetings, and there he contributed greatly to the agenda at all times. So in that sense he was effectively a full Minister.

It was during this time that Brian's office in Leinster House was next door to mine, as Leader of the Seanad. It wasn't long before he developed a routine of popping his head around the door most mornings to say hello — 'Well, how is the Senator today and how is the Seanad, and how is the Leader of the Seanad?' he would say to Eamonn McCormack, Lisa and myself. If there was time, he would come in, close the door and we would have some very interesting conversations. I became very close to Brian during this period. In a way, it reminded me of the time so, so many years ago when, as a young boy, he had come to his Aunt Mary to learn Latin.

I will just explain a little further here. My brother Brian Lenihan Snr and his wife Ann moved to Dublin with their young family in the early 1970s: Brian had decided that it would be the right place to make a go of re-forging his political career. As a result, Brian Jnr, who was then aged 12, was enrolled at the Jesuit College at Belvedere, in order to begin his secondary education there. However, his mother Ann was a little concerned when she learned that the boys who would be going into Belvedere Secondary from Belvedere Preparatory School had all had a good grounding in French, Latin and Greek at primary level, whereas young Brian had had no such instruction. There was nothing that could be done at that late stage about Greek, but Ann enlisted my help for the Latin and Grandma Lenihan's help for the French.

So that 12-year-old boy would come on his bicycle once a week to me in my home in Arcadia, Athlone. As I write, I can still clearly see his lovely round face, big, earnest eyes and remember his impish sense of humour. We both enjoyed those lessons so much. Brian would do whatever homework I gave him and a bit more besides if he could. He was always wanting to forge further and further ahead in *Longmans' Latin Course*, whereas I was taking the more cautious, teacher's approach of doing things bit by bit. Anyway, we would do the hour together and then young Brian would get on his bike and take off, with his homework for the next time. Likewise he would go to his Grandma Lenihan, and I know she found him to be the same as I did: bright and interesting and imaginative — although she would have preferred him to be taking the fresh air rather than be inside learning French! So we both packed him off full of knowledge, and when he went into his first year in Belvedere, he found that he was more than equal to the boys who had come through the Prep School.

For me, that pupil/teacher, nephew/aunt bond which had been forged so strongly then was to be forged again even more strongly during those years when our offices were door-to-door in Leinster House. And that is doubtless why, when Brian's death would come, it had such a devastating impact on me, since not only had I lost a dear nephew, but a very close colleague and friend as well.

As time went on, my own experience of the workings and daily processes of the Seanad would bear out many of the conclusions we had reached in that early review of its purpose and its contribution to Irish public life. I found that, as Senators, we could often participate very actively in the process of legislation making. A proposed Bill relating to any new piece of legislation can be brought either firstly to the Dáil and from there to the Seanad, or vice versa, i.e., it can go to the Seanad initially and then wend its way to the Dáil. I was always on the lookout to secure some of the particularly significant Bills for ourselves if possible, and with the excellent assistance of Eamonn McCormack, would keep in constant contact with the offices of the various Ministers, in order to ascertain whether something would come to the Seanad first — we would sometimes even demand that this should be the case. Michael McDowell was Minister for Justice during this period, and he brought many of his Bills to the Seanad first, where he always got a good hearing. Many of these then went on to the Dáil, having been improved in the Seanad debates.

In many senses, I discovered, the Seanad was a forum far more conducive to the collaborative and considered debate which lies at the heart of an effective legislative process. It was a much more intimate chamber than the Dáil, and this in itself made reasoned and careful deliberation far more possible. For me, the Seanad continues to be an invaluable environment for good Ministers to engage in useful debate and range and wide in their second stage in the forming of a new piece of legislation. I have no doubt that the five years which I spent there as Leader was time well spent.

Chapter 15 ∾

A CHRISTMAS VISIT TO ABBEVILLE

On one occasion during my second year in the Seanad, Senator Terry Leyden, whom I have already referred to as a great friend and supporter, came to me with the suggestion that he and I should go to visit Charlie Haughey at his home in Abbeville — by way of a social call, really, in the run-up to Christmas. It was December 2003 and we were already in the last few days before the Dáil and Seanad would be breaking up and everyone dispersing for Christmas. Terry and I had been members of the Shadow frontbench together from 1982 to 1987, which Charlie had headed up as Taoiseach-in-waiting. Those years had been a bonding experience for us, as had the rest of our time under Haughey's leadership.

Initially I wasn't so sure about this plan to visit our former leader, but Terry was quite insistent, saying that he would make all the arrangements and that he would drive, and so on. He rang Seán Haughey, Charlie's son, and ran the idea past him. At this stage, it was a well-known fact that Charlie's health had begun to deteriorate and that he was mostly housebound. Having consulted with his parents, however, Seán quickly got back to Terry, saying that both his father and his mother would be delighted to see us. And so a date was set for 16 December.

At about five o'clock on the evening in question, Terry and I duly set off from Dublin. I remember well that it was a very dark and bleak winter's night. When we arrived at Abbeville, Charlie Haughey was waiting for us, with the door to his home open. We went up the stone steps and inside, there was Maureen, also waiting. I had long liked and respected Maureen Haughey for the unassuming way she conducted her public life and the fine job she made of rearing her four children. She never partook in political debate in a public forum and was more than happy not to be in the spotlight.

They showed us into their living room. I had brought a bottle of nice champagne, which had actually been given to me as a gift, and which I could not see myself using. Terry had brought flowers for Maureen, which she promptly arranged in a pretty vase. At the back of the living room, Charlie had a small dispense bar — nothing lavish or ostentatious, but it certainly served its purpose well. He had two bottles of white wine already chilled for us, and once he had served us each a glass, and Maureen too, we all sat down to talk and chat, and sip, and talk again. Early on in the evening, Charlie refused Terry more than one glass, saying to him, 'You're the driver and you cannot take any more.' But he, Maureen and I continued to drink the delicious white wine, and we all talked vivaciously and spiritedly of the various events of the moment.

Charlie was as keen and witty and entertaining as he always had been and, as our conversation ranged far and wide, touching on many personalities, political and otherwise, he dispensed the type of acerbic comment that only he could, with regard to some of these individuals. At one point, for example, we were talking about Bertie Ahern, who had recently, when referring to the cabals of people who were against him, made the gaffe of calling them the 'kebabs'. I said that I thought sometimes Bertie came out with that kind of malapropism for effect, just so that he would be perceived to be not particularly articulate. Charlie thought about this for a few minutes, however, before he said, 'No, Bertie wouldn't be smart enough to say something like that for effect.'

We discussed many things and Terry and I very quickly became aware that Charlie was fully up to speed with all that was happening in the Dáil and indeed in the Seanad. At one point, he complained that when he watched the Oireachtas report at night on TV, he couldn't hear what the Cathaoirleach of the Seanad was saying, telling us that we had better tell the man in question to speak up. This greatly amused me and Terry, because we each had voted personally for Rory Kiely to be our

Cathaoirleach. But we both chose not to share this fact with Charlie, fearing he would castigate us for it. Old habits die hard indeed!

So the conversation flowed freely, as did the white wine, except in Terry's regard — and I could see him getting more miserable, since he was forbidden from imbibing any more. We stayed until around nine o'clock, and then we got up to go and both Charlie and Maureen came to the door with us. We exchanged kisses and good wishes and then away we went, back to Dublin, and Charlie and Maureen went back into their home together.

I thought Charlie appeared to be in good health — he was certainly in good form — but Terry thought he looked tired and he may have been right for, by that time, the shadow of ill health already lay on him. I remember Terry saying to me as we travelled back, 'Well, I'm sure we're the subject of mild gossip now between Charlie and Maureen', to which I replied, 'I don't think he'd bother!' In any case, both of us were very glad that we had made the visit, and it was the last time I would see Charlie Haughey until after his death in June 2006, when I went again to Kinsealy to see him laid out.

Now, this visit may not seem of such great significance, but for me somehow it was. It seemed to represent a sort of closing of the chapter of Charlie Haughey and my involvement with the man I had known and worked under, and who had had such an influence on my early political life, in appointing me firstly Shadow Minister for Education and then Minister for Education. From those actions on his part, so much of my later political life would flow.

That December visit to Charlie and Maureen's home, the cosy scene and the ambience of Christmas, also evoked in me many memories of the loved ones and friends no longer in my life — Enda, Brian Lenihan Snr, and so on. It seemed to me that many ghosts came out of the shadows that night and nodded approvingly, before fading away again, as we talked and remembered — many ghosts whose lives too had been so strongly influenced by Charlie Haughey. I am glad I got a chance to see him again when he was coherent, his mind and his talk intelligent, for it was only a few years later that cancer would take a hold on him. He had the good fortune to die at home, surrounded by his very devoted children and his ever-loving wife. Really, when it comes to the end, there is not much else one can hope for, but to pass away surrounded by dear ones who can reassure you with their love and care. And thus it was for Charlie Haughey.

Chapter 16 ∿

BENCHMARKING AND BEYOND

My years as Leader of the Seanad were busy and, I liked to think, productive in many ways. As I have said, I was determined to work hard and make the most of this honour and opportunity. Being out of the immediate spotlight, and away from the overwhelming demands which go with full participation in the Dáil, allowed me more distance and time to reflect on some of the developments and trends in Irish society related directly to the governance of the country — and to anticipate where these might take us.

One such trend which preoccupied me greatly as the years passed was how we moved from the emergence of the Programme for National Recovery between the government and the trade unions in the late 1980s, to a situation in the mid-2000s and beyond where, with the introduction of benchmarking, what had started out as a social contract between representatives of workers and representatives of government, was to become like a full government system in itself.

I have talked in an earlier chapter at some length about how in 1987 and 1988, the social partners and the government came together to hammer a way out of the extremely difficult financial situation, and how this gave rise to the Programme for National Recovery and other related social contracts. Every few years thereafter, there was a renewal of these programmes, each with their various titles. From 1991 to 1994, there was the Programme for Economic and Social Progress (PESP); from 1994 to 1996, the Programme for Competitiveness and Work

(PCW); from 1997 to 2000, the Programme for Prosperity and Fairness (PPF). As the programmes developed, they became more varied and allowed for the inclusion of other interest groups, such as the voluntary sector, the disadvantaged sector, and so on. I was a firm proponent of these programmes and enthused over them a great deal. And yet, I also found myself thinking on many occasions that they were usurping the role of Cabinet, the role of the Dáil and the role of the government itself.

Those of us in various positions in government were being reduced to rubber-stamping these programmes, just as the wider trade union working membership was reduced to rubber-stamping, just as the employers' representative bodies such as IBEC were similarly reduced to rubber-stamping. Were we, in effect, sidestepping democracy and thwarting the opportunity for what should have been very full Dáil debates on many issues of key importance? It was undeniable that, during the periods when the country needed to be sorted out financially and socially, these programmes had fulfilled a very important and meaningful purpose and made a wonderful contribution. IBEC representing industry, ICTU representing workers, the many other sectors and skeins of life which made up different legs of the various programmes: all of these were a vital part of the texture of Irish life right throughout the nineties and into the new millennium. As the years passed, however, by the time we were mid-way through Bertie Ahern's second term as Taoiseach — around 2004 or 2005 — the whole texture of these programmes became ridiculous, as benchmarking was introduced and began to assume an importance which was completely disproportionate. This was the period when private sector workers were deemed, in terms of remuneration, to have swept ahead of those in the public service and other trade union members generally.

I am not entirely sure who the creator of benchmarking was, but it quickly became an obsessive and ridiculous giant beyond our control. Senator Joe O'Toole put it most succinctly in an address at the INTO Congress in April 2000, as he sought to encourage his trade union membership to avail of benchmarking and thereby clinch whatever was the then three-year programme waiting to be ratified: 'As far as the INTO is concerned, the move from traditional review to the benchmarking review is no more than going to a different ATM . . .' And so it was. If you were in the public service, if you were a member of a trade union, if you were a member of the Dáil or the Seanad, you got money. Initially, you had to show that you had increased your productivity or how you might otherwise have earned it. But, of course, that was soon forgotten and benchmarking became an established rite-of-passage whereby, year by year, the public service and trade union members simply got more money because the mantra was that they had to catch up with the private sector. Naturally, it very quickly got out of hand and many of the ambitious work targets set for each sector of workers were just never realised.

And so it was that in time the public sector grew out of control. In 2010, all of this culminated as we know in the present Agreement — loosely called the Croke Park Agreement. The name has nothing to do with the GAA, but refers to the venue where this agreement was drawn up between the government and the trade unions! The agreement was in essence a commitment by public servants and their managers to work together to change the way in which the public service does its business, so that both its cost and the number of those employed within it will fall significantly, while continuing to meet the need for services and improve the experience of service users. On the other hand, Croke Park did also offer some measure of protection to public service workers, in forbidding compulsory redundancies and providing guarantees that, following the downgrading of pay which had been necessitated by the very difficult financial times of 2008 to 2010, there would be no further reductions in this regard. And I think there must be many a public servant who is glad of these aspects of the arrangement, even though the high days are over and everyone is back to earth with a bump.

In fact, Brian Lenihan, as Minister for Finance, did not fully approve of the Croke Park talks. On a particularly crucial day in the process, Brian was in Brussels, but keeping in touch with me by telephone. I gave a short interview on the plinth to RTÉ. Afterwards, Brian Cowen telephoned me in anger — although he did keep his calm — and more or less told me to mind my own business.

Croke Park has doubtless served a purpose. We have come a long way, from the Programme for National Recovery to the minimalism of the Croke Park Agreement now. Along the way, many, many good things were done to enhance the quality of life for all in Ireland. But in the end, like a lot of arrangements, these programmes grew into something too stylised, too stultified and far too satisfactory for a certain number of people in Ireland — those in the public sector who gradually lost touch with the harsh reality of the daily struggles and risks being taken by many of those in private industry.

Chapter 17 ∾

| BACK IN THE DÁIL

As 2006 drew to a close, preparations on all sides were already underway for the forthcoming General Election, due to be held at some point the following spring or early summer. My own term as Leader of the Seanad would be coming to an end around the same time, of course, but all of my focus in terms of the future was firmly fixed on one goal: to win back the votes of my Longford–Westmeath constituents and my seat in the Dáil. I knew that Donie Cassidy, as the incumbent who had won the seat from me, would be equally determined to reassert his claim, and it was clear that the rivalry was going to be intense. This time, however, I was more than ready for the fight and had no intention of allowing any interference in my territory.

As early as December 2006, and with as ever the invaluable support and assistance of my friend Mícheál Ó'Faoláin, my son Aengus and some other close friends, I took the bold step — which to some extent required me to put my money where my mouth was, as they say — and invested in a huge poster campaign. I was determined to get back my seat, to prove once more to my constituents, my family and myself that I could do it. There was a dual carriageway down to Kinnegad, but from Kinnegad to Athlone was still the old single-lane road which passed through the various villages. We took over a very, very big JCDecaux billboard opposite a small petrol station on the straight run into Kilbeggan. This was prime territory for me, which had been robbed from me by the tactics of the 2002 election, but on this occasion I was going to be sure to stake my claim well ahead in the game.

We got terrific studio photographs taken and the huge billboard duly went up. On the day of New Year's Eve 2006, Mícheál Ó'Faoláin and I drove out beyond Kilbeggan and then turned the car around and drove back, and the immense image hit us full force in the face — you couldn't miss it. From then on, of course, it was bang, bang, bang! Donie would put up a poster and I would put up another one. Soon everyone's posters were up and the campaign had started in earnest. It was tough but we were single-minded, and I roamed far and wide, canvassing and garnering support wherever I could. Throughout my five years in the Seanad, I had worked hard to ensure that I would have a staunch body of supporters upon whom I could call once the election date was set. Many weeks in advance we had also written to everyone who had had any dealings or contact with me, reminding them of the upcoming election and that I would be counting on their support and seeking their 'number one' vote.

Meanwhile, there was huge tumult within Fianna Fáil in spring 2007, particularly during the months of March, April and May. Bertie Ahern had been called to the Mahon Tribunal to account for various 'dig-outs' that he had got and, in particular, to explain — though it couldn't easily be done — how, in all the years he was Minister for Finance, he had never had a bank account. Now, in a way I understood in part why his outgoing expenses were so high. He had separated from Miriam as we know, but he felt of course that it was his duty to ensure that she and his two daughters could maintain a certain standard of living. He also had the expenses associated with a home for himself, in addition to the living quarters above St Luke's. These costly matters had to be provided for.

Around that time, Bertie gave a memorable television interview to Bryan Dobson. It was a very skilful, clever interview, during which just the hint of a tear was discernible in his eye, although of course he did not openly cry. Many people liked him so much that they wanted to believe everything he said. He spoke candidly, it seemed, about the various people who had given him 'dig-outs' — such as Paddy 'the Plasterer' Reilly — and although there could have been a comic side to it, with some of the names these people had, the public listened and seemed to be interested. Even so, clouds were beginning to gather above Bertie during these months and it seemed that his 'Teflon' coating was in danger of melting. He knew the election was to be called soon, and it was his dearest wish to be able to guide Fianna Fáil to victory for a third time.

Soon there were a number of stories circulating about the so-called 'men in grey suits' having to go to see Bertie and telling him, 'Listen, if you don't do something and snap out of it, we're going to be lost at the polls!' At one point too, on his return from a work trip to the Far East, Brian Cowen paid the Taoiseach a similar visit. Soon after, Bertie appeared to rally himself and pronounced that he was ready to push forward with the 2007 election campaign, as the figurehead for Fianna Fáil. In early May, the General Election was called for the 24th of that month. As campaigning began in earnest, there was a certain sense of unease at first, but as momentum grew, Bertie's strengths once more came to the fore.

So for all of us now, it was full speed ahead to Election Day. My two sons fought a fantastic campaign with me and it was such a great comfort to have my own on the stump with me, so to speak, now that there was no Enda. Aided and abetted also by all of the party people and my friends in Longford–Westmeath, and with the stalwart guidance of my valiant Director of Elections, P.J. Coghill, I was able to canvass very strongly and, as it would turn out, very effectively too. Bertie Ahern did a repeat of the tour of Ireland which had been so successful in 2002, but this time there was not the same atmosphere of loving adulation from the people. He did come to Athlone, however — two days before the vote — and many people turned out to meet him. I felt that he was in his own way trying to make up for what had happened with me in the previous General Election, and it seemed clear that his coming to Athlone that evening had a very good effect on the voters from my point of view. On Election Day itself and to my delight, I had a very good return indeed, with a great poll result. I got over 8,000 votes, and was the second highest in the count next to Willie Penrose for Labour. It was a huge result and one in which I took terrific pleasure.

Fianna Fáil as a party would win through at that election too, in spite of all of the doubt and uncertainty which hung over Bertie's continued dealings with the Mahon Tribunal. It was of course a relatively narrow victory. In retrospect, I am convinced that that would have been the General Election for us to lose and for Enda Kenny to win. Had Fine Gael/Labour got into government in that summer of

2007 (and they very nearly did), all of the subsequent brutal budgets would have been theirs to impose and any bail-out of the country by the Troika of the IMF/European Central Bank/EU would have been carried out under a Fine Gael/Labour regime.

Three weeks after the election, on 14 June 2007, the Dáil reassembled. Séamus Brennan had enticed the Greens to come into government with us, while Bertie had done his usual love-in with the Independents, whom he always made sure to keep onside. And thus the new government was in place. I had just turned 70 and did not at all expect that I would get any frontbench position, junior or otherwise — and neither did I want one. I was more than happy to have at last the opportunity to enjoy being a vigorous backbencher, a position which I had not held before because during all the earlier stages in my political career, I had either been a Minister, a Minister of State or a frontbench Spokesperson, or in equivalent roles in Opposition. One way or another, my work in politics had been a juggling act between dealing with national issues and doing my best to try to keep my constituents in Athlone and elsewhere happy. As a frontbencher, I had often been in the firing line. Now I was in the rearguard and able to do the firing myself. Although I never fired just because I wanted to fire!

Meanwhile, Bertie Ahern had asked Brian Lenihan to take on the role of Minister for Justice and Brian was truly delighted. As was I on his behalf — we were all very pleased that he had come into sunshine at last. Otherwise, the financial storm clouds were gathering in earnest by this time. Bertie, however, played bravado, saying that people who spoke in sombre tones about such matters were only seeking to wreck the economy, and so on. But, with the tribunal continuing all the while its relentless review of Bertie's finances (or lack thereof!), the miasma of uncertainty was over Fianna Fáil. The true extent of the country's troubles was yet to be revealed, of course.

For the time being, however, I settled into my nice modest office over in the building '2000', as we called it. Lisa Foran, who had worked with me in the Seanad office, came with me and I was glad to keep her. She was somebody I knew and trusted, and she similarly liked and trusted me, and we worked very well together. So I was set fair for life in government again — this time, as a sturdy, outgoing and hardworking backbencher.

I was very busy in my constituency at this time, having set up a constituency office in Athlone which was run by the very capable Breda Browne. Breda and her husband Seamus have always been among my loyal friends and supporters. By this time, the mobile phone had for some years been proving to be a very useful tool for those in public life in particular, because it meant easy accessibility and easy follow-up. Now that I was once more a TD, I made fastidious use of the system of Dáil questions, of which I would generally put forward at least half a dozen per week, if not more. I also took a very keen interest in the debates at parliamentary party meetings. I always contributed where I felt it would be helpful and expressed my discontent where I felt an issue was worthy of complaint. I hugely enjoyed those encounters and they remain as clear to me now as they were at the time. In the whole of my political life, in fact, I don't think that I missed more than one or two parliamentary party meetings, and only then because I was away from the Dáil on business of one kind or another.

When I first got back into the Dáil in 2007, I decided that I would speak on those matters of legislation in which I was particularly interested. We would have about a week's notice as to which legislative points were to be on the agenda for the following week, and I would select those for which I had specific ideas or direct experience. However, I didn't ever write out scripts or have them prepared in advance. I just rang up the Whip's office, got my time slot and then went along to speak at the arranged time. As time went on, I was pleased to note that more and more of whatever I said was being reported in the daily reports of the Dáil. But I was especially pleased to now have the chance to express myself freely — which I could not do when I had been a Minister. Mind you, even then, I had never allowed myself to be too caught up in the protocol of not saying this or not saying that. But being a backbencher now gave me great freedom and I explored it to the full.

As well as my constituency and Dáil commitments, I had another important role to fulfil within the new government: one which I was initially tentative about but which I found to be both worthwhile and satisfying. When Bertie Ahern as newly re-elected Taoiseach was selecting his Cabinet and making his other appointments, he had telephoned me one day to ask if I would be the Chairperson of the All-

Party Joint Committee on the Constitutional Amendment on Children. 'You were a great success in Education, Mary,' he said. 'And I know that you genuinely have children's interests at heart . . .'

Of course, I was extremely honoured to be so invited, but I had inner qualms about chairing an all-party committee, knowing how difficult it can be to chair a committee of any kind. However I duly accepted and the various parties put forward their nominees. For Fine Gael, the big guns were Alan Shatter, Frances Fitzgerald and Michael Noonan, who was appointed Deputy Chair of the Committee; for Labour, there was Brendan Howlin and Alex White; Sinn Féin nominated Caoimhghín Ó Caoláin, who, notably, would not miss a single meeting of the committee. Paul Gogarty was appointed from the Greens, while for Fianna Fáil, we had such heavyweights such as Maria Corrigan, Thomas Byrne and Seán Ó Fearghaíl. In general, it was the Opposition deputies who were appointed to the key positions in the committee — there was a lot of flux within the Fianna Fáil ranks, but that I fully understood, as they of course would be heavily committed elsewhere with all of their various frontbench obligations.

The date of our first meeting was 22 November 2007. I was very conscious of the huge responsibility of being in charge of an all-party committee with a mandate to bring about a consensus wording relating to the Constitutional Amendment on Children. It was a responsibility not only because our brief was a highly important one, but also because I would be required to mediate between and manage a number of big political personalities, while ensuring that we made steady progress on all of the key issues.

After our initial tentative meeting that November, we agreed that the first official meeting of the committee would take place in January 2008 and so in effect our work began then. We were very lucky to have secured a fine Secretary to the committee in the shape of Ann Marie Fahey. Ann Marie was a civil servant attached to the Houses of the Oireachtas, and as such, well-versed in dealing with various committees. She was also someone who approached her work with such professionalism and dedication that I can honestly say she was one of the finest civil servants I have ever met.

At that first meeting in January 2008, once we had set up our business stall, so to speak, I proposed that we would meet on a given day and at a given time on either a weekly or fortnightly basis, depending on the pace of business and the agenda which we had set ourselves. I had seen the committee system at close quarters in Leinster House, and I was strongly of the opinion that much of it was nothing more than grandstanding: members hauling in public figures so that they could upbraid them, get a couple of soundbites in the media and be in the spotlight as heroes or heroines for a while, without very much of any concrete value being achieved. So my suggestion was that we would carry out our business in private as far as possible, except where there was a clear demand for a particular meeting to be conducted in public. In that way, we went about our business quietly and efficiently, with nobody to bother us as we did so. It was a highly effective move, and one we were soon glad to have taken at such an early stage.

Let me go back in time. The need for a constitutional amendment on the rights of children had been first mooted in 1993 by the then Judge Catherine McGuinness, when she headed the Report of the Kilkenny Incest Investigation. At the conclusion of the report, Judge McGuinness put forward her belief that, until there was a change in the Constitution regarding the situation of children and their protection, needs and rights, deplorable matters, such as the one she had just adjudicated on, would continue to erupt into Irish life. After 1993, the issue would come to the fore again from time to time with ferocity, when a particularly terrible case of the abuse of children within their own family unit would come to light. Everybody would wring their hands and the combined call for a change in the Constitution would be reignited — only for the issue to inevitably die down again. This is the way of public life in Ireland and something which is, I am sure, replicated elsewhere throughout the world. When an issue is current and in the media spotlight, everybody will complain, remonstrate and demand that action should be taken. As soon as the issue disappears from the headlines, so do the complaints. And so it was also with this contentious issue.

At his Ard Fheis speech of 3 November 2006, Bertie Ahern had pledged his commitment to a Constitutional Amendment on Children. In his successive Ministerial capacities, Brian Lenihan had drafted the detail of the wording of such an amendment as he saw it, and now I was tasked with the job of bringing about that consensus wording.

Why was there a demand at all for a change in our Constitution with regard to children, one might ask? Weren't children already in the Constitution? Yes, they were, but always as an appendage of schools, of the community, of a family — never in their own right, as citizens of the land. The role of the family was regarded as paramount — and in many ways rightly so, of course — but this meant that the rights of the family effectively trumped the rights of the child, which in turn had led to decades of timid and tentative incursions by Health Service executives, by Health Board members, by social workers, all of whom were essentially very reluctant to intrude or intervene, even in dreadful cases where children were clearly being abused, out of fear that in doing so they would be acting against the Constitution, and that charges could be brought against them.

This unwillingness or inability to take decisive action, even when it was clear that something urgently needed to be done, was evident in very many legal cases involving severe abuse, and in report after report. And yet still everyone dithered and dithered about doing something, and the reason for this failure to act was because there was and is and will always be an extreme right-wing element in Ireland which — even though the headlines scream of the shameful abuse of children — will regard any such intrusion as being against the Constitution and contrary to the fundamental rights of the family.

Happily for me, at the very beginning of our deliberations, we became convinced that the only way forward was to ensure that we *equated* the rights of parents with the rights of children, in other words, that we made both equal. Now, perhaps that smacks of Charlie Haughey's long-ago law on contraception — an Irish solution to an Irish problem! But we were convinced that it was the only way forward. It is completely right that the family should be the paramount source of care and support of the child — and that the child is best brought up against the background of his or her family and is best disposed to make his or her way in life with the support, love and care of his or her family — but that is in the normal course of events. This notion of what is right and correct in normal circumstances does not allow for the abnormal or aberrant, and this was what we, through our consensus wording, were set up to address.

In the course of our discussions, other key points of relevance to our central focus also emerged. One of these, about which I felt particularly strongly, was that the voice of the child should be heard in all matters relating to court cases concerning him or her — such as, for example, where parents wished to part or were involved in acrimonious disputes for custody arrangements. According to the child's stage of emotional maturity and/or age, his or her voice should be heard, should be listened to and, if possible, acted upon. Of course, within the committee, but particularly within the parameters of the legal opinions offered to us, there were huge disagreements on this issue. We were reminded, for example, of the expense of providing a mentor for a child in such cases and other such financial considerations, but I remained very convinced that it was a strong point and one that I wanted to see implemented.

In total, the committee produced three reports. The first report, issued on 11 September 2008, set out a proposal 'to give legal authority for the collection and exchange of information concerning the risk or the occurrence of endangerment, sexual exploitation or sexual abuse of children'. The issue of the handling of 'soft' information and the need for the vetting of people working with children had of course arisen initially out of the Holly Wells and Jessica Chapman case in the UK in 2002, where a school janitor had been appointed, despite having a history of initiating inappropriate contact with children at a previous school. Subsequently, and rightly so, it became regarded as essential that proper vetting systems and as well as systems for the effective passing on of relevant information should be in place in all environments in which children were to be found. It had been thought that this item on its own would require a constitutional amendment, but having gone through the matter fully and with the benefit of the input of our legal advisors, the conclusion was that a very detailed piece of legislation would suffice.

Our second or interim report was published on 7 May 2009, and presented a proposal 'to give legal authority to create offences of absolute or strict liability in respect of sexual offences against or in connection with children'. The final report was issued on 16 February 2010 and set forth our proposal 'for a constitutional amendment to strengthen children's rights'. Each of these three reports was well received and the work of our committee was seen to have contributed significantly to the field of legislation on children's rights.

However, having explored and identified the key issues, our clear emphasis now lay in finding the wording and this is where the really intense work was carried out. At Michael Noonan's suggestion, it was decided that each party would work on bringing forward their own proposals, and that these proposals would then be merged and meshed to see if we could bring about a consensus one. Now, taking into account all of these elements as well as addressing the key issues we had identified for inclusion and clarification was a difficult balancing act indeed. But the end result of all of our hard work and patience was the satisfaction of knowing that the legal clause which we finally issued managed that difficult balancing act, while contributing in some new and important ways to the very worthwhile objective of strengthening and clarifying the rights of children under our Constitution.

Chapter 18 ∾

RECESSION AND A RECKONING

By late spring 2008 the Mahon Tribunal was taking more and more of a toll on Bertie Ahern, not only in a personal sense but also in terms of party confidence. There was increasing disquiet among the Fianna Fáil rank-and-file members about some of the revelations which were emerging, and the patently lame excuses which Bertie was offering to the tribunal. Although it seems clear that Bertie had hoped to stay in office longer, as the summer months approached, some of the 'heavy suits' in Fianna Fáil went to visit him and he was persuaded that it was time for him to hang up his boots, so to speak.

Bertie Ahern stepped down as Taoiseach on 6 May 2008. At that time he was still in many senses riding high in the Irish public's affection and esteem. Before his departure, he did a 'lap of honour' in relation to all the work he had done over the years in connection with the Peace Process. He went to Westminster, where Tony Blair invited him to address a combined House of Commons/House of Lords; he then proceeded to Washington where he spoke to Congress, also on the Peace Process. Few could fault him for wishing to finish on a high, but meanwhile at home, throughout Europe and indeed in the States too, the financial storm clouds were gathering relentlessly.

I just hope that the massive work Bertie did to erase the Northern problem will in due course be truly acknowledged as the huge accomplishment that it was. Of all of the attributes which he showed in relation to this issue, one of the most admirable was his endless patience, particularly in talking and dealing with David Trimble, as the two of them progressed along the path to peace together. Equally, Bertie's dealings with George Mitchell, himself a hero in the whole Northern context, were truly impressive also, and these two men were a very formidable duo when it came to resolving many issues along the way.

But I have a fear that events later on in Bertie Ahern's political life will overshadow his crucial work in the North. This shouldn't be overshadowed and I hope it won't, for nobody can ever take from what he did. I will never forget how, during those particularly dreadful years in the 1990s, all of us, both North and South, would wake up each morning, wondering what the latest awful atrocity would be, and we would so often be faced with the endless pictures of women sobbing at gravesides, sobbing and sobbing. I hope in time it will be for that magnificent Good Friday Agreement that people will remember Bertie.

As to Bertie's successor, it was the same scenario this time as so often in the past in the Fianna Fáil Party. The incumbent was already in place. Brian Cowen, who was bequeathed to us by Bertie, was to be the next leader and therefore the next Taoiseach. There was no contest for the leadership, no tussle for the job: Brian was seen as the natural successor, it seemed. He had proved his mettle — or so the perception was at the time — during his tenure as Finance Minister since 2004, and the Fianna Fáil grassroots wanted him, the organisation wanted him and the TDs and Senators wanted him. The only puzzle in all of this was — and it was a question which would only emerge much, much later — did Brian Cowen himself want the leadership? It is easy to imagine in retrospect that perhaps he didn't — that in fact he sleepwalked into the job, buoyed up by the acclaim of all of those who thought he was the right man for the role, and by the goodwill of Bertie Ahern, who liked to represent that he been the one to provide the party with this ready-made successor.

But real doubts about Brian Cowen's accession would only begin to emerge later. For the present, on 14 May 2008, the new Taoiseach sallied forth to enjoy a triumphant homecoming in Tullamore and Clara. There was the famous scene in Clara with the hundreds — no, thousands — of people on the open green, and Brian Cowen, clearly in his element, singing and generally being part of the joyful occasion, flanked by his wife Mary and their two lovely daughters. I know the media enjoyed having a snide laugh at it all, because I think it was something unfamiliar to them and which they felt uncomfortable with: after all, the media is Dublin-based.

This was an early indicator of the uneasy relationship which would soon develop. The media liked Brian Cowen as a person, but they never warmed to him as Taoiseach, and Brian in turn would make no effort to get on with them: he simply refused to acknowledge the value of trying to do so. More or less from the off, he took the line, 'They know me as I am: I'm plain; I'm ordinary; I don't put on airs and graces and I'm not trying to be something I'm not.' Now, these are all very noble and fine sentiments, but they just did not, and do not, fit the bill for a Taoiseach in today's world. As I know from my own experience in public life, the truth is that the media have to be indulged — not to an enormous extent, but they have to be taken into account. By his own admission at the time, Brian Cowen couldn't give a fig about them.

Having said this, it is important to stress again that Brian's appointment as Taoiseach was hugely welcomed by all elements of Fianna Fáil: the parliamentary party, the National Executive and of course the wider organisation. In hindsight, it remains to be seen whether we were at fault in thinking that Brian Cowen could deliver a continuation of the good times of Bertie, when confronted with what would be some very bad times. Perhaps it was just that we all felt comfortable with him, and we thought, 'He's the guy for us — he's the guy for Fianna Fáil.' As it would turn out, he wasn't, and I think early on, Brian recognised this himself.

Anyway, the new Taoiseach went about forming his new Cabinet. For days beforehand, the rumours circulated as to who would be appointed, particularly in relation to Brian Lenihan — Brian would be Tánaiste; he would be this; he would be that. When the big day was finally upon us, we were all ensconced in our backbench seats when Brian Cowen led his Cabinet into the Dáil. Immediately after him came Mary Coughlan, so we knew she was Tánaiste. Next came Brian Lenihan, which meant of course that he was Minister for Finance, because the Minister for Finance always takes the place next to the Taoiseach and Tánaiste. As Brian sat down, he looked satisfied and happy. So we were set fair from that day for four more years of government — or so we imagined at the time.

One of the first tasks facing Brian Cowen as Taoiseach was the Lisbon Referendum, which turned out to be the first of two Lisbon referendums. As we know, the issue at hand was the Lisbon Treaty, which sought among other things to streamline and simplify the processes of the European parliament, making them more accessible and comprehensible to the member states. To my mind, it was all very well thought out and had many excellent strategies to it. For most of the other European countries, the process of subscribing to the treaty was relatively straightforward, as it was a matter which could be decided by a vote in parliament. In Ireland, however, the Crotty decision in 1987 had established that any significant changes to European Union treaties would require an amendment to the Irish Constitution and should be taken to a national referendum before they could be ratified by the State. Whether we liked it or not, we were saddled with this requirement and that would mean a full-blown campaign in preparation for a referendum.

Despite our efforts, however, on 13 June 2008 there was a majority 'No' vote against the Lisbon Treaty. There was consternation throughout the land. What was to happen now? It was an almost fatal blow to Brian Cowen at such an early point in his reign as Taoiseach — how was he going to pick himself up from this? But rally himself he did and he went to Brussels, and more or less told them that we would have another referendum. Meanwhile, at home the debate raged. Had the people not spoken, and had they not said 'No'? And how many times had we had referendums on abortion, only to get the same result? Yet it was clear almost immediately that there was going to be another Lisbon referendum, although a decent period of time — more than a year — would elapse before it actually happened.

The second time around, the 'Yes' campaign was more focused and determined. In political circles, we all set about our business with intent, canvassing locally as if for a General Election. In civic society too, the chambers of commerce and many other various groupings got together — such as Young People for Europe and Women for Europe — and began to preach loudly the message of Europe. In fact, they all began to fight the extremely active, vibrant campaign which should have been fought for the first Lisbon referendum. There was huge relief all round when Ireland voted 'Yes' on 2 October 2009. But in the interim, as we know, financial disaster had struck the country on an unprecedented scale.

Brian Lenihan had not been long in his new role in the Department of Finance when he realised that Ireland was heading downwards fast. Realising the gravity and urgency of the situation, he consulted with Brian Cowen and others in the Department, proposing to bring forward the 2009 budget to October. It was decided that this Emergency Budget, as distinct from the usual December budget, would be delivered to the nation on 14 October 2008.

Before this however, on 30 September, we had the Bank Guarantee. By now of course, everybody is well acquainted with the Bank Guarantee. There have since been very many public debates held and documentaries produced and economic treatises written about it, so, in a sense, what is there left to say? So many eminent commentators rushed out their bestselling books at the time, purporting to know what happened that night and to give advice as to what action should have been taken.

For us ordinary backbenchers, who were not party to the Cabinet's urgent deliberations (although the matter would go to a vote in the Dáil afterwards), the drama of the night of 29 September can only be guessed at. The late-night calls to Cabinet Ministers; the representatives from the banks occupying — literally — the Minister for Finance's office and later that of the Taoiseach too; the overriding necessity to save the nation from grinding to a standstill, to keep the banks open and, as Brian Lenihan would say, 'the ATM machines turning over', so that people could still get out their money.

It is very easy now, post-event, for people to remonstrate and say what they would have done had they been in the Department of Finance or the Department of An Taoiseach in the throes of the urgency and the pressure of that night, when these momentous decisions were taken. I doubt very much if they would have any made better choices, in spite of what they might claim. When they came, begging to be saved by the Departments of Finance and An Taoiseach, the banks were just at the point of going to the wall. What would have happened in Ireland if the ATM machines had not worked the next morning? There would have been chaos, of course, and wholesale and outright panic!

There had been the earlier bank crashes in the US: Lehman Brothers,

Fannie Mae and Freddie Mac, Merrill Lynch. There were the English banks too. But somehow nobody believed that our Irish banks, such as Bank of Ireland and Allied Irish Bank — up until then well-respected — could have been engaged in nefarious pursuits. Yet they were, and what they had been mostly hotly in pursuit of was the modus operandi of the Anglo Irish Bank, which was apparently the golden success story of the banking world, inspiring envy in the other ordinary, more pedestrian high-street banks.

On a human level, I believe that that night of huge burdens on Brian Lenihan and all the many stresses of the time which followed took a massive toll on his health, and may even have sown the seeds of his pancreatic cancer. I do not think I am being fanciful when I say this, because there is a clear link between physical illness and emotional stress. As I have said, the burden placed upon him that night was enormous and in some important senses, he was alone in taking the decisions he had to take. Of course, Brian had at this stage a very wonderful advisor in Dr Alan Ahearne from NUI, Galway: a calm, good man who I am sure was able to be of great assistance to him at that dreadful time. And I know that Brian Cowen was a worthy comrade with him too. But the enormous scale and the import of the choices he was confronted with, along with the very poor, patchy and inconsistent advice from the Department of Finance advisors — all of this added up to a huge cauldron of worry and concern for Brian Lenihan. In the end a decision had to be taken by him on whom the crown had been laid, and which now had become a crown of thorns. This is not at all how it appeared at the time perhaps, but in hindsight, that is how it seems to me and to others who, like me, were on the periphery of the whole process.

The legislation which led to the bank bailout was passed in the Dáil and the Seanad on 30 September 2008. In a vote in the Dáil, Fianna Fáil, Fine Gael and Sinn Féin supported the proposed measures; Labour voted against. On 2 October, the Credit Institutions (Financial Support) Bill 2008 was enacted. Brian Lenihan took that Bill himself right through all the stages in the Dáil, and then straight on into the Seanad, where he was ably assisted by Martin Mansergh. There was confusion and chaos all around, and parliamentary party meetings were in disarray. Amid the turmoil, Brian Lenihan's was the one calm, lucid voice, as he strove to explain in plain language what was happening and make clear the serious nature of our predicament and the action which needed to be taken.

Hot on the heels of the Bank Guarantee and all the associated chaos which ensued, came the Emergency Budget, just two weeks later. By this time we in the parliamentary party were well prepared for the bad tidings it would bring. But we also knew that it would be crucial as the first step in the massive cutting back in national spending which would be necessary to try to get our situation under control.

One of the most memorable elements of the Emergency Budget was a seeming attack on the older population around the issue of medical cards. Heretofore, the system had of course been that anybody over the age of 70 was deemed eligible for a medical card. It was a measure which had been heralded by Charlie McCreevy in December 2000 and had come into effect on 1 July 2001: it had been blithely agreed to, even though the associated costs would clearly be horrendous. There was no doubt that some of this was quite unfair in a sense: there were some really well-off older people who could well afford their own medication and doctor visits, but who were eligible for the card anyway under the prevailing system. As soon as the news of the proposed cuts broke, there was huge public outcry. The over-70s were not having any of it! They marched in protest, occupied a disused church in Dublin and then paraded outside the Dáil: they were certainly not taking it lying down. There was uproar at subsequent parliamentary party meetings, until eventually an equitable solution and compromise of sorts was found. It was decided that if, through pension or payment, a person had a combined income of over €1,400 per week as part of a couple, or €700 as a single person, they would not be deemed entitled to a medical card. Everyone else over 70 would still be eligible.

Although that very contentious issue got sorted out satisfactorily in the end, it left a very bitter aftertaste for many people, and the impression of a government bent on attacking first of all the older population. This was compounded by the increasingly taciturn nature of Brian Cowen's public appearances and in his dealings with the media. Taken together with the first Lisbon defeat, the trauma of the Bank Guarantee and the brutal cuts of this most recent budget, it all added up to not a very pretty picture for Fianna Fáil at the time.

Accordingly, there was a growing sense of dismay within the ranks of the parliamentary party. This was not the Brian Cowen we knew of old: the 'hail-fellow-well-met', ordinary bloke who could appeal to all elements in our society. He still was this person, of course, but it seemed that the sophistication required by his new role on public occasions and in his dealings with the media was lost on him. He was the same highly intelligent, savvy and responsive fellow as before, but somehow the sense of finesse needed was now missing.

A contributory and disturbing tendency which, we noticed, had begun to permeate Brian Cowen's public appearances and media interactions was the civil service 'speak' which peppered his discourse in such situations. Let's say he would be out launching something or at some other kind of public function, and he was asked a question by the media — which question might have been harmless in essence if there was no big story or issue ongoing at the time — the Taoiseach would slip immediately into civil service jargon, giving a convoluted, complex answer which would require a lot of work on the part of his listeners to try to understand and to get to the nugget of relevant information.

I for one just couldn't make any sense of the turn his conversation and discourse had begun to take, because I had never known him to be like that before. In Athlone, we had a very great affection for Brian Cowen — whenever he visited our town, he was always well-regarded, greatly welcomed and we enjoyed basking in the neighbourly glow of having the Taoiseach living in the constituency beside us. I remember particularly how he had come to Athlone Institute of Technology to launch various of our initiatives; he also came to visit local industries and schools, and so forth. Each time, I had found him to be a good and effective person to deal with. Now, however, in that troubled period of his reign as Taoiseach, I was startled and dismayed by the change in his demeanour and indeed personality. It was as if he didn't want to be where he was, but that he was struggling on anyway.

All the while, Brian Lenihan was doing his utmost to steer some kind of course through the awful financial storm of the recession that was upon us, trying at the same time to remain calm and keep outright national panic at bay. After the Emergency Budget of 14 October 2008 came the Supplementary Budget of 7 April 2009, followed by another budget in December that year. I will always hold fast in my memory the image of Brian as Minister for Finance, standing there with his budget book in his hand in the Dáil to deliver that budget of 9 December 2009, setting out in his fine, measured, easily understood words what Ireland had to do now and what we could hope the future would hold for us. Of course, he said that we would round the corner, and that over the hill, there would be salvation for Ireland. In hindsight we can see that that has not come about up to now, but of course Brian Lenihan had to have words like that. How on earth could he have stood up in the House and delivered a dirge of gloom and despondency and thereby sown utter despair in the hearts of the Irish people? It was only right that he should seek to lift the spirits of the nation. But it was a very difficult task and, as I have said, one that he had to do alone.

Around this time, I noticed that Brian Lenihan began to telephone me frequently, not to talk about the difficult decisions he had to take, but rather by way of unburdening himself to his trusted aunt, of relieving the pressures he felt building up in him. I was glad to act as a sounding board for him and to provide an older person's perspective and just to listen too when he needed that. The routine became that he would telephone me either on a Sunday afternoon or a Sunday evening: we would often speak together for over an hour. Also, during the week, even though he would be busy, as would I in my own fashion, he always found time for a quick cup of tea or a brief discussion with me.

The thing about Brian was that no matter how busy, how strained or how tired he was, if he met me or anyone else he knew well in the corridor at work, he would always make sure to stop and talk and first exchange pleasantries and family news, before lapsing into more serious mode. I suppose in a way this lightened his load and leavened his mind, serving as a reminder of normal, everyday life, in which he too had to participate like everyone else. He also made the time to be as friendly and affable and outgoing as ever with those in the parliamentary party, so many of whom were confused and deeply riven with doubts by this point.

Chapter 19 ∾

| DARK DAYS

Despite all the gloomy forebodings, the budget in early December 2009 was carried in the Dáil and received a mixed, but reasonably favourable reception in the press and with the public. In the weeks which followed however, a terrible stroke of fate befell Brian Lenihan. This was his illness. By that Christmas Eve, he would already have confirmation that he was suffering from pancreatic cancer, the deadly disease to which he was to finally succumb, eighteen months later.

People have often asked me, how did it begin? What were the first signs for Brian that all was not well? Well, it seems that it had started with a stomach ache, which he put down to having eaten something at an official dinner which didn't agree with him — perhaps some chicken or fish or something of that nature. But when the discomfort persisted, Brian went to see his local doctor, who referred him immediately to the Mater Hospital. The first impression there was that it might be a hiatus hernia, and a number of tests and other investigations were carried out. Forgive me for being detailed, but people do ask these questions.

I remember speaking to Brian's brother Conor Lenihan on the telephone on 19 December or thereabouts, and we assured one another that a hiatus hernia was not that serious and that Brian would be okay. But by Christmas Eve we knew the worst — and the worst was pancreatic cancer. I'll never forget the utter despair which swept over the Lenihan family that Christmas Eve. All of us were devastated: Brian's wife Patricia, his two lovely children Tom and Clare (I don't know how much the children knew at this stage about the potentially fatal outcome of pancreatic cancer), his mother Ann, his sister Anita, his brothers Conor, Niall and Paul, and his two aunts. I felt it so keenly because as I have mentioned earlier, he was my dear friend and my dear work colleague, and our friendship went far beyond an aunt/nephew relationship. All of us spent a very unhappy Christmas Eve and Christmas Day.

Things were not about to get any better. On 26 December, even as we struggled with our grief, reeling from this terrible blow, TV3 chose to tell the world about Brian's cancer, in a startling, 'breaking news'-style intervention by their political correspondent, Ursula Halligan. She broke the news, not just to the nation, but to the extended circle of Brian's family and friends. Yes, we had been alerted just a day or two before Christmas, but there had been no chance for Brian and his family to tell the other very important people around them about what was happening. And for us to see it being featured so openly and graphically on our TV screens, with what seemed to us a lack of sensitivity and finer feeling — that was very hard to bear. TV3 defended themselves meanwhile, by saying that the public should know and that it was a matter of public interest. Of course we were more than aware of the need for those in public life to be accountable in such situations, and Brian had always intended to give an account of himself after he had had the privacy of spending the few days of Christmas with his family.

Accordingly, as New Year 2010 dawned, Brian went on the *News at One* show with Seán O'Rourke and gave a lengthy interview, in which — I don't use the words lightly — the sheer nobility and the hugely open and generous nature of the man was laid bare. Can you imagine how difficult that must have been for him? Yet he spoke with such grace and elegance that it appeared effortless. But of course, effortless it was not. He would have been so conscious of his wife and children; of those in his wider family circle; of his friends; of his party colleagues. He would have been so aware too of the pall, the sense of pessimism that had descended on the people of the country, on learning this news on top of all their other troubles at such a difficult time. Yet in that interview with Seán O'Rourke, Brian explained with such courage and composure exactly where the tumour lay — at the neck of the pancreas and on a major blood vessel — and that therefore he could not undergo an operation.

There is not a family in the land that has not had some experience of cancer within their ranks or among their dear friends and their close circles. Cancer is here to stay for the foreseeable future and despite all the advances — and there have been many leaps forward in such research — pancreatic cancer remains the one whose diagnosis will strike a chill into everyone's heart. It knows no mercy; it takes no prisoners. Whether discovered early or late, it is lethal.

In that period immediately after Brian's diagnosis, it seemed for me as if all of the raw and hitherto submerged grief, which was still deep inside me from the loss of Enda, had suddenly come to the surface again. I felt alone. I felt bereft. I felt as if life was coming to an end. And part of me raged. Why couldn't it have been one of us, who already had a good few years of life behind us? Why did it have to be this 50-year-old man, blessed with a terrific intellect and so many leadership qualities, seemingly full of vigour, who had now succumbed to the malign influence of this deadly disease?

Brian started his chemotherapy almost at once. Yet he continued all the while to put in a full day's work every day in the Department of Finance. During that period, he came in to the Department at 7.30 a.m. and often would not leave until midnight, day by day. He would frequently go into work again on Saturdays and Sundays. There was so much to be done: so many files to read, ponder and initial; so many measures to be planned, so many next steps he had to take. Yes, he was constantly overworked and of course some people have said that if he hadn't worked like that, his illness might not have been able to take hold. Was it the tension and the pressure of the huge financial burden Brian was struggling with, was it all of this which brought about the cancer? It is impossible for anyone to know.

As Brian continued his treatment and kept working so hard at his job, we began to feel that perhaps, just perhaps he might be one of the very few who would not be beaten by this cancer. Of course hope always springs eternal in the human heart and I, like many, many others, hoped that somehow Brian would surmount his illness. He was undoubtedly a fighter and I felt that such a strong spirit as his might be able to stave off any further inroads by the cancer. All the while, I could only imagine how Brian's wonderful wife, Patricia, was able, despite her own demanding job, to keep up her children's spirits at home as they continued their studies. At the time, Tom was doing his Leaving Cert and Clare was shaping up for her Junior Cert. As an aside, I remember well how, as part of his Honours History course for Leaving Cert, young Tom decided to do a project on his great grandfather and my father, P.J. Lenihan. To that end, he came down to Athlone to meet with George Eaton, who had been Company Secretary of Gentex — the two of them had a very useful and interesting conversation with one another. As part of the project, Tom also interviewed me at a later point. I never saw the end result of the project, but I'm sure it worked out really well because he was fascinated by his subject, as well he might be.

It was to be an enormously difficult year for the Lenihan family in 2010. As well as Brian's continuing struggle with pancreatic cancer and its bleak prognosis, we would lose my brother, Paddy, that autumn, in the month of October. Paddy had been battling illness for some time. Years before, he had been diagnosed with Parkinson's but, with the help of a very effective regime of medication, he had been able to withstand this difficult disease very well. However, in the twelve months preceding the summer of 2010, his health had taken a distinct turn for the worst. He had developed various problems with the veins in his legs and other chronic health difficulties. Taken in isolation, none of these conditions was serious, but together and in conjunction with his Parkinson's, it all added up to a poor state of health. At one point, Paddy went to Roscommon Hospital for about four weeks and we all visited him a lot during that time.

The whole Lenihan family had a great affection for Paddy. As I have mentioned in the opening chapter of this book, he was the younger of my two brothers, at 15 months younger than Brian Snr. Paddy was always regarded as, not so much the wild one, but the different one — and I think it was perhaps because Brian was so serious and so much the older brother when they were growing up. I remember Paddy in those early years so well, because I was always really fond of him and he of me. After completing his schooling, Paddy had enrolled at UCD to study Agriculture. I can still recall clearly being brought as a schoolgirl to see him at one stage in the Portobello Private Nursing Home in Dublin, where he had to stay for about four or five weeks, having had a very bad flu which had turned into pleurisy. Following this bout of ill health, Paddy had seemingly decided in his own mind that he had had enough of academic life and of what he saw as the strictures of life in Ireland — and so off he went of his own accord to work in England, without telling anyone that he was so doing.

One day, Paddy had telephoned my father out of the blue from England, to say where he was and what he was doing. As you can imagine, my mother and father had been in a fierce state of worry about him since his disappearance. Anyway, he explained to my father that he was living in a town called Worksop in the North of England, and that he was working down the mines earning his living and was quite happy. He said he was in decent digs and gave my father the name of his landlady, who, he said, was very good to him. I remember vividly how concerned my mother was on hearing that Paddy was working in the mines, as, with his record of ill-health and pleurisy, she was sure that he would be very prone to any of the miners' diseases which were so prevalent in the UK of the early 1950s.

My father would often have been in England on business for Gentex at this stage, and so he decided to go up to Worksop one evening to meet Paddy. My mother was very relieved to hear after this visit that Paddy was enjoying himself, and that he liked the work and had made some good friends. The experience had also clarified in Paddy's mind the realisation that he wasn't cut out for academic life and that he wanted to continue with the path he was now on.

I took it upon myself then to start to write to Paddy. In turn he would reply to my letters — although usually after a long interval! — telling me among other things that since he had been away, he had learned some wonderful poems by the folk poet, Robert W. Service, and in particular, 'The Shooting of Dan McGrew'. I wrote to ask him if he could send me the words of this poem, as I wanted to learn it off by heart as a future party piece. Paddy duly obliged and by return of post, I received the words of what I referred to as 'Dangerous Dan McGrew'. Once I had learned these and had all the words and various intonations off just so, I sprang a surprise rendition upon my family. They were completely amazed, particularly when I told them that Paddy had sent me the poem. It was a funny little interlude, but a measure, I think, of the friendship and rapport we shared.

After he had been in England for a few years, Paddy started to come home for summer holidays. He was always tall, but now he had broadened out and was a fine, strong young man — the hard work in the mines had seen to that. He certainly seemed to have toned down his wilder inclinations: again, perhaps that too was down to all the hard work. I guess that even then, when there would have been a shortage of workers in the mines, you had to be on top of your game to keep your job. On one trip home, during the time we were all still living at the Hodson Bay Hotel, Paddy met Brid O'Flaherty, a fine young Connemara woman who had trained in Cathal Brugha Street in Dublin as a chef and was now head cook in the Hodson Bay Hotel. She and Paddy hit it off well, but he went back to his work in the mines in Worksop and she stayed in her job directing the kitchens in the Hodson Bay. Soon, however, Paddy started to come home more regularly and we all knew that the reason was his attraction to Brid O'Flaherty. And so it was no surprise when he eventually came home for good, married Brid and set up in business with the Athlone Transport Company, which I helped him to run. Paddy drove the haulage lorries, while I kept the books.

When he came back to his home town, Paddy got involved in Fianna Fáil and went on to become a member of the Fianna Fáil National Executive. He famously fell out with Charlie Haughey over Neil Blaney and the republican movement. Of a strongly republican bent himself, Paddy had taken the part of Neil Blaney at a National Executive meeting. After this incident, he decided to leave the Fianna Fáil organisation and continued on his political path as an Independent Fianna Fáil Councillor on Roscommon County Council. Was this a cause for any embarrassment to my father or Brian Snr, who were both then advanced in their political careers? No, not a bit of it!

I always loved Paddy dearly, and all in all, he was a really good brother to me. He and Brid went on to have a lovely family: Pádraig, Gráinne, Caoimhín and Finbarr. Young Caoimhín was autistic, at a time before the causes or effects of autism were known about as fully as they are now, and Brid and Paddy and all of the family would have immense challenges to face in this regard. A lovely young man, tragically Caoimhín died very young in a swimming pool incident. Pádraig, who is my godchild, joined the Irish Army and then went on to become a lecturer in history in both NUI Galway and the University of Limerick. Gráinne (my dear friend, whom I mentioned at the very opening of this book) became a secondary school teacher after a few years of adventuring in Algeria and various other exotic locations. Finbarr qualified in medicine and now practises in Edinburgh.

Anyway, back to the late summer of 2010, and before Paddy's deteriorating health necessitated his admittance to Roscommon Hospital, there had been an earlier happy interlude for the whole family. It was during one of the holiday weekends in August, and Paddy was still at home, king of his own domain, at ease and happy to see the family, and Brian Jnr in particular, who had come down to Athlone with Patricia, Tom and Clare for a few days. The occasion was the re-launch of my father's sailing boat, the '67', at the Lough Ree Yacht Club, and I had asked Brian to do the honours at the event.

Just to explain, my father had had a very fine sailing boat which he left to the Lough Ree Yacht Club for the use of young people who might not have the means to go sailing: he had asked that the club would provide sailing lessons in his boat for what we would now call disadvantaged young people. The club had duly carried out his wishes for some years and it had all worked out very successfully. Following a conversation between myself and Alan Algeo, Commodore of the yacht club, we had decided to have the boat refurbished, and this was the rationale behind the re-launch.

Brian duly performed the honours at the Lough Ree Yacht Club. Before he did so, Harman Murtagh, on behalf of the club, bade him welcome, in a most wonderful and moving address. Harman is a renowned historian and art collector and his father and mine had been friends long ago, not from political circles, but through sailing and the common bond of living in Athlone.

After the ceremony, we all went on to a lovely dinner in the Wineport Lodge. The memory of that dinner and of the happiness we shared on that August weekend will forever be in my mind, bright and strong. Brian was in great form and at the dinner he particularly enjoyed talking to our close friends, Hugh and Celine Campbell. Hugh has an encyclopaedic knowledge of European and Irish history, but needless to say, Brian was able to match Hugh memory for memory and word for word! Patricia was in great form, as were Tom and Clare, and the family had booked themselves into the Hodson Bay Hotel. In a way, I now realise that it was Brian's farewell to Athlone, although he would be there on two occasions yet to come, which I will tell of in due course.

On the Saturday morning after the launch of the '67', Brian walked from the Hodson Bay Hotel up the road to see Paddy, who lived in the first house on the avenue near the Hodson Bay Road. Paddy and Brian sat together for a good hour and a half, talking and talking — of history, of the world, of the family and surely many other things. Paddy, like Brian, had words at will, and that morning must have marked for them both a special watershed in their lives.

Later that Saturday afternoon, we all visited my son Aengus in his home at Barrybeg on the Roscommon Road. Brian was delighted to see Aengus and his wife Lisa and their lovely children. When Brian and his family left the following day for the next part of their trip — a week in London — he rang me to say how much they had all enjoyed themselves. It is so poignant to think now that this was to be one of their last holidays together as a family.

That weekend in August 2010 had a dreamlike quality for all of us, and particularly, I imagine, for Brian. The lovely trip on the lake; the launch of the '67'; the coming together of old friends; the rare let-up in public pressure; the delicious meal in relaxed company in the Wineport Lodge, and so on. For the rest of us, it was easy to forget that weekend that Brian was as ill as he was. I remember how I talked about it after he had gone back, with Aengus and Feargal and his wife Maeve, who had also come down for the weekend. We buoyed each other up, I suppose, saying that maybe Brian would be one of the very few lucky ones who managed to escape the coils of pancreatic cancer. But deep within me, I knew it would not be so, and that we were of course just fooling ourselves. As for Brian himself, there was something in his face at that time, always, which seemed to betray that he knew the end was coming and that he was now resigned to it.

Brian's next visit to Athlone would be for the sad occasion of my brother Paddy's funeral, in the second week of October 2010. As I have said, the family had known for some time that the end was near for Paddy, but we were all choked up with grief when he finally left us. Before he died, I had been to see him several times in Roscommon and also in Portiuncula Hospital in Ballinasloe. No matter how ill he was, there was always the lovely light in his eyes when he would see me coming into his room. That was my beloved brother, Paddy.

I feel it reflects so well on Brian Lenihan that, even at the height of his own very severe illness and indeed when he was nearing the end himself, he honoured his family commitments and came to pay the fullest of tributes to his uncle — by his presence in Flynn's Removal Home, by his presence at the Mass, at the graveyard and at the lunch afterwards. I will always remember the honour he paid Paddy.

Chapter 20 ✥

BÉAL NA MBLÁTH

I f that idyllic weekend of the Lough Ree Yacht Club event in August 2010 had been a magical one for us as a family, another occasion of great national significance was soon on the horizon. This was the commemoration of the death of Michael Collins at Béal na mBláth, on 22 August. Brian Lenihan would play a central part in these proceedings too.

In July 2010, about a month prior to the event, the Fine Gael TD, Jim O'Keeffe had issued an invitation to Brian, asking if he would speak at the forthcoming remembrance for Collins. Never before had a leading member of Fianna Fáil been asked to address the faithful at what is naturally a highly significant event in the Fine Gael political calendar. This was a huge invitation and honour for Brian and, with his own historical and legal knowledge, he was even more intensely aware of the implications of such a gesture. Naturally, he accepted.

After what would be a very memorable occasion in many ways, I wrote a short piece for publication, which appeared a year to the day in the *Irish Daily Mail*, and after the death of Brian Lenihan. Written as it was relatively soon after the Béal na mBláth event itself, I think it captures very well the atmosphere and tenor of that day, and so I include it here as it first appeared:

This Sunday twelve months ago, at around 9 a.m., we left Athlone to travel to West Cork. Anyone observing us loading up so early could see we were going somewhere for a purpose and yes, indeed we were.

Was it a GAA match? No — indeed that day Cork was meeting Dublin in Croke Park, so we were going in the wrong direction. In fact, we were going to Béal na mBláth in West Cork, where each year on the Sunday nearest the death date of Michael Collins (22 August 1922), the faithful gather to pay tribute to him. Mostly they have one of their own to give the address, occasionally they have asked an outsider but always with a purpose. On this occasion, their chosen guest was Brian Lenihan, TD, the then Minister for Finance.

During that previous week, the papers had been full of this invitation which had been issued to Brian Lenihan from the Michael Collins Commemorative Committee at Béal na mBláth, asking him to come and to deliver the yearly address.

A few days beforehand, Mícheál, a close friend of mine in Athlone, had called one night and suggested we should travel to Cork to hear the address and to be part of what we knew would be a forever-to-be-remembered, historic occasion. We enlisted another dear friend, Seamus, whom we asked to take the wheel and off we went, three Fianna Fáil people from Athlone, who wanted to travel to Cork to honour the death of Michael Collins. The weather was promised fair, but we loaded our umbrellas and our coats and set off through the soft undulating countryside of Offaly.

Athlone to West Cork is a long distance, but we hardly felt it as we moved onwards and onwards. As we neared Béal na mBláth, the crowds were swelling and the attentive and careful Gardaí were on duty everywhere. We pressed on, however, keen to get an advantageous spot, which we eventually did — very near the place where the talk was to be given and where the crowds pressed most keenly in anticipation.

Neither I nor my two companions had ever been to Béal na mBláth before. Yes, I had traversed all of West Cork further on and on, but had never taken the turn which led to this hallowed historic spot. Absorbing the scene, notwithstanding the huge crowds, it was easy to envisage what had happened in this narrow gorge 88 years beforehand. It was a spot tailor-made for an ambush, and which was now taken up by a simple platform where the Committee assembled. Bit by bit, we talked and mingled insofar as we could in the midst of such numbers, with crowds from counties all over Ireland, including a busload from Dublin West.

Shortly afterwards, well on time, Brian Lenihan appeared to the tumultuous crowds.

Brian spoke generous, strong words. He stood tall and well. It was easy for all of us who watched and listened to desperately disbelieve the stark health prognosis he had been given and to think that somehow he would surmount it. Anything seemed possible on such a beautiful sunlit day in that narrow West Cork spot. Today, as I write and speak, can I remember what exactly he said? No, but I can remember that it was stirring and strong, that the sun shone high, that the crowds applauded and sang and willed him to be well.

Long after the formalities were over, Brian lingered and talked personally with every single person who wanted to meet him. They pressed in and pressed in and shook his hand and kissed him — and I know he was as stirred as they were. It is as if their collective wish was to make him remain as he was — strong, good, firm and steady — and on that day, it seemed that all old animosities died away.

So how did the Commemorative Committee decide that Brian Lenihan should be their chosen guest for that great occasion? I have never heard the full story of why, but I do know that the retired Fine Gael TD, Jim O'Keeffe, was the purveyor of the invitation and I also know that it took Brian very little time to make up his mind to go.

There is an old Irish proverb: 'Briseann an dúchas trí shúile an chait'. You see, while we have been a strong Fianna Fáil family for many decades, my father, as a young man in University College, Galway, was on the side of Michael Collins and took part with other students in manoeuvres in Athenry on behalf of the Treaty side. There was never any secrecy about it. My mother, in compensation if you like, came from a strong, strong republican family in Sligo. So we were reared in a family where the two traditions were spoken of in an easy, non-threatening way.

We set off for home and Athlone again. Back through all the lovely counties, and we made no stop until we came to the fine midland town of Birr. Mícheál and I decided that one drink was in order and that we would get our non-drinking friend a mineral, so we repaired to the County Arms and watched the 9 o'clock news. As we watched, we relived the scene once more. It is now the 89th anniversary of the death of Michael Collins.

Do we remember what Brian said on that day? No, we can't remember the exact words, but we have so many perfect pictures in our minds of the shining Cork sun, of the strong stirring words Brian spoke and of the tumultuous surging crowds. But most of all, we remember that we came back to Athlone with hope in our hearts.

Of course as we all know now, it was not to be, but we have forever those memories of that Sunday Cork visit and the generosity and love of the Cork people of that region who came out to meet him with full hearts and hopes, and who gave Brian an honour which he never forgot for the rest of his short life.

Chapter 21 ⌒

| IRELAND GETS A BAILOUT

B y late autumn 2010, despite the imposition of budget after brutal budget and the enactment of a series of aggressive cuts in government spending, it became clear that a new crisis point had been reached for Ireland. Put simply, by the beginning of November, it seemed that no-one in the international financial markets was prepared to lend to the Irish banks, and so other European Finance Ministers were putting Brian Lenihan under increasing pressure to accept a bailout from the IMF/ECB/EU Troika, fearful that 'panic' in Ireland might spread to other countries such as Spain and Portugal.

The reason for this critical lack of confidence in Irish banks has been summed up by Morgan Kelly, the eminent Professor of Economics at UCD, as 'the certainty that [Irish] bank losses would far exceed the estimates of [the governor of the Irish Central Bank], Patrick Honohan'. Appointed by Brian Lenihan as Governor to the Irish Central Bank in September 2009, and thereby as the government's chief financial advisor, Honohan was effectively in a position to take control of important aspects of our economic policy, such as the banking and finance sector. An inherent weakness in Honohan's position, however, was that as well as his other offices, he was a member of the Council of the ECB, and thereby bound to follow their directives in key matters. And so a potential conflict of interests — between what was good for Ireland and what was good for the ECB — lay at the heart of any decision-making process he undertook.

As Finance Minister, Brian Lenihan however was determined to hold out for as long as he could against the pressure of seeking a bailout, in order to get the best possible terms from the Troika for the

Irish people. He knew that in some ways, we were in a stronger negotiating position than might have first appeared and he was intent on exploiting this advantage, however small it might be. It was a very difficult position to be in, and he was very well aware of that.

I remember so clearly a telling incident of the night of 17 November 2010. I had stayed late in the Dáil and was in the canteen with Terry Leyden, having something to eat. It was about nine o'clock. I saw Brian Lenihan come in and, once he had ordered a salad or something light for himself, he joined us at our table. Not long afterwards, Brian's Private Secretary Dermot Moylan came into the canteen, looking harried. Dermot came straight over to where we were sitting and told Brian that Patrick Honohan, the Governor of the Central Bank, was on the phone from Frankfurt and wanted to speak to him urgently.

Brian duly went away to take the call. When he came back about twenty minutes later, he was quietly fulminating. It appeared that Honohan had wanted him to call a Cabinet meeting that night, in order to say that we were going to accept help from the IMF. Brian had replied that it was not he who called Cabinet meetings — that this was only within the remit of the Taoiseach — and that therefore he couldn't do it. Clearly, he had no desire for his hand to be forced in such a way.

All hell broke loose the next day, 18 November when, speaking live from Frankfurt, Patrick Honohan did a radio interview on RTÉ's *Morning Ireland*, in which he said that the IMF were coming in and that Ireland would need a bailout of 'tens of billions'. That Honohan should have made such a statement without the input and agreement of the Cabinet or the Taoiseach was remarkable in so many ways. Uproar ensued, as, for example, Ministers Dermot Ahern and Noel Dempsey, who had both attended public functions some days earlier, had been put in the excruciating position of denying that the Troika were coming in — because to their knowledge, nothing official had been ratified to suggest otherwise. Brian Cowen and Brian Lenihan were livid, of course. As I say, they had been holding out so that the best deal could be secured for Ireland and for some time had been trying to keep public speculation as to a possible bailout under tight control, knowing how easily this would paint us into a corner, and how dramatically such a development might affect the confidence of the markets and the public too.

In hindsight, Patrick Honohan's intervention on that fateful day has been widely regarded as deeply controversial. He had made a statement that was clearly at odds with what had been, up to that moment, the public position of the government. In doing so, he had left the government in an impossible situation. In an article which appeared in *The Irish Times* in May 2011, Morgan Kelly summed up the episode most incisively: 'Rarely has a Finance Minister been so deftly sliced off at the ankles by his central bank governor . . .' I must agree wholeheartedly with his assessment here.

Thinking about that period and looking back on it now, however, I am still not able to reconcile in my mind the huge sense of shame that was supposedly associated with the fact that we had had to invoke the IMF. Was it not better that we got money to pay our nurses, doctors, teachers, Gardaí, council workers, than to beggar ourselves completely and renege on our debts? That would never have been an honourable way to go. As far as I was concerned, we were part of Europe, we had chosen to be part of Europe, and better it was that we now made use of the monetary facilities available to us through the European structure, to put our house in order while we could. In my view, it was not the Bank Guarantee which weighed so heavily upon us, but rather that we were paying out far more — in wages and subsidies and everything else, per week, per month, per year — than we were ever taking in. It was that financial imbalance in our domestic set-up which got the better of us in the end.

So, in the bleak situation we found ourselves in once more during that winter of 2010, further austerity measures were clearly required. And of course the unenviable task of formulating and implementing these fell on Brian Lenihan's shoulders. Accordingly, he brought us the budget of 7 December 2010. Looking back on it now, it is incredible to contemplate how much Brian had to deal with during the three years of his tenure as Minister for Finance, and how much he managed to pack into that time in terms of the number of emergency measures and strategies he put in place. Between 2008 and 2011, he guided us through four budgets and enacted no fewer than 24 pieces of 'fire-fighting' legislation, which he himself introduced into Dáil Éireann with the very able and loyal assistance of Martin Mansergh, his second-in-command. In addition to this, there were the hugely significant events of the Bank Guarantee, the IMF bailout, the arrival of the Troika to somehow be negotiated — and Brian was the one everyone looked to here too.

In seeing through all of these practical measures and concrete scenarios, Brian was fuelled by a determination to somehow get us as a country back on the straight and narrow, while attempting to inject some measure of optimism into the picture and to maintain a sense of the wider historical perspective of all that was happening. And it was all done of course against the background of his fatal pancreatic cancer. How did he do it, you might ask? He was only able to do it because he was so deeply imbued with the highest qualities of selfless service to his country. There is no doubt in my mind that Brian put his country before himself.

During all of these difficult times, Brian had scant support around the Cabinet table. To be fair, he had welcome support in his health difficulty from Brian Cowen, but he was given very little backing from his Cabinet colleagues as regards the path of financial rigour he was trying to take. The truth of the matter is, Brian arrived in the Department of Finance as, in his own words, the whole construction industry in Ireland was coming to a shuddering halt. He came into the picture too late — and yet in a way, this is what saved him in the eyes of the public and the party, because he had not been around for the construction boom, for the spending excesses and for the wayward policies.

The problem was that Brian Cowen never explained. Some might say that it would have been difficult for him to do so, since he had been Minister for Finance during some of the critically important years. But now, in the immediate aftermath of the Patrick Honohan/Troika matter, an explanation or a state-of-the-nation address of some kind was needed more than ever. Yet, despite ever more persistent entreaties from the parliamentary party, Brian Cowen did not see fit to go on national television and relay it as it was. I must say however that when I spoke at a parliamentary party meeting at that time, I myself did not encourage him to do so, because I thought he would be uncomfortable in such a situation, and would not cut a reassuring figure for either the Irish people or for the party. I have mentioned earlier the curious habit he had, when faced with the cameras, of lapsing into 'civil servant speak'. When he did this, he became like another person, and no longer the Brian Cowen we knew so well. I don't know what that was based on. As far as I could see, it wasn't fear that he would say the wrong thing: Brian was, and remains, a very clever, able man who could, if he set himself to it, devour a brief in very short time and gain from it the salient points.

The fact was that the always uneasy relationship between Brian Cowen and the media had been going from bad to worse, particularly in the months leading up to the dire circumstances in which we found ourselves in the winter months of 2010. This was reflected in the increasing prevalence in the papers, on an almost daily basis now, of unflattering, unappealing photographs of the Taoiseach, in which he had clearly been caught in off-guard moments while in the public eye. Of course, this can happen to any public figure, but, in my own experience, when you are a Minister or otherwise frequently in the public eye, you need to be conscious at all times as to how you might appear. Are you sitting up straight, are you smiling at people, are you paying attention to the other speakers, and so on? It seemed, particularly to us Fianna Fáil backbenchers, that some of the newspapers were consciously on the look-out for moments when they could catch Brian Cowen on camera in unflattering poses, and certainly not at his keen best as we had known him.

At parliamentary party level, the mood was sombre and uneasy as we broke for the Christmas holidays. Of course, given all that had been happening and the increasingly negative 'spin' the media were putting on Brian Cowen's general demeanour and apparent failure to confront things head-on, some may wonder how he had managed to keep the rank-and-file of party faithful on side for so long anyway. The truth is, however, that Brian had always managed very well at parliamentary party level. I always thought he presided over the weekly party meetings with great honesty and integrity. Chairperson John Browne would guide these meetings in the main, but the Taoiseach would always be there and would often take the opportunity to get to his feet to deliver what would be a sort of a 'state-of-the-nation' address — but at party level, to us backbenchers. Particularly if there was a topic or a piece of legislation which we felt needed further clarification or explanation, he would take great pains to address our concerns and often be rewarded

by our applause. In this context, Brian Cowen was invariably very frank
and open, as well as very honest and straightforward. If only he had
been able to find the means to translate this very successful approach
into the wider context of public life and the media spotlight, I have
often thought! He spent a lot of his political capital at those party
meetings and it was the reason why so many were able to keep their
faith in him for so long.

Even from the early days of Brian Cowen's reign however, a group of
dissenters had formed themselves. Of course, there will always be a
group of dissenters in any political party. This is something I have
observed at every stage of my career in politics — in Charlie Haughey's
time, where dissension became an art form of sorts; under Bertie
Ahern, albeit in a more hidden, less obvious incarnation; and now in
Brian Cowen's government, where it was very vocal and open. Here it
was headed up in the main by John McGuinness, who felt he had been
slighted by Cowen when he had been relegated to the backbenches
from his role as Minister of State in the Department of Enterprise,
Trade and Employment. The origins of the friction between the two
men could be traced back to 2008 and a trade mission to China where,
within the earshot of some Irish officials in attendance, McGuinness
had voiced displeasure at some of the actions of the Taoiseach. This had
reached the ear of the Taoiseach and naturally he didn't like it and no
doubt said so, which sowed the seeds of a very dogged determination
on John McGuinness's part to gather others to his cause of growing
dissent. I have to be utterly frank here. The media encouraged and
applauded John McGuinness: he was fodder for them and he was built
up to be a person who had the potential for startling, wonderful ideas,
if only he would be allowed to give free rein to them. Another
important skein to his dissent, and which no doubt appealed greatly to
the media as well, was his belief that civil servants were pampered,
overpaid good-for-nothings, and indeed this was the dominant theme
in the book he published at this period.

There were others who spoke frequently at parliamentary party
meetings in a way which was not sympathetic to the Taoiseach. Tom Kitt
was one of these, although always in a gentler fashion than John
McGuinness, and you would often feel that he really didn't have his
heart in the argument when he stood up to make his point. Tom had

been Chief Whip under Bertie Ahern, and Chief Whips in a governing party are always fairly powerful people. When Brian Cowen had taken over, he had seen fit to dispense with him as Chief Whip, offering him a role as Minister of State instead. Tom, however, wouldn't accept the role, and it seems clear that he too felt he had been slighted. Another dissenter was Mattie McGrath, who ultimately would make the decision in 2011 to run as an Independent (when, against the grain, he won a seat). The truth is that Mattie is one of those people who will forever be a dissenter against the status quo, whatever it is. But it seems that he has proved himself to his electorate and in the game of politics, that's what matters. And there were other dissenters who came and went, such as Michael Kennedy in Dublin North — a fine, rugged, 6-foot-4-inch individual, a real grassroots man, who was clever and able.

By Christmas 2010, a feeling of revolt and discontent was beginning to take hold on a wider level within the party, however, and not just among the few diehards who had for whatever reason always had their gripes. Yet another difficult budget had compounded the many tensions at backbench level. Although there was a recognition of the necessity of such measures of austerity, there was also an awareness that we were growing increasingly unpopular as the various remedial measures were being put in place. Among a greater and wider membership within the party at large, there was now a conviction that we could not face into the upcoming General Election with Brian Cowen as leader. A series of by-elections were immediately pending, which we as a government felt we couldn't move to fill, because we were not sure we would win them — sitting governments never do. Relationships were beginning to sour badly also between the Greens and ourselves around this time.

The whispering against Brian Cowen became more vehement and more open. On two separate occasions John McGuinness proposed and was seconded by Noel O'Flynn — a Cork deputy, who by now had become very anti-Cowen — that the Taoiseach should resign as leader of our party. Brian Cowen always withstood them. He was very ably backed up by Mary Coughlan as his Tánaiste. Mary Coughlan had, to my mind, been a wonderful Minister for Agriculture for the farming community. The Fianna Fáil Party in general, and indeed those she dealt with in a wider, European context, had fully embraced her approach and liked her immensely. However, under Brian Cowen's government, her sojourn in the Department of Enterprise, Trade and Employment had been less successful: it seemed that her carefree, jousting manner did not find the same echo in the Kildare Street offices. The Taoiseach soon transferred her to the Department of Education, where she seemed happier.

For some time in parallel to all of this, the party faithful had been urging Brian Lenihan to take over the role as leader of the party. Yet one of Brian's main priorities was to do his utmost to maintain a good working relationship between himself and Brian Cowen. After all, this is the requirement of our Constitution — that the Taoiseach works in close conjunction with his Minister for Finance — and in this case, both men wanted to deliver on that to the best of their abilities. There was no doubt that if, at any stage during this period, Brian Lenihan had come forward and said he was going to challenge as Taoiseach, he would have won the day. But, as Shakespeare said, 'uneasy lies the head that wears the crown', and Brian Lenihan was always deeply conscious of this. More important, because of his own upbringing and the way his father had been, he always felt that loyalty to a leader was hugely important and this indeed is a key tenet of Fianna Fáil political life. And of course, underpinning everything was the terrible reality of his illness.

In spite of all this, the Fianna Fáil National Executive decided to go ahead with some early conventions, believing that we were very near an election — which we were, as it transpired. It had been the intention to fill Longford–Westmeath before Christmas but we held off until 3 January 2011. Brian Lenihan came down to chair our convention and, for me, it was particularly poignant to have him there as Chairperson, when I of course was a candidate. He did a great job all round and spoke brilliantly when the actual nomination of candidates, including myself, was made.

After the business of that day was concluded, Brian, Mícheál Ó'Faoláin and I sat down to have something to eat and to talk together. I felt Brian was in good form physically. He didn't show any signs of tiredness even though it had been a long afternoon, but he seemed weary in spirit about the ongoing battle within Fianna Fáil. As I have said, Brian was highly conscious of his sense of loyalty and duty to the

Taoiseach. But he was equally aware that, if we went to the General Election with Brian Cowen as our leader, the Fianna Fáil Party was going to be beaten to a pulp. As an active member of the parliamentary party, I was privy to all of the backroom gossip and knew that Brian was being pushed to throw down the gauntlet and to become leader. Many times on the telephone, he and I had discussed the imponderable — could Fianna Fáil under him or indeed under any other leader, salvage any seats from the tsunami which we instinctively felt was to come upon us? Brian knew in his heart of hearts that he hadn't long to live, and yet this pressure was being piled upon him.

That whole period of Christmas 2010 was a cobweb of worries and anxieties, and I could not help thinking back to the heartache the previous Christmas had brought, with the awful news of Brian's diagnosis. I knew that others in our close circle would be feeling the same, especially Patricia, Tom and Clare. It will be very hard for any of us in our family to ever think of Christmas as a good time again.

Chapter 22 ∾

| 'WE ALL PARTIED'

We went into government in the summer of 2007 under the leadership of Bertie Ahern, with high hopes for our third consecutive term and the future. By February 2011, four months short of our second four years, it was all over for us. In the General Election of that month, we were overwhelmed by a tsunami of defeat and would emerge deflated, humiliated and badly beaten. The magnitude of our losses was historic in our own party terms, and worse than this still perhaps, the Fianna Fáil 'brand' was soon being widely denounced as 'toxic' — all at once we had become the untouchables, it seemed. So, what happened to the bright morning on which we had embarked? What went so badly wrong?

In hindsight, there were many reasons the shine wore off us and of course it is crucial to try to identify and analyse some of these. Yet I felt and continue to feel that an important element in our defeat was the fact that we were simply too long in government. The fact is that the people and the media just got fed up of us. In simple terms, we had been around for too long and people were tired of our faces, weary of our voices and they just wanted a change. As I have said earlier, I always felt that the General Election of 2007 was the one for us to lose and for Enda Kenny to win — and of course he very nearly did. I continue to believe too that, even if the last General Election had been held in late September 2010, rather than February 2011, the Fianna Fáil Party could still have salvaged something. We would have been saved the bailout in November 2010 and the Troika coming in. Yes, we would still have lost the election, but we would not have suffered the virtual wipe-out at the hands of an angry electorate that February 2011 brought us.

There was the question too of how much better we might have fared, had we gone to the polls with Brian Lenihan as our leader. I spoke to Brian several times in the weeks after Election Day, following his own win in Dublin West: he was the only Fianna Fáil deputy elected in Dublin. He was much preoccupied with the question of whether he should have gone for the leadership, as many had been pressing him to do. But as I have said, his loyalty would not allow him to do it, and so we will never know what a Brian Lenihan leadership of Fianna Fáil might have achieved. It must be said of course that Micheál Martin, who took over as leader just before the election, fought a valiant fight for our party.

All of this aside, there were many other key factors which led to the decline in our political fortunes. The biggest of these was the terrible blight of the global recession which hit us with full force in 2008. I have talked about the bailout of the Irish banks which was first put into force that September, and many have seen this as a pivotal moment in Ireland's downward decline. It was a very stark choice which faced Brian Cowen and Brian Lenihan that night, and it will always be my belief that they made the right decision for the people of Ireland at that time. Financial turmoil was sweeping the world on a massive scale — the US, Europe, the UK and so many other countries were beginning to feel its effects too. We were hardly going to be left out of that dreadful global experience. The debate will rage for a long time yet, as to why Brian Cowen as Minister for Finance for the four years previously had not been more attuned to the problems which were in the offing. It appears that the Central Bank and the Financial Regulator had had little inkling either, beyond issuing a few bland speculations that there was to be a downturn in the Irish economy, but which could be negotiated without too much difficulty; that there would be a soft landing for us. Soft landing, indeed!

Of course, the troubles in the Irish banks arose because everyone wanted to copy Anglo Irish Bank. They were giving out stupendous business loans and 100 per cent mortgages to anyone who asked, and so the other banks began to grumble and wonder why they couldn't do the same. We saw the echoes of that in the 2011 Presidential debates, when Mary Davis was castigated — unfairly, I thought — for being on the board of the Bank of Ireland's ICS Building Society, which was granting

'100 per cent plus' mortgages. Anglo Irish was of course engaged in very dodgy dealings, lending massive amounts of money to speculators and to property gobbler-uppers. Yet for so many at the time, it seemed that this bank and Seán FitzPatrick were doing wonderful things. I remember being at a function some years prior to 2008, and somebody saying to me, 'Do you want to meet Seánie? He's the real man of the moment!' I can recall replying, 'No, not particularly: I don't want to meet him.' FitzPatrick was like a god whose toga people wanted to touch and clutch onto. But he turned out to be a false god and the emulation by fawners of what he represented was destined to contribute to our downfall.

The prices of houses rose and rose. Young people queued for hours to put down a deposit on a very ordinary semi-detached house which they now regarded as nirvana. The price of a property which might have previously been going for about €200,000 was now creeping up to €500,000 and the banks were starting to grant these '100 per cent plus' mortgages. At the end of the day, of course, the banks can be blamed for the speculation in which they engaged, but at the same time they were responding to demands from the people themselves. It is the people who pressed for such financial facilities. Everyone wanted the bigger house, the next holiday, the private school for their offspring, and so it went on and on. There was just no end to it, and we were all living in a bubble. I remember very clearly the words of Brian Lenihan, in an interview on *Prime Time* in November 2010 — for which he would later be greatly reproached by some: 'I accept that there were failures in the system. I accept that I, as a member of the governing party during that period, have to take responsibility for what happened. But let's be fair about it — we all partied.' And he was right — we did all party, and for too long. And in many senses, Brian Lenihan merely inherited the legacy of what had already been happening for some years.

Regulation of the banks — or the lack of it — is where so many of our difficulties lay. When I was at the Cabinet table between 1997 and 2002, I remember a huge ongoing debate on this subject — the general consensus was that the lighter the touch a government could have in terms of financial regulation, the better. But that was utterly wrong. And once the Central Bank and the Financial Regulator realised that those in political authority were not keen on 'nanny' regulation, they too went soft on regulatory standards and guidelines. For all the time leading up to the disintegration of the banks, the Central Bank kept saying we were headed for an easy time and that we would get out of any troubles which arose without too much hassle. And houses were still being built and the construction taxes continued to flow in, and everything seemed well. Shortly into his term as Minister for Finance, Brian Lenihan appointed Matthew Elderfield to be the new Financial Regulator and he was regarded far and wide as an excellent appointment, and as somebody who held out great promise for us. But in a sense by that stage, much of the damage occasioned by a lack of stringency for so long had already been done.

In my view, the whole idea of loose regulation goes back to a key tenet of the Progressive Democrat philosophy. I am not saying this in the hope of somehow exculpating Fianna Fáil from our share of the blame — far from it — but certainly in the earlier days, particularly during the time I was in Cabinet from 1997 to 2002, and could observe all that was going on, there was a great sense of mutual understanding and collaboration between Mary Harney and Charlie McCreevy. Now it was very naturally the case that these two Ministers should operate well together, given their points of confluence in terms of political values and outlook, their long years of working together, and the fact that in the past they had been comrades-in-arms against Charlie Haughey. In fact, when the PDs first formed their party in 1986, it had been expected that Charlie McCreevy would become one of their number. But he had stayed put and I often think it was because of his love and remembrance of his dear mother, who was an avowed and everlasting Fianna Fáiler.

Despite never joining the PDs, Charlie McCreevy remained a neo-liberal at heart and therefore, during the time they worked in Cabinet together, he and Mary Harney were essentially the nexus of much that happened there. It was always my strong impression that it was in essence they who decided budgetary policy, and that they would only allow the Taoiseach in at the end of such deliberations, so to speak. It often seemed, to me in any case, that coming up to Budget and Estimates time, the parameters and the small print of the Budget and Estimates were often worked out between Charlie McCreevy and Mary

Harney, and that Bertie was sometimes peripheral to the fine detail of
such things. This is not in any way an attempt to incriminate Mary
Harney — far from it — she was and is a very fine person, but her
mantra and the mantra of the PDS was always to cut taxes as much as
possible. But of course, you can't continue to cut taxes all the time and
still keep education and health services intact. It just wasn't feasible, but
every year it seemed more and more that the Holy Grail was to get as
many people as possible out of the tax net.

Some of our policies on tax would ultimately work to compound
the problems associated with the construction boom. An initiative
which was introduced during Albert Reynolds's time as Minister for
Finance was to be continued with gusto by Charlie McCreevy, as parts
of Ireland were carved out, in which tax rebates would be made
available for any developers who came in. One of these was the upper
Shannon area, where all around County Leitrim, tax rebates were given
and this led to the building on a large scale of estates of holiday houses
'on spec' — these would become the ghost estates which haunt our
countryside today. Soon the demand arose for similar measures to be
put in place for those of us living in the mid-Shannon area as well and
in other parts of the country. We all wanted the same thing, so it is a
pointless exercise to actually blame any one particular person. We all
thirsted for these tax benefits and the cry became, a tax rebate for this,
a tax rebate for that. But such tax breaks meant a corresponding
depletion in the resources of the Exchequer in the long run, and that
was a dangerous thing.

As well as this, one of the key sources of our subsequent difficulties
was, as I have said earlier, the construction boom in itself. Bertie Ahern
loved the construction 'buzz'. I remember one day, as I was coming out
of the lift on the fifth floor of Leinster House with him, he drew me to
a window and said, 'Look at the number of building cranes there are
out there,' — there were perhaps 20 or so on the horizon — 'Isn't it
wonderful?' Yes, of course it was — it meant almost full employment
and, as the construction taxes kept coming in, much of the consequent
spending was *good* social spending. But the difficulty was that at a
crucial point, no one shouted 'stop' on construction, and spending got
out of control and policies became increasingly wayward.

If I were to pick out one other key governmental transgression of the years preceding the downturn, it would be the policy of decentralisation. In a way it is easy for me to explain what this policy meant in practical terms, because Athlone had been a benign focus for decentralisation long before it ever became known as that. Decades ago, in the late 1960s, when Brian Lenihan Snr was Minister for Education and Charlie Haughey was Minister for Finance, the then government took a decision that they would relocate sections of some Departments to rural areas. In this move towards decentralisation, Athlone became the new base for a huge section of the Department of Education. A few other urban centres also benefited from such an initiative. This, however, was the selective decentralisation of very specific parts of Departments — those which could be easily detached and operated as separate entities from their main units.

Some years later, when we came in under Charlie Haughey in 1987, he and Ray MacSharry proposed a further wave of decentralisation. Again, this concerned the operation of carefully chosen areas of certain Departments being transferred to towns where there had already been some decentralisation. For example, Social Welfare went to Longford and Sligo, while Athlone became the new base for another tranche of the Department of Education. For Athlone, this move to decentralisation would represent an important economic boon, because we now had up to 600 civil servants whose lives were based in our area. Of course, there were those who commuted from Roscommon, Longford and Offaly every day, but in the main, most of the civil service workers who came to Athlone made their homes and reared their families there, sending their children to school and then college and so on, in our area. As with towns such as Sligo and Longford, Athlone was a fine area to which to bring decentralisation, because it had a good transport structure, great secondary schools and a third-level educational institution. All in all, Athlone was well able to successfully accommodate such initiatives.

The programme for wholesale decentralisation set out by Charlie McCreevy at the end of 2003 was a very different proposition altogether. Firstly, Charlie unfolded his proposal in a budget speech, without having first run it past the civil servants in his Department. In one sense, I can understand why he followed this policy of nondisclosure in relation to his own Department colleagues — he probably wanted to make sure the public did not hear of it until he was fully ready; he also wanted to cut off any incipient refusals from his civil service staff. But the announcement had no place in a budget speech: it was not a budgetary measure, after all. Yet Charlie knew that he would make the maximum impact if he announced it as part of his budget and so this is what he did.

Charlie McCreevy's plan was wholesale decentralisation, in that complete Departments would be moved to rural towns and some relatively remote areas. He saw the advantage in this as being — and there was a grain of truth in this — that such decentralisation would bring an economic boost to the areas in question through the presence of so many civil servants now basing their lives there. He also believed that such an initiative would inevitably shake up the various Departments and enable their revitalisation and reorganisation in a positive sense. This I can fully understand.

There were some successes in the Charlie McCreevy decentralisation, of that there is no doubt. The Pensions branch of the Department of Finance was transferred to Tullamore, and that certainly seems to be operating well. The relocation of another branch of Education, the School Building branch, was similarly relocated to Tullamore and seems to be very successful too. But by and large, the whole escapade was ill-judged. The result was widespread uproar from many quarters. In terms of the public and political response, there was absolute delight on the part of those whose town or area was mooted, and absolute fury from those whose town or constituency was not being considered. There was a never-ending series of delegations from Opposition deputies and from government deputies too, who lost no time in beating down the doors of Charlie McCreevy and the Taoiseach to make known their determination to get decentralisation at any cost. Because Athlone had already been an important focus for this policy, I did not get involved as such myself but I could understand in some senses how people felt. And so there was a veritable mayhem of desire and uproar, as the cry resounded throughout the country: 'We want to get a portion of decentralisation too!' That is how foolish we all were.

But of course the biggest obstacle to the policy's overall success — and one which clearly had not been anticipated at the planning stage —

was the refusal on the part of many civil servants to go along with the proposed relocations. They dug in their heels and obstructed these moves in any way they could. They simply said 'no' and no trade union or Ministerial dictat would make any difference to this decision. (And it should be said that no trade union dictat was forthcoming in any case.) If they didn't want to go, they simply wouldn't go. And so gradually, bit by bit, decentralisation ran into the sand.

When looking at where we as a government went wrong in the years leading up to the downturn, it would be naïve to deny that there were aspects of our collaboration with our political partners in government which contributed to a lack of effectiveness. As we have already seen, Fianna Fáil had a long-standing coalition arrangement with the PDS which had been sustained through a succession of governments. There were certainly positive sides to this collaboration. Bertie Ahern and Mary Harney had forged a very strong and good relationship together, which went back to 1997 and continued through 2002 and then 2007. The two genuinely liked one another and Mary Harney proved a loyal and workmanlike comrade for Bertie and Fianna Fáil to have in government. In 2004, Mary had looked herself for the punishing portfolio of Health, leaving the Department of Enterprise and Employment behind her, where she had had many successes, and had at one point been able to oversee almost full employment in Ireland.

Mary Harney said that she wanted to bring about a journey of reform and recovery within the health service, but little did she know of the daily vicissitudes which awaited her. Michael McDowell was also a great colleague for us to have in the coalition. During my Cabinet years 1997 to 2002, I found him as a member of Cabinet and indeed Attorney General to be rock-solid, professional and always helpful. In 2002, when Michael became Minister for Justice, I experienced for myself as Leader of the Seanad the breadth of his intellect and his forensic attention to detail. My fellow Senators and I were fortunate in that he brought many of his important Justice Bills, once they had cleared Cabinet, to the Seanad rather than to the Dáil.

In 2006, Mary Harney surrendered the leadership of the PD Party and Michael McDowell took it over. The PDS, such as they were throughout the country, felt perhaps that the constant barrage against Mary Harney in Health would not augur well for their party in the forthcoming election. In the General Election of 2007 they got a scorching, returning only Mary Harney and Noel Grealish in Galway. Subsequently, the PDs disbanded in 2008 and Mary continued in office as an Independent member of the Cabinet. There were some terrific PDs who lost their seats during that election, but for me, the person who was most sorely missed from political life was Liz O'Donnell. Yes, she was glamorous and wonderful, and she was also sound and steady and had a lot to offer.

While we had the benefit of these strong and very worthwhile connections among the PDs, there is no escaping the fact that some aspects of their central philosophy and the concrete measures which this engendered — such as policies on taxation and financial regulation — undermined our effectiveness during a crucial time in government.

We had another partner in the coalition during our last term in government, in the form of the Green Party. What did those of us on the backbenches, the rank-and-file of Fianna Fáil, make of the Greens, you might wonder? In the beginning, all looked well. Bertie was able to claim that Fianna Fáil had always been a green movement and that by going into coalition with the Greens, we were in fact going back to our roots! Not many of us actually believed that, but in the heady, triumphant mood of forming a new government, many were prepared to suspend their disbelief.

John Gormley was leader of the Greens, and he was dogged, single-minded and joyless. I realise it might seem an odd thing for me to say, but there was very little of humour among our Green partners. As time went on, from 2007 onwards, there was very little to be humorous about, but even from the beginning, they were persistent and dogged. They unstintingly got their points put forward in the Joint Programme for Government, as had always been the way with our coalition partners, but we soon began to feel more and more uneasy and stifled as their partners. Yet it must be said too that Brian Lenihan consistently drew from the steady support and friendship of Eamon Ryan at Cabinet.

I hope that some of the reflections and observations above go some way to clarifying my views on what went so wrong for us as a country and for Fianna Fáil as a party in recent years. As I have said earlier, the

2011 General Election dealt us a massive blow, not only in a substantial loss of seats, but also in terms of severe damage to our reputation and standing as a party. While I believe that this vilification of our party is grossly unfair to our rank-and-file and the many members who have always conducted themselves honourably and given of their best to the Irish people over many years, it cannot be denied that some of those who held key positions have not always acted with the same integrity.

The twists and turns of the Mahon Tribunal, and its successive revelations over the 15 long years for which it ran, could not but have a devastating effect on the credibility and public reputation of Fianna Fáil and those who headed the party. I'll never forget that day in early April 2004 when I appeared before the tribunal myself to give evidence. I had been summoned there to give my account of that pivotal meeting which Tom Gilmartin said had happened in the Dáil in February 1989, and after which it seemed that he had been asked, in a bare-faced and blatant way, for a huge sum of cash for access to Ministers. The tribunal had written to everyone whom Gilmartin said he met in the Dáil on the day in question, but, as Jody Corcoran remarked in a lead article in the *Sunday Independent* just prior to the day I was to testify, it seemed that I was the only one who remembered meeting Gilmartin on that occasion. As it transpired, I was the only one prepared to tell the truth.

Appearing before the tribunal was very intimidating and I was glad to be accompanied and represented so ably there by my dear friend and legal advisor, Hugh Campbell. The court room was in a huge complex of buildings. When you were called, you had to put your hand on the Bible in front of you before you gave your testimony. I was in the Seanad by that stage, where as I have said, I had the excellent Eamonn McCormack as my Private Secretary. Eamonn would later tell me that, the day after I had been at the tribunal, an up-and-coming government member at the time had stopped him as he was passing, saying, 'So, what do we make of your lady, running up to the tribunal, causing trouble for the Taoiseach and inventing stories?' Eamonn had simply replied, 'She told the truth — and if you don't tell the truth in a tribunal, it is perjury.'

Eamonn and I had already discussed this, and had decided that this is what he should say to anyone who brought up the matter with him.

The one person who never mentioned the tribunal to me was Bertie, which I suppose in hindsight is pretty damning in its own way. He said nothing directly to me, but I knew he was very annoyed about it. Typical of Bertie, his way of dealing with it was to have others say that my testimony was all an invention: that I was losing it and didn't know what I was talking about. In light of this, I was very pleased that when the final report of the tribunal was in due course made public, it stated, in relation to my testimony: 'The Tribunal in particular noted, and accepted, the clear recollection Mrs O'Rourke had of the meeting and, in particular, her vivid memory of Mr Flynn having invited her to join the meeting and the manner in which he effected his albeit perfunctory introduction to her of Mr Gilmartin. The Tribunal was satisfied that Mrs O'Rourke's evidence in relation to the meeting was entirely truthful.'

While others had allegedly forgotten all about it, the details of that particular day in February 1989 were etched clearly in my mind. There wasn't a meeting as such — it was more that Pádraig Flynn had had Tom Gilmartin brought into the Dáil and was doing his 'Mr Big' act, hauling Ministers in to meet him by way of demonstrating his own importance to Gilmartin: 'Here is the Minister for Education', and so on and so forth. No wonder I remembered it so clearly, with the declamatory way in which Flynn was carrying on! I was called in and there were five or six others in the room — it was more of an informal gathering than an official meeting. There was Ray Burke, Bertie Ahern, Pádraig Flynn of course, Brian Lenihan Snr (by the time the tribunal came around, Brian was no longer alive), Gerry Collins and me. As Pádraig fetched me in, he was saying in a big, booming voice, 'Mr Gilmartin, this is our lady Minister, the eminent Mary O'Rourke for Education — what do you make of that, now?' Gilmartin had a kind comment for me — he had remembered that my mother had recently died and he said, 'I have already said to Brian here and I would like to say to you too, I am sorry for your recent loss. The Scanlans were a fine family.' So Gilmartin registered with me because of this: as I said at the tribunal, you remember people who sympathise with you.

I didn't stay very long after this introduction, but left to go about my business. According to Tom Gilmartin's later account, a little later that day outside the room where we met, a fellow had come up to him and said, 'You are going to be helped — sure, look at all the Ministers you have met. You will be helped every step of the way, but we need money for access.' Now I didn't see that person myself, as I was no longer there by that time. And I genuinely had no idea what Pádraig Flynn was doing that day — I thought he was just being Pádraig Flynn: a big, bombastic buffoon.

Over and above the Mahon Tribunal and all that it brought to light about certain individuals in the party, I can attest to the fact that in a more general sense there has been in recent years a degree of disintegration in the social cohesion and sense of individual and collective responsibility within Fianna Fáil. One field in which I experienced this for myself was the whole area of party fundraising — an activity which has always been a knotty issue for political parties in general. Before going any further however, it is appropriate that I should emphasise that fact that all political parties undertake various fundraising activities. They need to keep their parties afloat, and in Ireland, particularly as regards the larger parties of Fianna Fáil and Fine Gael, fundraising has always been a necessary and unavoidable part of the political process.

My own experience of party fundraising goes back to 1993, at a time when Fianna Fáil and Labour were in government together under Albert Reynolds as Taoiseach. I was Minister of State for Labour Affairs to Ruairi Quinn as Minister for Employment and Enterprise — a collaboration which, as I have said earlier, I very much enjoyed. During this period, Bertie Ahern was Treasurer of the Fianna Fáil organisation. It was well-known in the party generally that we were very much in debt at Fianna Fáil Head Office.

One day when I was working in my office in the Department, I received a telephone call from a man who introduced himself as Tony Kenna. He said that he was ringing at Bertie Ahern's behest and was asking for an appointment with me. We duly fixed a time and day for a meeting and he came to see me as planned. His tale was that Bertie Ahern, as Treasurer of Fianna Fáil, was trying to drum up financial support so that he would clear the debt at the party's HQ. To that end they were asking all of the Fianna Fáil Ministers to become engaged in a fundraising effort. Tony then proceeded to put two possible courses of action to me, emphasising all the while that the first one was the more desirable. This was that I would host a dinner party in a private house for, say, 10 or 12 carefully selected guests, and at which either Albert Reynolds or Bertie Ahern would be in attendance for the evening. I would act as hostess, and each guest would come along, eat their dinner and socialise, and then leave an envelope with a donation for Fianna Fáil at the end of the night. The alternative course of action Tony was proposing was that I could run a golf competition within my constituency, the proceeds of which would go to Fianna Fáil HQ.

My immediate response was to ask, regarding the first option, whether I myself would be expected to cook the dinner for the glitzy event in the private house. Tony quickly assured me that no, the owner of the glamorous house would arrange for the cooking of the glitzy dinner: my job was just to be there as a Fianna Fáil Minister, to be pleasant to everyone and, putting it crudely, to rake in the cash for the party. I didn't like the idea of it then and I don't like the idea of it now. However, as regards the alternative option, the difficulty for me was that I knew nothing whatsoever about golf. Despite the fact that I was brought up in the Hodson Bay Hotel in Athlone, right in the middle of a golf course, I had never so much as taken a golf club in my hand! To be honest, I had always thought of golf as a waste of time and effort — you hit a ball and nobody hits it back to you; you walk after it and you hit it again: where was the point in that? Before all of the diehard golfers descend upon me in outrage, I have to stress that this was just my own take on golf and I didn't expect everyone to feel as I did!

Anyway, I told Tony Kenna that I would have a think about these options and let him know of my decision in due course. That weekend at home, I discussed the matter with Enda and Mícheál Ó'Faoláin. The three of us decided against the dinner party possibility — none of us liked the sound of it at all. My difficulty with it was that I would be required to hold out my hand and take the envelope. Although being in a posh house with glamorous people eating a glitzy dinner might have had a certain appeal, I just didn't see myself in that role. So we decided that we would run the golf competition. Enda had in fact played golf some years earlier and Mícheál was himself a dedicated and indeed a very good golfer.

When I went back to Dublin the following week, I contacted Tony Kenna and told him that we had opted to raise funds for Fianna Fáil through the running of a golf tournament and competition. It was definitely the preferable option as far as I was concerned, also because it struck me that at the time, plenty of people from all sorts of organisations — GAA clubs, charities, and so on — were running such events. In fact, such competitions and indeed golf clubs in themselves, had become all the rage in those days. In Athlone alone, we had the new Glasson Golf and Country Club.

And so in 1993 we ran the first of our golf competitions. The inaugural one was held at the Athlone Golf Club and went very well indeed. So that there would be no confusion about it, the letter of invitation we sent out to potential participants and attendees, with my letterhead, stated clearly that any proceeds from the event would not be going to the local Fianna Fáil organisation or to me as constituency representative, but towards clearing a debt at Fianna Fáil's national HQ. On that occasion, we raised about £20, 000 for HQ, and the event was deemed to be both a commercial and a sporting success.

From then on, we ran a golf competition each year. We built up a database of keen golfers, who were willing to participate and we kept adding to that list as time went on. Every year, the said Tony Kenna would come down to Athlone to take part himself, and I grew very fond of him and his lovely wife. There would always be a key Fianna Fáil figure in attendance too — Bertie Ahern, Charlie McCreevy, Brian Lenihan, Séamus Brennan, or any of the other luminaries within the party — who would come to lend their support and sometimes their own golfing skills to the national effort. We kept this up on an annual basis, and each year faithfully sent between £18,000 and £25,000 to Fianna Fáil HQ, meaning that over the entire period, we raised somewhere in the region of £200,000 for the national party through the golf competitions. My belief at the time was that all the other TDs and Senators were doing the same. It was only later that I discovered that lots of people were running golf tournaments, but for the benefit of their own local organisations — in other words, that they were using the funds to forward their own political careers. I know it sounds naïve on my part now, but at the time, I was truly innocent of what was happening on this front. As leader, Bertie Ahern ran an enormous golf competition every year for his own constituency office in Drumcondra and for his local political organisation. This set an example of course for every other TD and Senator, and many thought they should do the same, until gradually there were just a few of us left running annual events for national Fianna Fáil.

I am not relating any of this in order to blow my own trumpet or boast about my virtuousness, but because I think it is indicative of the times in which we were and are living. I understand that other political parties, such as Fine Gael, have also run golf competitions of a similar kind for funding purposes at both national and local level. Of course, nobody finds anything wrong in that. To this day, however, I am glad that I took the golf competition route and steered clear of playing hostess at the glitzy dinners. That is a practice which has certainly been called into question in recent years, with stories abounding of dinners being held all over the country, where large cheques were handed over — it has become the stuff of tribunals, as we know. The whole question of political fundraising is one which I feel very much necessitates further discussion and analysis in a more general way. But in terms of our own party practices over the years, what bothered me about my own experience was the lack of clarity in the way things were done at times, and, as I have said, I believe that this contributed to a general breakdown of social cohesion and accountability within the party.

As this book testifies, I have been a member of Fianna Fáil for all my adult life, and indeed in my earlier years too. I have earned my living and worked hard and to the best of my ability as a public representative, and I have always been proud to be a member of Fianna Fáil. I find it utterly outrageous that it is considered nefarious to be a member — even a grassroots member — of our party, and as I write this today, this seems to be the common thread emerging in the media and in public discourse. I rail against the fact that there are many writers and commentators who in my opinion could be accused of breaching the code of incitement to hatred, in the way in which they write and talk about Fianna Fáil. 'Toxic', 'disreputable', 'underhand': all these adjectives about us are heaped one upon another. I feel it is strongly reprehensible and grossly unfair to the ordinary men and women throughout the country who are the foot soldiers, unpaid, of the party of Fianna Fáil. How dare people cast aspersions upon them?

It is as if over all of the years, the pent-up hatred of the success of Fianna Fáil has cut loose and commentators are giving vent to it, and in a way that completely lacks proportion or even-handedness. Micheál Martin, our current leader, is doing his best to bring the party back up from the abyss into which we plunged after the General Election of February 2011. He has some task ahead of him, particularly in the chilly, unforgiving political climate in which we now find ourselves.

Chapter 23 ❧

'SLEEP THAT KNITS UP THE RAVELL'D SLEAVE OF CARE . . .'

After losing my seat in the February 2011 General Election, I picked myself up pretty quickly, reasoning that I had had a great run of it. It was a consolation to me also to know that Longford–Westmeath had at least returned one Fianna Fáil TD in Robert Troy — unlike in so many other constituencies, where there was no Fianna Fáil TD at all. While I knew that my time as a Fianna Fáil aspirant or TD was now at an end, I certainly did not feel in any sense that life was over for me in a more general way.

The night I came back from my final defeat, I made up my mind that I was going to write this book, and in the days and weeks which followed, I took up my tape recorder and started to record some of my thoughts and put some order on the various key events in my career. Indeed, during that period in February and March 2011, I was chiefly obsessed with two things: gathering material for my book and, even more intensely, my nephew Brian and his struggle with his illness. By day, I was working on the book, at night I was hardly sleeping and waking up very early, thinking about Brian and waiting for his next call — and there were many of those.

In mid-March 2011, just a month after the February election and all that it had brought, I was contacted by Professor Ciarán Ó Catháin, Director of Athlone Institute of Technology, who told me that the Institute wished to confer a distinguished fellowship of life's work on Patrick Cooney, myself and two other local business people, Dr Donald

Panoz of Elan and Stephen Grant of Grant Engineering. The professor explained that Paddy Cooney and I were being so honoured for our lives of political endeavour, and for all the efforts we had made on behalf of the college during our years in politics. I have to say, it gave me a psychological boost to be so contacted, especially so shortly after the events of the previous month, and I was delighted to accept this honour.

In due course, I was contacted by Dr Eoin Langan, Head of the Business School at AIT, who had been nominated to read the citation on me at the ceremony. He came out to see me and we went through various points together. The date for the event had been fixed for Tuesday, 29 March. I was asked to give a list of the names of people I would like to invite to the ceremony, and the college sent out the formal invitations on my behalf.

I asked my two sons Feargal and Aengus, with their wives Maeve and Lisa, and their children. I asked Gráinne, my friend and niece; my two sisters-in-law Eithne and Maureen; Mícheál Ó'Faoláin and his wife Maura (who were unfortunately away on holidays and so could not attend); Hugh and Celine Campbell; Niall and Angela McCormack; John and Mary Butler; Seán Rowland; Breda Browne who had run my constituency office in Athlone and her husband Seamus, also an old and long-standing political friend. I also asked Brian and Patricia Lenihan, Ann and Anita Lenihan and my sister, Anne, and her husband. Anne's husband, Seamus, was not well enough to come so they had to decline with regret, likewise Ann and Anita. Patricia could not attend either, but to my delight, Brian said that he would be there, and I was happy to know he was coming.

When the big day dawned, I went to the college in good time, looking forward very much to the ceremony ahead. It was a solemn event, as well it should have been, bearing in mind the huge honour which was being bestowed upon us. Paddy Cooney and I metaphorically clung to one another: both of us were, as I have said, the political nominations and we had much in common, in our love of Athlone, our love of politics, and most of all in our work and love for the college. As I have mentioned earlier in this book, my interest in the college, and that of the Lenihan family go back a long, long time. I had always been very proud of the fact that during his time as a TD for

Longford–Westmeath and when the locations for Regional Colleges were being decided at Cabinet level, my father pushed to have Athlone chosen as one of the sites. Hence the long link between me and this establishment. In an important, emotional way, my abiding love affair with AIT was cemented on that Tuesday in March 2011, when I received my fellowship from them in front of my friends and family.

I was honoured that Brian came, and in fact it was to be his last full public engagement. The college was understandably also very proud of the fact that he had taken the trouble in his last illness to come along that day. They put on a wonderful lunch buffet and we all enjoyed ourselves. I have great photographs of that special afternoon. Brian telephoned me later that day when he got back to Dublin to say how proud he was of me.

Brian had brought with him a young man called Brian Murphy, who had worked as a researcher and speech writer in the Office of the Taoiseach, under Bertie Ahern and later under Brian Cowen. He was a fine man whom we all held in fond regard around the Houses of the Oireachtas. Brian Jnr's wife Patricia had thought that it would be better for him to have a companion with him for the drive to and from Athlone, and hence Brian Murphy had come along too. I was not to know until a couple of weeks later in fact, when Brian Murphy rang me one evening to thank me for the event, that when they had left the college, Brian said to him, 'I'll show you Athlone.' It seems that they had driven all around the town, as Brian had pointed out the old River Bridge, the Batteries, the Napoleonic fortifications, the house on Retreat Road where he had been brought up as a child, the Marist Brothers where he went to primary school, St Mel's Park, and all the other old familiar places. It was as if he knew it would be his last trip to Athlone, the place he always regarded as his home town.

Meanwhile, during those months of February and March, Brian had been in and out of the Dáil a couple of times. He rang me on one occasion, deeply upset because he had just learned that Micheál Martin, the new leader of Fianna Fáil, wished to relieve him of his duties as Finance Spokesperson. Now perhaps Micheál was suggesting this out of a wish to spare exertions on Brian's part, but Brian did not want to give up his position like this. I told him to go and see Micheál and to say that he wished to stay on for as long as he was able to do so.

He took my advice, and evidently he won that little joust, as when the frontbench was announced, Brian was the Spokesperson on Finance. It would have been a travesty if he had not been, but it just shows you what can be done to someone.

We continued to speak many times on the telephone, mostly on Sundays or during the week at nights. Bit by bit, I noticed Brian's voice getting weaker. I remember discussing this with my son Aengus one evening, and the only way I could describe it was to say that his cousin's voice had become like that of a very old person — faint and far away, with no vigour in it at all. I didn't say this to Brian himself, but I knew then that he was coming to the end. Even so, I didn't realise that it would all be over so quickly for him.

Time moved on and soon it was April, which was a beautiful, bright, sunny month with a lot of warmth. April 2011 was the summer of 2011 — we got no fine weather after that. That month was warm, with golden evenings and for Brian it must have been particularly poignant, as he knew time was marching on. He helped his young son, Tom, who was studying Law at Trinity, and told me one day on the telephone, 'I'm so glad I'm at home with Tom. I'm so glad I'm able to talk with him and help him through some of his studies.' Clare, his daughter, was studying for her Junior Cert, and as such probably did not require much help, but encouragement and parental interest are of course always useful, no matter what stage of life one is at.

Then one day, about ten days before he died, Brian called me and said, 'Mary, I'm sleeping all the time. I sleep twelve hours and I get up and then I want to sleep again.' Trying to be reassuring, I told him that sleep is good for one, which of course we all know. I remember quoting to him that line from *Macbeth*: 'Sleep that knits up the ravell'd sleave of care ...' I have always thought these are the most beautiful words, and so apt too, because of course you can go to bed careworn and yet wake up refreshed. Brian immediately asked me to say the line again, and, when I did, he said, 'You were always a good teacher.' As I write now, the tears flow fast and I remember again the earnest 12-year-old boy whom I tutored in Latin all those years ago. This was the last conversation I had with Brian.

In many ways, I am glad that I didn't see him again. I am glad that he spent his last days with Patricia and his two children, as they lay down with him that last Tuesday, Wednesday and Thursday. Brian died on Friday, 10 June 2011. I am glad that my last memory of him is of the happy man who came to the IT in Athlone for the presentation of my fellowship. I am thankful that he had that happy day and that I have that happy memory.

As I write these lines, I can see Brian in his seat, midway down the room in that assembly hall, on the right-hand side, where all my invitees had gathered. I can see him later at the lunch we had, talking to everyone, moving about, deep in conversation with many people and particularly with Paddy Cooney and Harman Murtagh. Most of all I can imagine him driving around Athlone with Brian Murphy, revisiting the places and the happy days of his youth in his home town.

| NEW LIFE AGAIN

After Brian died, it was a long while before I felt ready to do any public speaking or appearances again. I suppose his death brought back to me afresh all the pain of losing Enda and also my dear brothers Paddy and Brian Snr. I found myself dwelling a lot on death and all those I had lost. It is something which still preoccupies me, I have to say, as I cannot help thinking that so many of the men in my life went too soon, before their time — although of course I still have my two lovely sons, Feargal and Aengus, who are a huge consolation to me.

In time, however, I got back into the swing of things and my new life beyond politics, and was able to enjoy the various opportunities to speak in public which presented themselves. Since my retirement from active political life, I have given a lot of public lectures — people write to me, having heard me on the radio, for example, asking if I will speak at various events and public functions, such as book launches, art exhibitions, openings and literary festivals. This year I spoke in Mornington Church in County Louth, where they have a very good pastoral council who organise such things. For the six Wednesdays of Lent, they had six speakers, of whom I was one, as were journalists David Quinn and Colm O'Rourke. I spoke from the altar on my own perspective on life and what needs to be done by the Church, something in which I strongly believe. As far as I see it, the Church has to get simple again: it has to be all about the parish priest and the local parishioners, because my feeling is that it is some of the Bishops with the high hats, and the pomp and circumstance that have alienated people from religion.

For this and many other reasons, I have always thought that separating the Church from the school system is a good idea. Since my retirement from politics, I have been a very enthusiastic member of the National Board of Educate Together. I am excited by the fact that we are now venturing into secondary level education. We hope to gradually extend our secondary level remit into areas where Educate Together primary schools already exist. So I remain hugely interested in education.

I have also recently accepted an invitation to become a patron of the Cappagh Hospital Trust, and am looking forward to working with them. In addition to this, I am Honorary President of the Haemochromatosis Society, which furthers research into the condition to which my brother Brian lost his life.

Since 2011, I have also made some enjoyable forays into media work. Of course as a politician, I always had a lot of dealings with the media, but recently I have had the opportunity to undertake such work in an altogether different role. In the summer of 2011, I did a stint as guest presenter on Vincent Browne's *Tonight* show for a week. In 2009, I had appeared on TV3's *Midday* programme a few times, and on the back of this, Andrew Hanlon offered me the chance to do the Vincent Browne show for one of the four weeks of Vincent's holidays. As it turned out, I loved it! I was nervous enough until I got going and then my nerves just evaporated.

For my week on *Tonight*, I picked the themes and the panel, in as far as possible. Bertie Ahern agreed to be on the first show, which was a bit of a coup because he doesn't do much television. I rang him to say that I was doing the programme and that I wanted to talk about the North, about which I felt there hasn't been enough coverage here. No matter what can be said about Bertie, his achievements in terms of the Peace Process cannot be taken away from him. Albert did a lot of work in this respect too of course, and Bertie kept up the momentum, because he believed in it so much. Anyway, he immediately said he would do the interview and we got very good feedback on that show. I also managed to get Liz O'Donnell, David Trimble and Alex Maskey from Sinn Féin to participate in that session.

Another night that week, I had a 'Women Authors' show, when Deirdre Purcell and others joined me to talk about writing and how they had come by the inspiration for the plots and characters in their novels. That was a very interesting night. I also did a session on Education, in which Seán Sherlock participated on behalf of Ruairi Quinn, along with some other really good people, like Gemma Hussey. We did a programme entitled 'Fiscal Woes of Ireland', for which I didn't choose the panel, but I was able to meet and speak with them, and be briefed beforehand and that session went down well also.

All the shows went out live, which was scary enough, of course. If you are a teacher or in public life, you know that if and when things go wrong, all you have to do is keep calm and just pick yourself up. And I had great guidance and support from the production team, especially Lisa Marie and Lynda. Vincent Browne had left a script with guidelines for all of the guest presenters, which said things like, 'If you find the dialogue going dead, jump up and say "So, what do you think about *that*?" and they will all say "What?" and things will take off again'.

Later last year, I was asked to make a bid for the Irish Presidency — various TDs, Senators and members of the public suggested it to me. But I knew I couldn't do it. Imagine being told to 'stand there, don't say that, move four paces that way' and so on! I did give it some serious thought, but I decided pretty quickly that I would feel too corralled and hemmed in as to what I could say and not say, do and not do. I prefer my life now to be familiar and ordinary and low-key. In a more general sense, I feel that Fianna Fáil were right not to run anyone in the end — I know that Éamon Ó Cuív doesn't think it was a good decision, but I do.

While I didn't go in for the Presidency myself, I did do a lot of work for RTÉ during the campaign as a political analyst — something which I very much enjoyed. I thought a lot about Brian Snr during that 2011 campaign: some very vivid memories came back to me. I also found myself reflecting that, if circumstances had been different, Bertie Ahern would have been a likely contender for President. I think he would have been good in that role. As for the successful candidate, I know President Michael D. Higgins well — he was Opposition Spokesperson for Education when I was the Minister. Michael D. would always have been ideological, a little bit like Garret FitzGerald — although more likeable, in my view.

I will always have an abiding interest in politics and I will always welcome the opportunity to have my say and continue to participate in public debate and have a voice. Politics has remained and will continue to be my biggest passion in life outside of my family.

One of the things I am enjoying most about no longer being so actively involved in public life is that I have been able to spend much more time with my sons and their families, and with other friends and family members also. Feargal now lives in Dublin with his wife Maeve (née Barry) and their two children, Jennifer and Sam, who are aged nine and seven. Feargal was married previously to Muriel Moroney, a lovely young woman. They met and married very young, but separated after seven years and then got a divorce. Each of them has since remarried and both are very happy. Feargal and Maeve and the children come down to Athlone a lot to stay with me.

Aengus lives in Athlone with his wife Lisa (née Dunwoody) and their four children, Luke, Sarah, James and Scott. Lisa, who is originally from Dublin, calls quite often when she is in town: she will bring the smallest lad, who is only two years old, to see me, and he will say, 'Mary, go Mary in car!' I am very blessed with my two daughters-in-law, Maeve and Lisa, with whom I get on very well: they are like daughters to me. I love them for themselves and as the spouses of my sons and the mothers of my grandchildren. And I love all the grandchildren, of course: they have added a real texture to my life.

At the end of August last year, I went on holiday with Ann Lenihan (Brian's mother) and his sister Anita: we went to Madeira for a week. I would regard Ann as my closest female friend. That was a lovely week: the hotel was great; we relaxed by the pool every day, went to the beach and did some sightseeing. We also talked a lot about Brian which did us all good — it was a kind of catharsis, and we got some of the grief out of our systems. Ann has had a very rough ride in life — the tough times I have had are nothing compared to what Ann has endured. She lost her husband; she lost a little boy, Mark, at five years of age; and she lost her first-born son, Brian. How do you cope with that? She had a small stroke herself from which, thankfully, she has made a great recovery. Ann is a very lively woman, and she has always been that way. I loved that holiday we had and I think it resuscitated me a bit.

Dr Seán Rowland, the founder and director of Hibernia College in Dublin, is among my dearest friends, and we meet frequently. He comes down to see me in Athlone or I go up to Dublin to meet him. He is truly a sterling friend.

Summer 2011 was intertwined a lot with family, between all my grandchildren, my sisters-in-law and the occasions of my eldest granddaughter Jennifer's and my grandson Luke's Holy Communions. And in mid-July 2011, Brian's Month's Mind was held in their family home. Now it is over a year since Brian died. Even very recently, I was speaking with Dermot Moylan, who had been Brian's Private Secretary in Finance. Dermot referred to that period working with him as a 'golden time', despite the huge daily pressures of the national economic troubles, political uncertainty and Brian's failing health. He concluded by saying, 'There was never a day I didn't want to go to work for him and with him.'

In so many ways, it is my children and my grandchildren who have sustained me in recent times. I love my sons and their families so much. As for my age, I don't dwell on it. I am a very active person and I like to keep my brain occupied too. I have tried to keep myself healthy, both in body and in spirit. I believe in goodness and I believe in love. Love helps to keep you vital and positive. And there is nothing like grandchildren — they just love you to bits and they make all the difference. It's compensation — it's new life again.

INDEX